GLOBALLY ACCLAIMED IN S

ADAM

WITH **KAZIMIR KOLESNIK**

7P.M. AUG. 16, 17 LA·MAMA

SHIBUYA

パントマイム

PRESENTED BY ADAM DARIUS JAPAN, COSPONSORED BY THE JAPAN FOUNDATION AND BRITISH COUNSIL.

FOR FURTHER IMFORMATION, PHONE 479·0232 ADAM DARIUS JAPAN

The Adam Darius Method

Few performing artists in any field have been seen in as many diverse cultures as has Adam Darius. Born in New York City on May 10th, 1930, he began his career as a ballet dancer and choreographer, working with a number of ballet companies in North America, Europe and Asia. Evolving an original fusion of dance and mime, he has established himself in over 60 countries as the unparalleled dramatic mime artist of our time, influencing and inspiring countless people of every background and orientation. No one who has seen him in performance can fail to notice that in addition to his unique expressive powers, he is, as well, a ballet dancer of spiritual line and sculptural beauty.

Director of The Mime Centre in London, Britain's only intensive training for the mime arts, he is the author of *Dance Naked In the Sun*, *The Way to Timbuktu* as well as this latest book, *The Adam Darius Method*.

Choreographer of the internationally acclaimed *The Anne Frank Ballet* and the provocative evening length *Marilyn*, his career has encompassed a colourful spectrum of world theatre.

In *The Adam Darius Method*, he has recorded his long sought after codified technique, a technique that frees the psyche while controlling the physique in order to produce the total actor.

This book will serve as a constant reminder for those who have personally studied with Adam Darius. And for those who have not, the following pages will open the door into the vast mansion of theatrical experience inhabited by him.

The many rooms of his creative habitat will undoubtedly fascinate for they include not only expressive mime technique and an in-depth analysis of movement, but also a wide range of allied practical subjects essential to all those for whom the theatre is a career.

The Adam Darius Method will, unquestionably, enrich the lives of all those already on the stage as well as the many more young people who dream of one day joining them.

By the same author

DANCE NAKED IN THE SUN
THE WAY TO TIMBUKTU

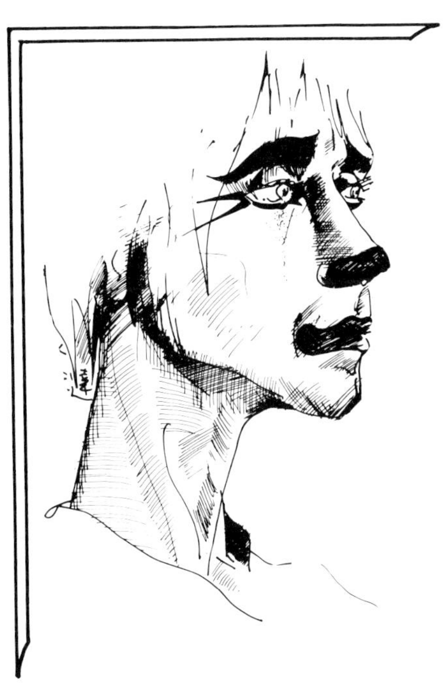

THE ADAM DARIUS METHOD

a technical and practical handbook for all performing artists

by
ADAM DARIUS

Latonia Publishers · LONDON

First published in Great Britain 1984
by Latonia Publishers
104 Monarch Court
Lyttelton Road
London N2 ORB, England

Designed by Susan Ryall

ISBN 0 9502707 2 5

Printed and bound in Great Britain by
Butler & Tanner Ltd, Frome and London

To Burton

June 5th, 1926–April 22nd, 1983

Cherished son, husband, father,
brother and nephew

Dear brother,
Life is encased
in its boundaries of time,
but love knows
no restrictive barricades.
We are dreadfully impoverished
by your passing,
but immeasurably enriched
from having loved and been loved
by you in your good and generous life.

Contents

With Gratitude

I would not, nor could not, begin this book without thanking the following people for their contributions to this book or to my life. They are rather intertwined.

Firstly, to my father, who though no longer physically here, is a permanent tenant of my mind, the landlord of my body. He gave to me, my life, his love.

To my mother who is the unremitting loving thread throughout the entire tapestry of my existence, my endless thanks. Across the widest seas the permanence of her concern for me never wavers. She, for me, is a reason why *mother* is a sacred word in virtually every language.

To my aunt Minnie Stark, for her devotional belief in me since the days of early boyhood, my continuing gratitude. More than my favourite aunt, she is my beloved friend.

To my late brother Burton for having always provided me with his loyal support; the last conversation we ever had took place on the telephone in February, 1983 when, from his store of languages, he spontaneously translated from the Spanish the five poems within this book. To Burt, then, my remembered and everlasting love.

To my late and lamented friend of 15 years, the outstandingly gifted mime artist Nathaniel, my profound and abiding gratitude for his abundant contributions to the previous and future chapters of my life's book. His death, without warning at the age of 36, has left those of us who loved him, still staggering from the shock. The eulogy I wrote for and read at his funeral in July, 1983 is to be found, along with six photographs of him, in the Epilogue section of this book. Though the ashes of his beautiful body have been scattered on the pale green grass of our still grieving Indian summer, his life force continues in full focus.

To Riad Ismat, Syria's leading theatre critic and one of the Arabic world's ranking playwrights, my appreciation for his Epilogue to this book.

To José Luis Naranjo Ferrer, from Cuba, who saw me perform in Havana, my thankfulness for his five strikingly beautiful poems which grace this book. Each of the poems preceding a chapter is his response to different works in our repertoire.

To the great Indian poet of photography, Ashwin Gatha, my indebtedness for his cover photographs, both front and back, taken on Copacabana Beach in Rio de Janeiro, for the Taiwanese poster photograph chosen for the endpapers, for the recent photographs of me at practice in London as well as for the many technique illustrations, all posed by Kazimir Kolesnik.

(Only some of the technical exercises have accompanying photographs since the method in this book does not demand slavish imitation. On the contrary, within the given framework, the student must provide his own inventiveness.)

To Douglas Fairbanks, Jr., Dame Alicia Markova, Warren Mitchell and Kate Bush, my appreciation for their thought provoking reflections in the *Conversations* section of this book.

To Dr. Alberto Testa, Italy's pre-eminent dance historian and, as well, distinguished critic and choreographer, my appreciation for inaugurating my many performances in Italy, birthplace of the commedia dell'arte.

To Natsuo Amemiya of the Japan Foundation in Tokyo, my thankfulness for initiating our recent appearances in the land of the rising sun.

For the endpaper poster as well as the line drawing of my face and hands, I thank that most original of artists, Naoki Okamoto. Moving from the far east to the nearer west, my grateful admiration to the superb English artist Chris Gunton for his drawing of Marita Phillips and clown portrait of myself.

To Marita Phillips who remains my sequoia tree of comforting embrace, a deep révérence for her Introduction. Great-great-great granddaughter of Czar Nicholas 1st of Russia and Alexander Pushkin, sister to the Duchess of Westminster and Duchess of Abercorn, she is, her historical lineage notwithstanding, a commoner in the equally apportioned distribution of her gifts. Founder of The Mime Centre, she is, herself, a mime artist of international repute, actress and lyricist. Most importantly, she is and will always be my cherished friend.

And to conclude these acknowledgments, I thank that fantastic new mime artist and dancer, Kazimir Kolesnik, for his unswerving allegiance to our shared goals. The recent acclaim he has earned in the Orient, Middle East, America and Europe establishes him in Britain as the most dynamic mime of his generation. I, personally, will go further and state that there is no male dancer in this country who possesses his cyclonic power and range as a dancing actor. This book, then, is my living and loving gift to him, the devoted torchbearer of my life in art. Our alliance is the homecoming harbour of my enduring voyage.

Dear reader, I now thank *you* for your interest in this book, so long in preparation.

Before the acquisition of technique must come the understanding that we are all, essentially, human beings, shipwrecked together on some mysterious morning beach, sprinkled at first by iridescent foam then later deluged by the tears and tidal waves of imminent dusk.

It is the artist's hallowed mission to salvage us from our island of despair, to lead us mercifully to the further and happier shore beyond, to guide, to pacify, to clarify and inspire us on this, our awesome and earthly journey.

Adam Darius
London
November, 1983

Introduction

by MARITA PHILLIPS

Few performing artists in any field have been seen in as many diverse cultures as Adam Darius. His cataclysmic presence has inspired and influenced countless people of every background and orientation. Now, at last, he has recorded his codified technique and in this book shares not only his principles of expressive mime, but a panoramic range of subjects essential to anyone involved in the performing arts.

Despite the fact that this book is packed with detailed instructions and fascinating information, it cannot remotely approximate the experience of seeing, firsthand, the creator of this system. His personality is electric and he electrifies those who partake in his class.

Each class is approached as if it were a performance. The same high standard is demanded in the physical framework and in the mental approach. Curtains are drawn, spotlights turned on, articles of clothing are not left lying around the studio, students sit cross-legged on the floor and there is an atmosphere of anticipation. Adam Darius demands absolute attention and he gives absolute attention. Within seconds a diverse group of people becomes a unified whole. As he so rightly believes and teaches, only within a framework of complete discipline can freedom of expression really blossom and be explored.

His technique is designed to free the psyche while controlling the physique in order to create the total actor. Every class begins with the students inflating and deflating, breath being the basis of life and movement. Adam Darius claps his hands and pianist and students simultaneously begin.

The exercises are first purely technical then either dramatic, poetic or tragicomic. The exercises end with either a sharp clap of Adam Darius' hands with him concurrently commanding "Rest," a snap of his fingers or him chanting, "Stay, stay ..." until he feels the echo of the exercise is complete. He, not the students, chooses when to end it.

There are no halfhearted attempts allowed in class any more than half hearted attempts would be acceptable on stage. Everything taught is geared to the theatre, but the classroom is the place to dare, to explore, to extend, to acquire technique and to cultivate creativity. It is all too easy to have brief moments of inspired improvisation but in order to develop and sustain those flickering moments of creativity it is vital to have someone, as Adam Darius, who both recognizes and encourages them.

He very rarely demonstrates an exercise as he is not looking for mere imitations of himself. He wants the students to work from within themselves and to express the thoughts or emotions in their own individual style.

Maria Callas, referring to her own training, stated, "The difference between good teachers and great teachers is that good teachers make the best of a pupil's means; great teachers foresee a pupil's ends." Callas' description of pedagogic greatness is applicable to Adam Darius.

As well as grasping each student's individual potentiality, he has impeccable, intuitive timing; knowing when to ignore a student, when to encourage, when to clamp down and when to challenge. Demanding as he is in discipline and standards, he is unreservedly generous in his praise when it is due. Unlike many teachers he believes it is as important to comment on what is right as what is wrong. For when students are creating and experimenting in a class, it is vital to be told what to retain, not just what to lose.

Few great performers are also great teachers. Adam Darius is both because he is analytical, articulate and totally generous with his vast knowledge. Many of the exercises he teaches are coloured by anecdotes and remembered experiences from a long career in the theatre; the mistakes, the moments of glory, the lessons learned, the artists he has worked with, his own teachers and the reasons why. It is also rare to have the opportunity to study with someone who is the supreme example of the art he teaches, physically, mentally and spiritually. He is relentlessly disciplined in his physical exercises and rules of health and diet. The integrity and dedication he applies to his work is almost of religious fervour.

There is an Indian tradition of total surrender of the disciple to the guru. The guru, in turn, gives shelter, guidance and instruction to the student. There is something of this same quality in Adam Darius. It is only possible to surrender to someone who both lives out his art and philosophy completely and gives out his knowledge and experience completely. It is from this temporary sense of surrender that Adam discovers, encourages and cultivates the seeds of every individual's potential.

Most people have a desire to move to music and express themselves physically but it is almost unique to find a teacher whose technique is based on free, individual movement. A deaf boy who attended a course at The Mime Centre wrote, "I always thought that being able to hear music was the overall reason for getting people to move. But today I felt a tingle, that so-called unlocked feeling, the secret of movement." Adam Darius unlocks mentally and physically. This is, of course, one of the greatest steps in an artist's journey.

My unreserved respect and belief in Adam Darius as a teacher was the overriding reason for my founding The Mime Centre in 1978. It seemed a necessity that people should have the chance to study with him over a period of time instead of just isolated master classes. This book will no doubt serve them as a constant reminder. For those unable to witness the teachings of the author firsthand, the following pages will prove an invaluable source of inspiration and information.

I can only add that I remain eternally grateful for having had the opportunity to study and work with one of the great teachers of the world, Adam Darius.

Photographs

Yesterdays

1 **With my father, New York State, circa 1933**
Collection: Adam Darius

2 **With my brother Burton, New York State, circa 1934**
Collection: Adam Darius

3 **In the title role of my ballet *Robin Goodfellow*, New York City, 1951**
Photographer: Walter Owen

4 **With my aunt Minnie and mother, Florida, U.S.A., 1971**
Photographer: Nathaniel

1

2

3

4

Arabesques through time

1 1948–On top of the Pyramid of the Sun, Teotihuacan, Mexico
Collection: Adam Darius

2 1983–Practicing 35 years later, London
Photographer: Ashwin Gatha

1

2

On stage

1 In *Les Sylphides* with Joyce Gearing and June Summers, International Ballet, Dublin, Ireland, 1953
Photographer: James O'Callaghan

2 In *The Village Idiot*, Tokyo, Japan, 1983
Photographer: Shige Morishita

1

2

3 In *Resurrection: The Nazi and the Nazarene*, with Kazimir Kolesnik as the Gestapo and myself as Christ, Havana, Cuba, 1982
Photographer: Prensa Latina

4 As **Puck** in **Benjamin Britten's** opera, ***A Midsummer Night's Dream,*** Göteborg, Sweden, 1961
Photographer: Stora Teatern

5 In ***Hearts and Flowers*** **with Marita Phillips, London, England, 1980**
Collection: Marita Phillips

4

5

6

7

6 In *The Mourners*, Rio de Janeiro, Brazil, 1977
Photographer: Fernando Uchoa

7 In *Death of a Scarecrow*, Bouaké, the Ivory Coast, 1976
Photographer: Gérard Payen

After the performance

1 **In Monrovia, Liberia, with dancers of the National Cultural Troupe, 1976**
Photographer: Wilson Paaper

2 **In Sumatra, Indonesia, 1976**
Collection: USIS

3 **In N'Djamena, Chad, with local actors, 1976**
Collection: USIS

4 **In Kaoshiung, Taiwan, 1981**
Photographer: Kazimir Kolesnik

5 **In London with Prince Charles and Marita Phillips, 1980**
Photographer: North Sullivan

1

3

2

4

5

On tour

1 **With Aborigines in the Northern Territory, Australia, 1971**
Photographer: Nathaniel

2 **In front of the Sphinx and Pyramid, Cairo, Egypt, 1976**
Photographer: Gazaros Demirdjian

1

2

3 **Poster of Kazimir Kolesnik and myself in Taiwan, the Republic of China, 1981**
Photographer: Ashwin Gatha

4

5

4 With local actors after a workshop, Dacca, Bangladesh, 1976
Photographer: Subha Barua

5 In Wat Pho, the Monastery of the Reclining Buddha, Bangkok, Thailand, 1976
Photographer: Honyiu Lok

6 Line drawing of myself by the artist, Naoki Okamoto, Tokyo, Japan, 1983
Photographer: John Freeman Group

7 With Kazimir Kolesnik at the Blue Mosque, Istanbul, Turkey, 1982
Photographer: Gutekin Cizgen

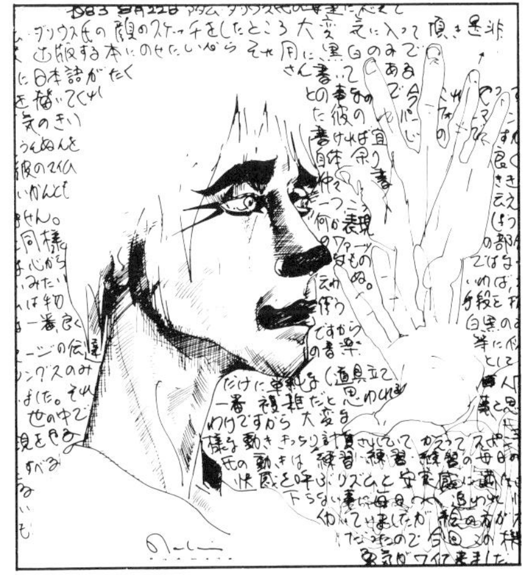

6

7

8 

8 **Backstage at the Kabuki Theatre with Umenosuke Onoe, Kazimir Kolesnik and producer of the National Theatre of Japan, Fumio Ohta, Tokyo, Japan, 1983**
Photographer: Shige Morishita

1 **At the Amazon, Belem, Brazil, 1980**
Photographer: Marita Phillips

2 **By the Neva, Leningrad, U.S.S.R., 1971**
Photographer: Nathaniel

3 **On the banks of the Nile, Cairo, Egypt, 1976**
Photographer: Gazaros Demirdjian

Three rivers

1

2

3

With Kazimir Kolesnik

1 Kazimir Kolesnik in *The Inmate*, Hong Kong, 1983
Photographer: Bruce Chan

2 Kazimir Kolesnik in *Prince of Darkness*, Tokyo, Japan, 1983
Photographer: Shige Morishita

2

1

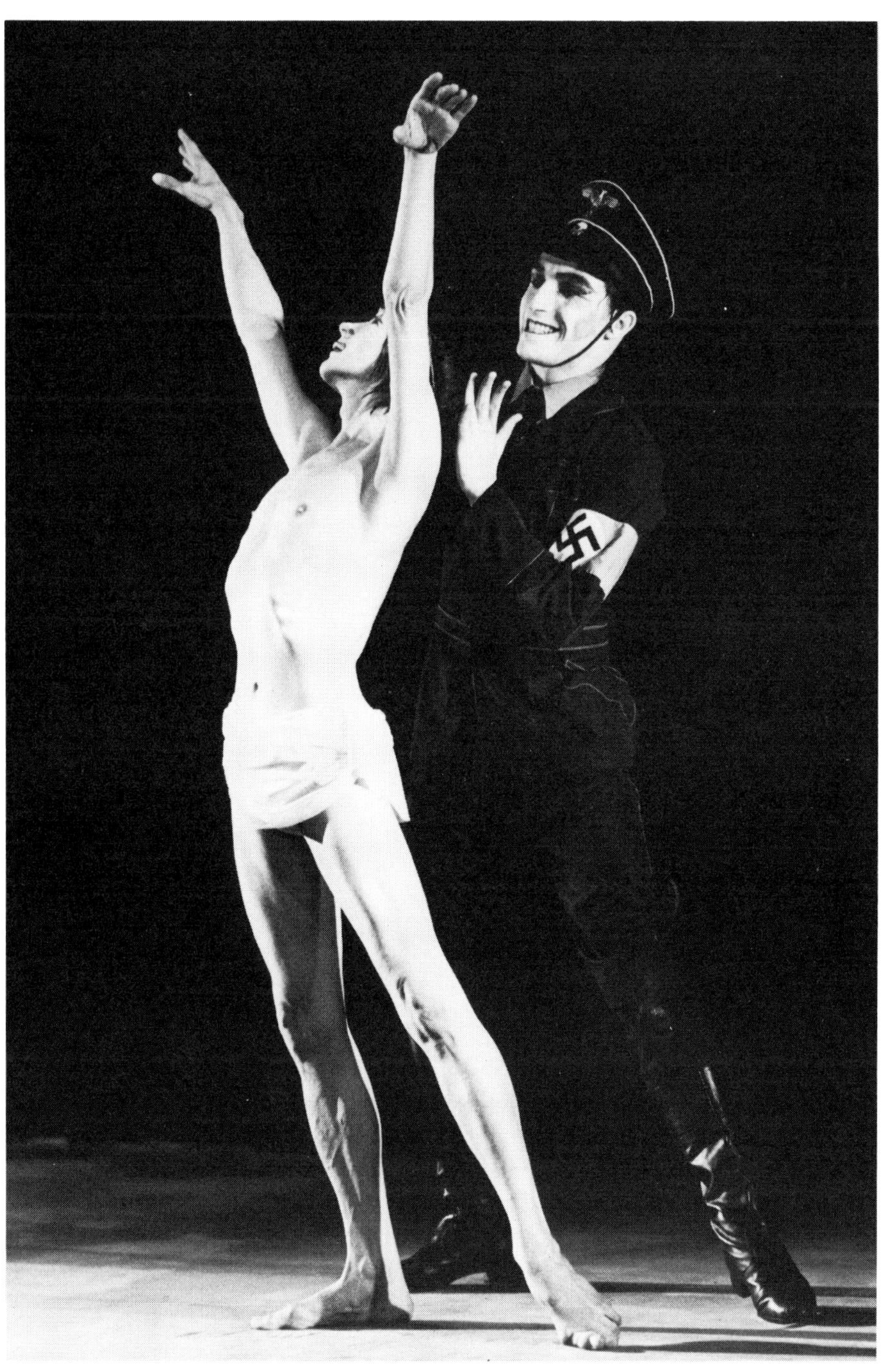

3 Kazimir Kolesnik as the Gestapo, myself as Christ in *Resurrection: The Nazi and the Nazarene*, Havana, Cuba, 1982
Photographer: Prensa Latina

4

5

4 Kazimir Kolesnik as the prostitute, myself as the judge in *Judge Closes Sex Shop*, Hong Kong, 1983
Photographer: Ivan Lau

5 Kazimir Kolesnik as Peter lifting Jane Carr as Anne Frank with myself as Otto Frank in *The Anne Frank Ballet*, the Dublin City Ballet, Dun Laoghaire, Ireland, 1981
Photographer: Tom Stokes

6 Kazimir Kolesnik as the Fox, myself as the Pet in *The Fox and His Domesticated Human Pet*, Tokyo, Japan, 1983

Photographer: Shige Morishita

Hands and feet

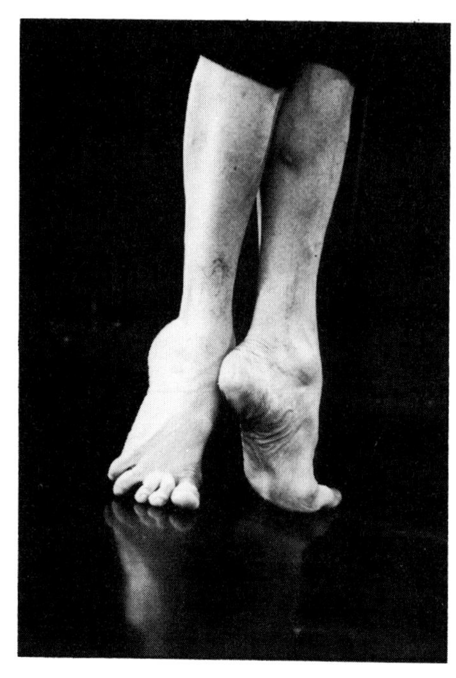

Maintaining my flexibility from fingers to toes, London, 1983
Photographer: Ashwin Gatha

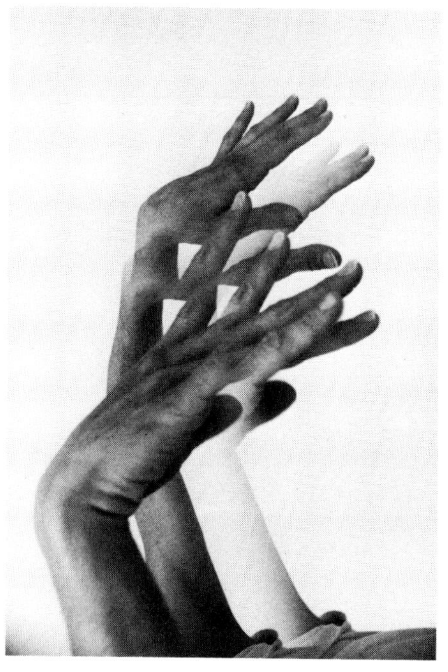

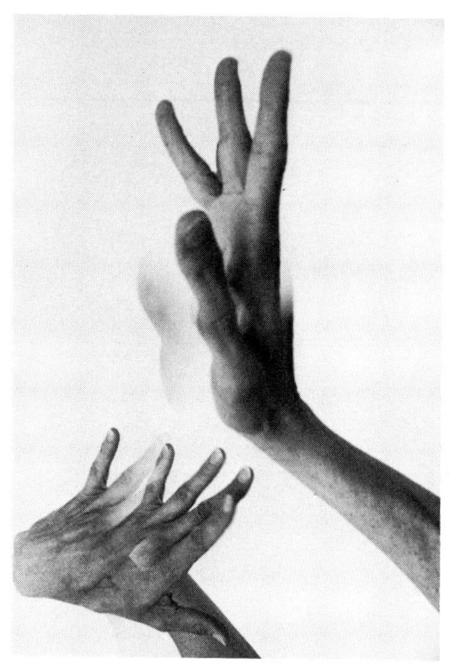

The daily ritual

Doing a barre at The Mime Centre, London, 1983
Photographer: Ashwin Gatha

My favourite guru

With Baby, Nathaniel's loving legacy. His, and now my, cherished dog first revealed to me the noble virtues of the animal kingdom; London, 1983
Photographer: Derek Bertram

The Adam Darius Method

1. To the Moving Actor:

A poetic and practical survey

THE RITUAL

The sun contains me,
there is no winter in my skin
and this man surges up out of
the brilliance of the streets
tirelessly and eternally seeking
to enhance his art.

He loves and glides with each step
and even with his back turned
invokes the magic of a hundred ports
as easy to reach
as death itself . . .

. . . but he believes in a smile
and tells us with every step;
Time is a knife of dust
without power.

José Luis Naranjo Ferrer

PREPARING

Defining mime

The great German writer Goethe noted in his essay on *The Last Supper*, "In Leonardo, the whole body is animated. Every member, every limb participates in all expressions of feeling, of passion and even of thought."

What the Renaissance's greatest genius felt about painting is no less applicable to the art of mime. The entire body must reflect the every nuance of the mind. No grimaces, charades or guessing games. Illusionary mime is a fashionable interpretation of the timeless original. Nevertheless, there is no disputing the historical definition, namely that mime is the wordless revelation of human emotions. It is not the mimicked circumference of an imaginary teacup or the splayed finger impasse against those invisible walls!

Illusionary mime technique is so absorbed in its depiction of man's pedestrian daily activities such as the handling of invisible objects that man's mind, mood and need are evaporated in the mechanical process.

These reservations notwithstanding, illusionary mime has its place in the sun, but it should not be confused with the actual source of light.

Throughout the recorded history of the world (and probably long before that), man has always been consumed with the need to express himself in relation to the supreme godhead as well as to his earthly neighbours. Long before speech was refined into an expansive vocabulary, man assisted his thoughts with gestures to either supplement or replace the spoken word. So, in a sense, mime or the wordless communication of feeling has always been in existence.

Times have irrevocably changed yet the man in the street still uses gesture and mime as additional methods of expression. When one asks directions for the nearest bus stop, the verbal reply is accompanied, without fail, by a pointing finger indicating the direction.

We are all expressive creatures or should be and those who bottle up their emotions soon find themselves with ulcers and other debilitating physical ailments. We long to communicate and since only a relative few can do so with superlative skill, audiences will travel long distances and relinquish sums of hard earned income to watch others do it for them.

In the riveting ritual of ancient Greece's great amphitheatres, mime was one of a number of total theatre techniques utilized to convey the intentions of an Aeschylus, Sophocles or Euripides. Vocal intoning, chanting, singing, dancing and miming were called upon either separately, in unison or canonically.

Walking amongst the ruins of the Theatre of Dionysus in Athens, the huge amphitheatre in Ephesus, Turkey, and the open air theatre in Dougga, Tunisia, one is humbled by the consciousness of a hallowed theatrical tradition in which our own participation seems, by archaic contrast, ephemeral.

Mime, as both a vehicle of human communication and theatrical expression, is inseparable from civilization. Mime, either as part of a collective artistic enterprise or as a complete entity in itself, reflects the corporate dream of mankind.

During my tours abroad I, who teach much, am taught more. Meeting Australian Aborigines, Liberians, Javanese, Taiwanese or Afghans, I see, repeatedly, that all men need to retain their self-respect and dignity, to feel that their life efforts are not in vain, that the rudimentary comforts will not be denied them and that the loving warmth of relationships is an avenue forever open.

The reader may well ask what such thoughts have in common with virtuoso theatrical skills. The answer is everything. The vehicle of mime has, as its port of call, humanity.

Donald Keene, Professor of Japanese at Columbia University, stated in a preface to one of his many books on the Orient, "The purpose of Noh drama is not to divert on the surface but to move profoundly, and ultimately to transcend the particular and touch the very springs of human emotions."

This is the humanity I had earlier referred to, at the very core of Japanese Noh drama and my own expressive mime technique as well.

On performing

The victory of great performing is achieved by initially surrendering. How can one triumph, it may be asked, by capitulating? The answer is that the outstanding performer acquiesces to the theme, the environment, the sound or music, his partner, to the very spirit of the creation. By succumbing to its totality, he rises above the individual parts.

The crest of a musical wave cannot be ridden until one has lain back and been submerged by its force. Similarly the performer must give in before he gives out.

Self-involvement is the first step towards magnetizing the public. People are always curious when confronted with self-absorption. Once an audience is captured, they must never be released. To lose an audience for a few moments is to risk losing them altogether. When the public enter a theatre, they bring in with them the countless competitive thoughts that have flooded their brains since awakening some 12 hours earlier. To keep at bay the crowding day's events for two hours is a feat requiring great inner immersion and power of distribution.

Humility and confidence

Agnes de Mille once said something to the effect that stage magic is not only having the power to move an audience but *knowing* that you can. Stage magic being the penthouse of an edifice, the basement is humility, the kind that will accept the constant dart-throwing of criticism. Not everyone is equipped with the type of resilient temperament that accepts the often barbed comments of teachers. Some students, when subjected to fault finding, go on the defensive. Instead of assimilating the correction they look for a reason why the teacher/director is wrong. This is sheer stupidity for the teacher will take his comments and offer them elsewhere while the director will choose not to work again with that person.

Confidence is not a commodity purchased over a counter. It is a result of slow progression resulting from doing well in class, in rehearsal then on the stage. Confidence, when watered by appreciation, grows. In exceptional cases it reaches the level of stage magic, mentioned earlier.

Insecurity is often the handmaiden of sensitivity. For this reason so many artists are precariously perched. Insecurity is the great common denominator apparent in students from every country and every social background. Insecurity is entrenched if a student is told often enough he's bad for he quickly gets worse. Conversely, if he's told with enough frequency he's good, quickly he gets even better. A simplistic equation but it works almost without fail.

The ripened artist needs a combination of humility and confidence. Humility alone will cut into the courage needed to take over a stage. Confidence alone soon sours into cockiness. Humility and confidence, strange bedfellows, need each other for warmth during the long, light night of theatre. Humility ensures the need to be better, preventing stagnation; confidence permits audacity, without which a performer does not electrify.

Maria Tallchief, once America's most dazzling dancer, was the inspiring muse to a succession of ballets by her then husband, the eminent choreographer George Balanchine. When their marriage ended and Balanchine changed from Henry Higgins to Henry the VIII, Tallchief faced the executioner's block, so to speak. "I will be listed alphabetically, if I must, but I won't be treated alphabetically," so stated the once queen of the American ballet world. But she had no choice in the matter and as she was given less and less to dance with longer intervals between appearances, her confidence eroded and with it her once prodigious technique.

Musicality

So many people think the word means keeping a strict tempo when moving to the music, not to be in front or behind the beat but with it steadily, as a human metronome. But true musicality goes far beyond a mirrored rhythm.

Genuine musicality occurs when the performer allows the spirit of the composer to borrow his body, to re-visit the scene, to make his presence felt. Genuine musicality goes way beyond rhythmic obedience. We are witnessing true musicality when the performer submits his will to the dictates of the composer.

Favouritism in school

Get used to it. Life plays favourites, the theatre even more so. I, myself, at the outset of a term at The Mime Centre, give everyone equal attention until such time as certain students require more attention at a particular point than others. For some, too much attention too soon is detrimental; attention too late for others is equally damaging. The teacher must be aware of an intuitive clock that allows him to ring the alarm for the right person at the right moment.

Some students become spoiled by the generous distribution of attention and if, for whatever reason, that focus is removed, they tend to feel rejected. But one day school days will end and the actual world of competitive theatre will take over. That world of intense determination and exposed nerve endings will not treat all and sundry with equality. Most will be overlooked, a few looked over and even fewer chosen, though even for the selected few there is no guarantee that it will continue. This is autocracy at work. Good schooling should prepare the student for such reality. So, if the teacher does, on occasion, ignore the student, he may well be learning a valuable lesson.

Creativity

Creativity is not as rare as we are led to believe. Children have it in abundance but lose it as, gradually, society instills its obligatory restrictions. Children, not yet fenced in by inhibiting regulations, gambol innocently through fields of fantasy. Adults, too often discouraged by conformity, trek aimlessly through the barren desert of drugs and alcohol.

The prerequisite of creativity is a continuous state of acute consciousness, particularly to the whispered inner voice. Messages are received, in whole or part, and must be transmitted immediately before slipping into the deep funnel of forgetfulness.

On not wearing a watch when working

Aside from the practical consideration of ruining the mechanism by constantly perspiring into it, the watch is a subconscious reminder of the next appointment or any other similar practical consideration. The movement artist should work in measureless space unencumbered by the distraction of the ticking clock. Overtime should be left to the union deputy.

On being interviewed by a school director

In an office interview, the student's answers should be succinct, not discursive, for let it not be thought that the interviewer has the time or inclination to listen to a stream of consciousness improvisation.

Is it necessary to remind the hopeful student to refrain from smoking during the interview or worse, to enter the office with a lit cigarette? Not everyone is enamoured of carcinogenic fumes.

As it is stating the obvious to arrive on time, I will only add it is always advisable to leave early for a scheduled appointment in order to allow enough leeway to get lost and still arrive punctually.

Don't call the director by his first name at first meeting. What is considered informality in one part of the world is construed as familiarity in another. If the director wishes, at a later date, to be addressed on a friendlier basis, that fact will be known in due course. The student, however, should refrain from this casual address over the telephone or at the first interview.

Soiled jeans made up of a patchwork quilt of coloured denim over the seat and crotch may well be fashionable but they are out of place in an office interview. Because time is always limited, some people judge a book by its cover. Don't be thrust back into the shelf unread.

The experienced ballet or drama student is aware of the following advice, but, unfortunately, there are always applicants less disciplined who aren't. For this minority, the words I'm about to write down are of paramount importance.

Do, upon arising, bathe or shower. Do apply a deodorant and wear fresh clothes. The human body, left unwashed, does not exude an irresistible fragrance. During a movement class it takes only one delinquent student, in this area of social responsibility, to disfigure the environment for all his colleagues. Not everything natural is necessarily beautiful, witness earthquakes, typhoons and active volcanoes.

Without giving the interviewer the feeling that you are being deferential (though if he has been or is a star, he is accustomed to it and if he hasn't been, he might appreciate what was missed), the student's answers should be emitted with an appropriate politeness. Bad manners are the quickest route to the nearest exit. No school director knowingly admits a bad apple into his bushel.

Ask questions if you will but never give the director the idea that *you* are interviewing *him*. That is, unless you wish to negate the purpose of your application which is, ostensibly, to gain admittance.

As well as talent, most school directors are impressed by a student's sense of urgency in wanting to gain admittance. Does the student fervently wish to be part and parcel of the school fabric or is his present effort, namely being interviewed, an optional one?

Any school is only an arrow, never the target. But that arrow, if aimed with immaculate precision, can take its archer closer to the next and higher rung of the ladder.

On not rehearsing with mirrors

I never rehearse in front of a mirror. If I were to, the moment I would see myself, I would pass judgment, thinking, that's good or that's not good. Either way, the response would interfere with my involvement, thus cutting it. The mirror acts as a magnet, drawing one's mind away from the dramatic issue at hand. Also, as one looks at oneself in the mirror, the head is not in the position it would be if one weren't looking, another good reason for avoiding one's moving reflection.

Ballet dancers, in particular, are guilty of being glued to the mirror, especially in class. After a while, balance and series of turns *sur place* become dependent on seeing the mirrored image. Since you can't take a mirror on stage with you, it's better to gain early independence from it.

On coaching a lady in walking seductively

When you walk away half hiding your face behind a Spanish fan, it's more than an invitation (which can be refused). It's a provocation (which cannot).

On antagonizing your director

Don't.

This single cautionary word reminds me of the time when I was appearing in the remote African country of Chad. The tourist brochure had a heading WHAT TO DO WHEN SICK. Under the headline it said, "Don't. The nearest hospital is in another country."

So for the tourist in Chad regarding sickness and for the actor in rehearsal resisting his director, an equally applicable warning. *Don't.*

On not reviewing the choreography at the last moment

If one is a member of a ballet company and the choreographer chooses to change anything from a passage to a detail, that is his prerogative though the dancer's dilemma. Ideally, though, choreography should be so digested that the movement becomes automatic, that the muscles, themselves, have memory. Justice cannot be done to choreography if the interpreter is fighting to remember what comes next. It is a fearful situation to be in as anyone who has been thrown on in a ballet company well knows. To be forgetful in a solo is nothing compared to an analogous situation in an ensemble. To make a mistake in a chorus is like waving a neon light during a blackout. Who can miss it?

The first time I was in Bulgaria was in 1965 when my then wife Marilyn Mather was a competitor in the Varna ballet competition (other contestants being Natalia Makarova and Natalia Bessmertnova). The great and noble prima ballerina Alicia Alonso offered to coach Marilyn in the *Nutcracker* solo which she was to perform in the open air theatre within a few evenings.

The night of the performance/competition was upon us and in front of a huge public and a jury including the Soviet Union's prima ballerina Galina Ulanova, Marilyn recalled neither my choreography nor Alonso's. Standing in the wings I was utterly helpless to come to her rescue. It was like a car bearing down on a child and not being able to yell, "Get out of the way!"

But with a wonderful sense of aplomb, Marilyn filled in the missing gap of choreography with the most spectacular step in the female vocabulary, the *fouetté*. She continued non-stop to do the spinning movement, a step that has struck terror in the hearts of the world's most notable dancers, until a new phrase of music reminded her of where she should be next. All the while, though, while she was in search of that next step, the audience was applauding her virtuosity.

Later in the evening Marilyn danced, with exquisite finesse, excerpts from my ballet *Madame Butterfly*. After it was all over, while Marilyn removed her make-up in her dressing room, I sat down on a bench feeling somewhat faint. Swirling about me were the multi-lingual conversations of the worldwide participants. My dizziness departed but not my reaction to the situation which caused it.

Choreography must be so assimilated that it seems to happen rather than be performed. Last minute changes interfere with automatic execution, with the instant memory of the muscles.

Automatic technique

One should have technique in excess, insurance technique, so that when circumstances reduce it, there is still enough left to suffice. A bad stage, missed lighting cues, a noisy audience, any of these can be very distracting and unless one carries around insurance technique, the performance will be visibly reduced.

Truly fine technique is automatic. If one has to think about how to do it, or can I do it?, that question hovers over the performance as a raincloud about to burst.

The verbal actor, having only to talk, does not court danger as does the dancing actor or total mime artist. To express elation balancing on one leg and on *demi-pointe* with the other leg raised towards the rafters, as in ballet, who would argue that this is not more difficult than expressing the same emotion curled up comfortably on a living room sofa as in a straight play?

It is clear that the physical artist requires a muscular technique that never answers back, that is unconsciously obedient. Without such automatic technique, every step on stage is to walk a pirate's plank.

On remaining positive if enveloped by the negative

Too often the student or even the performer finds himself within an indifferent atmosphere. The students around him are coasting rather than moving at full speed, the audience is resistant or the other members of the ensemble are caught up in an unenviable state of lethargy. It is in this artistic quagmire that one must pull out of the quicksand, quickly.

Never take on the neutral or grey tones of the environment. It is very easy, regrettably, to do so. Superimpose the high level of one's best intentions rather than succumb to the arid atmosphere of mediocrity.

On making-up

If life for most people is a restrictive bedsitter, for the actor it can be a palatial residence. A majority of people live in one room with only one visible visage for life. The actor, on the other hand, assumes many faces besides the one with which he was born. The man with a thousand faces lives upstairs as well as downstairs, in the attics of the past, in the basement of our beginnings and the living room of our present.

In making-up, we create the physical characteristics of the person about to be portrayed. This is the overt reason for the change about to take place. There are covert reasons, as well.

Everyone has limitations, physically, intellectually and emotionally. Often the transformation into someone more beautiful fulfils the actor in a compensatory way, while painting a nasty face, conversely, provides a reverse satisfaction. For undeniable ugliness exerts a mesmeric hold and the actor, during those moments, knows a fearful power. Neither great beauty nor grotesquerie can be ignored. The actor who traverses both poles knows the impact of acting in *extremis*. The meridian, afterwards, seems unchallenging by comparison.

The theatre gives licence to otherwise bottled emotions; it is a safety valve for the sealed off currents of both practitioner and public. Beyond the release acting affords actors, it is also the passport into the bewitched geography of denied experience. Watch as the face in the dressing room mirror turns myth-like in its metamorphosis.

On wanting to go on stage

There are many reasons why young people enter the world of theatre. Some of the reasons stem from neurosis. The person in question turns a disturbing force, usually from early childhood, into an alarm system that clangs incessantly for attention. "I will substitute the love of many for the absence of one." Sometimes this early deprivation enables the sufferer to commandeer a career.

But it isn't only a craving for affection or a low self-esteem that propels a person into overlapping pools of many coloured gels. There are many people who enter the theatre simply because they believe they have a talent and wish to express it through the vehicles of the world's finest playwrights, composers and choreographers. Or perhaps they wish to be their own creators.

To exhibit oneself, to counterbalance the early deprivation of parental love by demanding the later attention of the public's, to sing, dance or play an instrument for the sheer joy of it, to express oneself, to escape the separateness of our common isolation, to share one's reverence for life by revealing it—the motives for wanting to go on stage are as varied as the actors through the ages who have done so.

On space

Space is your invisible but ever present partner. Why move like Prometheus chained to his rock or Petrouchka confined to his cell when the space around us begs to be taken over and conquered? Move spaciously through space. Manipulate it, cut through it, sweep across it, gather it in all embracing arms, cut patterns through it with scissor sharp legs and melting arms, be master of the air. The audience will identify with your conquest for they, like the rest of earthbound humanity, yearn to sail, unhampered.

On never using a real knife in an improvisation

Using a lethal weapon in a rehearsed and set production is dangerous enough. Using one in an improvisation is an open invitation to a nasty accident. It takes only one second of a miscalculated move from the person with the knife or the person facing it, to plunge a scene from improvised theatre to the operating theatre.

The sheer stupidity of using a real knife as a prop is beyond my comprehension. There are enough uninvited accidents during a performance without giving fate the (blood) red carpet treatment.

On the difficulty of repeating an improvisation

Ignorance is sometimes bliss and doing an exercise hitherto unknown often permits us a confidence which disappears when a little bit of knowledge is present. A good improvisation in class depends on our secret knowledge and absence of restraint. To repeat a good improvisation a few days later is often a severe let-down. The spontaneity present the first time is now absent with no substitute security such as memorized text or choreography. The actor, remembering how well he did in his earlier improvisation, now feels derailed, his train having seemingly gone off the track.

How does one avoid the accident? Firstly, don't try to imitate or repeat the previous result. The content of the improvisation remains the same, of course, so re-create its form. With the theme as the stable tracks, arrive at the same destination by another route.

Begin the improvisation as if you had never done it before. Let the scene lead you, so to speak, through new terrain. When the train pulls into the station it will be, for the audience, a land of first visit.

Avoiding clichés

Unless those overexposed clichés of illusionary mime are dramatically justified, avoid using them. Walking on place and feeling the confines of imaginary walls prove to the audience only that the performer has taken some three lessons with someone who studied with someone who studied in Paris.

The scales of the pianist and the pliés of the dancer are executed in the privacy of a studio. Why should the mime do his lesson number one, two or three in front of the paying public? The audience has the right to expect that the performer has, indeed, been to school.

Wherever I travel, the wares of the local mimes are paraded before me. Whether in Madagascar or Egypt I know what I will see before they even begin. One of these days someone will surprise me and express in mime the world at large *beyond* those mandatory and invisible walls!

Creating a repertoire

The young mime artist in search of a repertoire must look into himself for an idea with which to build an item. Hopefully, if he has access to the creative spark, he will let that idea materialize, either bit by bit, or receive it fully formulated.

Actually, we are servants to the master that is creativity. If the master feeds us piecemeal, we must accept the crumbs (fragments of an idea). If the master offers us a full course meal, we should sit down at his table (the idea fully emerged).

Creative ideas make their presence felt in the most unusual places and irregular hours. Be grateful for the message and take it down whenever and wherever, be it in a bathtub, plane, kitchen sink, cinema or bed.

Keep your scenario simple and uncluttered. Don't try and cram in the rise and fall of the Roman Empire within three minutes. Always ask yourself if the idea can be conveyed without words in visual terms.

Once the idea has proven its validity by knocking again and again at the door of the brain, get a pen and paper and start writing everything down. With each section of the scenario, also write down the sound or music you think would be appropriate as the accompaniment for the action.

Finally, add the length of time you consider appropriate for that particular section of the scenario. As an example, here is an approximate scenario of an item brilliantly performed by a former Mime Centre student, Danitra Easton. It was her own creation, entitled *Hurt*.

SCENARIO	SOUND/ MUSIC	TIME
1. Young girl recoils in pain trying to avoid the wounding words of her mother.	Mother's voice in non-stop vicious, verbal attack	2 minutes
2. Momentarily escaping, the girl recoils from the barrage of her mother's hate.	Silence	¼ minute
3. Crying with her body, the girl spirals and twists away from the imprisoning walls of her environment. As the music ends, the girl determines a fairer future.	Jazz music	2½ minutes
		TOTAL: 4¾ minutes

The idea has now arrived, the scenario written down, the sound or music (or silence) selected with its length determined by what is happening dramatically. If you are technically inclined, you can make the tape without help. If not, assistance is needed. It is not a wise idea at this point to have a recording studio make the tape, for if the idea doesn't work out well in rehearsal, the considerable expense of a studio will have been avoided.

It is now time to choreograph. Listening to the music or sound again and again, physicalize the inner image phrase by phrase until gradually the outer shape is found. Being so close to one's own concept, it is often difficult to detach oneself for a more objective view. One's candid friends can be very helpful at this stage of creation.

Having seen a rehearsal, did they understand the narrative and the point of view or were they confused and if so, why? Where is greater clarity needed? Is there curvature of the thematic spine?

With refinements and adjustments being made, the item must be so rehearsed that there is no fighting for sequence of steps. Absolutely embedded into the memory, the steps must occur as automatically as breathing.

The young mime artist should avoid improvising on stage. If one night he happens not to be in the mood, the performance falls apart at the seams. Doing set choreography, a certain level is assured, in the mood or not in the mood.

The physical groundwork secured, immersion into the character is now possible. Generally speaking, a character evolves through cumulative rehearsals and performances. Rarely does one find it fully developed at a first rehearsal. Even intuitive performers, who have a solid grasp from the very beginning, find deeper nuances as they live with a role.

There is a certain point at which an item is ready to be performed. To rehearse it beyond a certain point in the studio is to keep the baby too long in the pram. The unknown aspects of audience reaction, greater space, bright lights and magnified sound will now give another dimension to the newly created item.

The premiére is, in a sense, a kind of baptism. Just as a child's personality is shaped by its growing experiences, so is a new item modulated by what happens to it in the course of contact with a succession of audiences.

Each completed item leaves the creator free to dwell on his next idea so that gradually a repertoire comes into being, a repertoire constructed with an eye to contrast, tempo and overall unity of style.

On structuring a solo performance

A good performance must begin auspiciously and end conclusively. The audience's attention must be arrested from the outset and then held until the very end. The very first minute is crucial in that you establish your right, or forfeit it, in those opening moments.

During the introductory item, the audience is assessing the performer, that is, evaluating him physically and temperamentally. Because of this scrutiny, the performer, as the gold prospector, must at once stake his claim.

In the first item proper, great intellectual demands should not be made, thus permitting the audience time to warm up and tune in. In a programme of many items, there should be a contrast of comic, dramatic and poetic repertoire. After a particularly dramatic sequence, for example, a lighter number should follow, one that is less draining emotionally. There is a saturation point in audience absorption which should not be pushed to overflow.

The last ten minutes or so of each of the programme's sections (Act 1 and Act 2) must be ascendingly climactic. Of the four very strongest items in the repertoire, two must close Act 1 with the other two closing Act 2.

In my own solo performance, to cite a case, *The Father Who Searched For His Long Lost Son* then *The Lovers* conclude Act 1 with *The Village Idiot* and *Death Of A Scarecrow* ending Act 2. In my double bill with Marita Phillips, *Hearts and Flowers*, that bittersweet elegy of shattered love, brings the evening to a close.

In my present duo mime performance with Kazimir Kolesnik, *The Resurrection* brings the evening to a harrowing close. Instead of Christ and a Roman soldier, we see Christ and the Gestapo, the Nazi and the Nazarene. To the sublime music of Wagner's *Leibestod* juxtaposed with the voices of German storm troopers and Adolf Hitler, the danger of resurrecting political evil is sledgehammered home to the audience.

The placing of repertoire items can make or break a performance. It is no different with a good meal. A dessert before a salad can ruin both.

Selecting a title

If using a placard, banner, scroll or any other material upon which the letters are printed, choose a title which gives an instantaneous insight into the number about to be viewed. However the title is announced, be it visually or aurally (the voice on tape), that title is the frame in which the picture will be set. That title must set the stage as clearly as a designer's sets do for a play.

If the title confuses or misleads, the audience will be distracted in their efforts to re-locate themselves. Once distracted, the public return only sporadically. They now have other things on their mind, namely the more pressing problems of rental increases, dental appointments, domestic quarrels and belligerent offspring.

There is no such thing as an unimportant detail. A fine performance is a huge mosaic of a thousand details, individually unnoticed but collectively the sum total of excellence.

And we must never forget that the eye and ear are always drawn to the isolated error. In the case of the critics, they are positively in search of it. A prima donna can sing 999 perfect notes but the single sour one will take over half the critics' next day review.

Making a statement

Within the domain of dance it is permissible to choreograph attractive movement for its own sake. In mime, on the other hand, a statement should be made and a point of view put forward. Dance can and often does make a statement, but it doesn't have to. On the reverse side of the coin, the mime *must* declare.

Select a subject about which you feel strongly. Does the finished product pose a pertinent question? Have you, the creative artist, made your comment? If the answer is yes to either question, you are moving in the right direction.

Time limit

Many years ago in New York I saw at the old Roxy Theatre that most exciting performer Josephine Baker, she of the banana necklace and not much else in her earlier Folies-Bergère heyday. With her extravagantly feathered headdress framing her face like a peacock, she sang a song, one of the lyrics being, "I could go on all night like this." *She* could but don't you!

First of all Miss Baker was referring to another area of human activity. Secondly, western audiences are not prepared to watch an all night spectacle. Make your point and finish. Don't go on for fifteen minutes when the statement merits no more than five. Self edit mercilessly. Many a fine item has been ruined by not knowing when the number is over.

So be sure to know when to call it a day, let alone a night. After all, there was only one Josephine Baker.

Tapes

When having tapes made for a performance, always clearly specify either *full track mono* or *two track stereo*. Any other system invites the possibility of unexpected sounds or the reverse, the loss of anticipated sound.

With regard to silences on tapes; some people prefer using coloured leader since blank tape sometimes picks up sounds after a while. A word of warning, though, if using leader on a performance tape. Check that the tape recorder doesn't contain a device that automatically stops the tape recorder when coming to the leader. If such a tape recorder is the only one available, a switch can be turned off which will prevent this happening.

It is risky to travel with only one set of tapes. Heaven forbid, they could be erased when passing through ultra-sophisticated machinery at terrorist-conscious airports. Or a valise could go astray. I carry one set of tapes in a large piece of luggage containing my other performance equipment with a cassette in my hand luggage. Better safe than extremely sorry!

Testing costumes and props

In a large scale presentation the first night is always preceded by a dress rehearsal, the purpose of which is to iron out any creases and wrinkles of the production. In a solo mime performance there isn't always this opportunity. Though what I'm about to write seems axiomatic, never wear a costume or use a prop in front of an audience without having worked with them full out beforehand in the semi-privacy of a studio.

Hats fall easily off the head, stitches come undone, props come apart, skirts are stepped on, trousers split in the crotch, naming only a few accidents that seem funnier on paper than they do when happening on stage.

Check, double check then triple check. When I used to do an item called *Balloon From A Forgotten Summer*, I always had a spare balloon (already inflated and secured with thread so that the air couldn't escape) waiting for me in the wings just in case the balloon on stage inopportunely burst.

Sometimes nervousness makes one think an all important prop has not been left in its proper place when, in actual fact, it has. This is another reason for a triple check. To perform at peak form one must have the security of knowing that everything is where it belongs.

Body make-up should be tested as well for if working with a partner, there is the strong likelihood that the body make-up may rub off all over his or her costume. Hot lights, exertion and perspiration have a way of encouraging body make-up to leave its imprint.

The time for an accident to happen is in a rehearsal, whether public or private. If the mishap occurs then, there is little chance it will happen in front of a thousand prying eyes.

Auditioning

Beware the four letter word NEXT.

If you are asked your name or the name of the selection about to be performed, speak up, speak clearly and with charm.

Establish from the first moment your right to try out for that part. Don't waste a single second in self-indulgent or discursive movement or text. Your preparation has been done in the wings or if in a room, before you entered; you have begun before you begin.

Set yourself off as a rocket. From the first moment you are either heard or seen, be already in orbit.

On making a check list

Until 1968 I never had a check list to which I referred before performances. What I needed to bring with me to the theatre was kept in my head. The situation forever changed when, arriving at the Aldeburgh Festival in 1968, I discovered to my dismay that I had left my wig (at that time blue) in London. Five hours away by train there was no possibility of getting hold of it.

That evening Benjamin Britten and Peter Pears were to be in the audience and I was denuded of the crowning item of my transformation. Worse still, my own curly hair had just been cut so there was little I could do with it. Depressed, I asked myself if my impact was dependent on a wig or artistic qualities. The question correctly answered, the depression lifted.

When the smiling blue eyes of Peter Pears and the warmth of Benjamin Britten's smile greeted me in my dressing room, I felt emotionally equipped to be at my strongest. Nevertheless, I never again went anywhere in the world without a packing list which consists of the following divisions:

PERFORMANCE
Costumes, props, make-up, tapes, etc.

OFFICE
Teaching material, Diners Club card, passport, plane tickets, clock, foreign change, stationery, publicity photographs, suitcase keys, current business correspondence, birthday cards to be sent to friends while on tour etc.

FOOD
Vitamin supply (*not the synthetic variety from the chemist shop*), *muesli with ground nuts, bran, powdered soya milk* (*healthier and more humane than cows' milk*), *honey etc.*

TOILET ARTICLES
All necessary personal articles as well as a portable clothes dryer, soap flakes etc.

CLOTHES
All necessary clothing for the trip, ascertaining what season one will be entering in that country and bringing along appropriate things to wear.

Years ago I dreamt on several occasions that I had arrived at a theatre without my dance belt. That nocturnal preoccupation has long since been retired thanks to a check list which never lets me down.

On the importance of programmes

The programme is the audience's preparation for the performance they are about to witness. It is their framework of understanding, so to speak. The artist in question may be superb, but if the audience know nothing about his background, they will not derive the same degree of satisfaction as they would otherwise.

The act of love implies preliminaries; its counterpart, sexual seizure, is stripped of introduction. A well appreciated performance, as the act of love, demands build-up. The programme is part of that psychological preparation.

I became convinced of the programme necessity after similar incidents in Australia and Russia. Touring Queensland in Australia, my performance one evening was no better or worse than on preceding nights, but the applause was noticeably diminished. Investigating the matter I discovered that the management had run out of programmes, leaving this particular audience in the dark as to who or what I was. To coin a familiar phrase, they didn't know me from Adam. Until new programmes were sent from Canberra, the response from the audiences remained muted. When the replacement programmes finally arrived, the audience reaction rose to the previous level of enthusiasm.

Six months later I was touring Russia, giving a performance in Tartu, Estonia, one of the 15 Soviet republics. After the first act the response was curiously subdued for a Russian public. Finding out during the interval that the programme supply had been exhausted, I had my interpreter read to the audience before the second half began, the one programme I carried with me.

At the conclusion of the evening there were 10 curtain calls, a very generous response which compensated for the earlier coolness. (Throughout Russia the average number of curtain calls I received at the end of the performance was 14, with 25 and 27 calls respectively on the opening and closing nights in Leningrad.)

The second half of my Tartu performance was not superior to the first half, the difference being, of course, the reading of the programme material. The audience knew where I came from, what I had done and why and how my work differed from other mimes. I was a guest, not an intruder.

I needed no further proof as to the necessity of programmes. There are certain impresarios who justify the absence of programmes by saying that if you're good, the audience will soon know about it. This is a fallacious way of thinking.

As the actor must prepare, so, absolutely, must the audience. For the actor acting as his own impresario, remember that about a third of an audience buy programmes so bear that in mind when ordering from the printers. Also remember that as printers are notoriously slow and generally deliver past the promised date, submit the programme copy well in advance of the performance dates.

On my own training

The artist's creation begins with training, a training that never ends, once initiated. My own preparation, at the outset of my artist's pilgrimage, included tutelage at the feet of many of the world's most respected dancers. They hailed from the Maryinsky Theatre in St. Petersburg, later the Kirov in Leningrad, from the Bolshoi in Moscow, from the Diaghilev Ballet and from the Anna Pavlova Company; supreme exponents of the Russian Imperial Ballet as Anatole Oboukhov, Pierre Vladimirov, Elizaveta Anderson-Ivantzova, Nathalie Branitza, Felia Doubrovska, Bronislava Nijinska, Alexandra Danilova, Aubrey Hitchins, Muriel Stuart, Igor Schwezoff, George Goncharov, Lubov Egorova, Lydia Kyasht and Olga Preobrajenska. These matchless torchbearers of that gilded age were my teachers.

When I think that Preobrajenska, at the age of 22, worked personally with Tchaikowsky in the world première of *Nutcracker* in 1892, then taught me sixty years later when I was 22, the historical link is concertinaed into startling immediacy.

I studied modern dance as early as 1949/50 at the New Dance Group in New York City long before it was mandatory for the classical and contemporary to merge. It was clear to me, even then, that the body instrument had to speak more than one language to be fully understood.

I was less happy studying jazz as for me it felt like shallow window display. Only when I used jazz movement dramatically in my own choreography could I come to honest terms with it.

In ballet, even in class, there was an atmosphere of aspiration, a soaring upwards towards some untouchable ideal. In modern dance there was a gravitation, an earth level practicality, manifesting itself in a more concave concept of movement. America's finest male modern dancer, José Limon, was among my teachers in that genre.

I had worked with Sweden's most celebrated director, Ingmar Bergman, before I had received formal schooling as an actor. This was in Strindberg's *The Bridal Crown* at the Malmö Stadsteater in 1952. Some years later I benefited from the teaching of Raikin Ben-Ari in Hollywood. For twelve years he had worked at the Moscow Habimah Theatre with Vachtangov, Stanislavski's most trusted colleague. In Ben-Ari's Hollywood drama studio, guest teachers included Shelley Winters and Nicholas Ray, director of the now cult star James Dean.

When France's most eminent actor and mime, Jean-Louis Barrault, presented me at his Théâtre Récamier in Paris, that, in itself, was another lesson, though not of the formal variety. For the enthusiasm of this no longer chronologically young actor was a reminder that extended youth begins in the mind. The body, as obedient servant, takes dutiful orders from its master.

Regarding my mime training, I studied with no one, but rather, evolved over many years my own approach. I could not accept the optical trickery and visual ventriloquism that I saw around me, as true mime. At the very base of my mime technique are, of course, the combined arts of the actor and dancer.

My training continued as I went on stage in such ballet and theatre companies as Ballet der Lage Landen (Ballet of the Lowlands) in Holland, the Malmö Stadsteater and Stora Teatern in Sweden, the Scandinavian Ballet in the Canary Islands, Mona Inglesby's International Ballet in Britain, the Royal Winnipeg Ballet in Canada, the Israel National Opera in Tel-Aviv and the Israeli Ballet (my own company) throughout Israel. More recently there have been the Rio de Janeiro Ballet in Brazil and the Dublin City Ballet in Ireland.

Additionally there had been much television participation throughout the world from expected countries like the United States and England to such unexpected countries as Tunisia, Bangladesh and Indonesia, to single out only a few.

My actor's instrument had been well stretched in theatre productions from Las Vegas to Gothenburg where I acted Puck, in Swedish, in Benjamin Britten's opera, *A Midsummer Night's Dream.*

All the previous learning of my life was released through the vehicle of my solo performance with which I subsequently toured every continent (that is, except Antarctica where I have yet to perform for the tuxedoed penguins, black and white first nighters in their blindingly light theatre of ice).

Until 1975 I always practiced in a class as is the usual habit of dancers everywhere. Few dancers practice on their own as do musicians and singers. Besides the space required, dance upkeep necessitates a militaristic rhythm of enforcement. Few people can sustain this kind of self-inflicted punishment for long.

I never even entertained the idea that my dance technique, which is the physical foundation of my work as a mime, could remain intact without the supervision of the teacher/general. Then during one very busy week in 1975 I decided to save time by practicing in the little studio within my flat, instead of travelling to central London then wasting even more time by pleasant but irrelevant chitchat in the dressing room.

As I began my exercises alone I didn't think I would last the hour let alone the week. With a variety of inspiring music on a tape recorder, I survived not only the hour but also the week and the ensuing years.

People have repeatedly told me that I seem technically stronger now than formerly, observations which make short shrift of the constant reminder that we are heading downhill as we approach 30! Working alone, I challenge myself with the exercises my body and manner of movement require. The number of exercises I execute in one hour is the equivalent of a much longer time span since there is no stopping for explanation or demonstration as in group classes.

Also, in explanation of my augmented strength, is the fact that my self-image as an artist is not dented by the battering of ballet company managements as is the lot of even Royal Ballet principals. Conversely, my belief (without which technique rapidly disintegrates) is regularly nurtured by new audiences.

In my daily workout (with usually the week-end off when I concentrate on correspondence and other writing) I approach the exercises in a performance frame of mind. If I think of it as just another workout, my motivation might weaken. Spotlights are turned on, deluding me into thinking that a performance is in progress!

Daily training is a battle in which, at best, there is only a truce. Victory is only momentary since the war begins all over the following morning.

How do I feel, still practicing after 38 years? Tom Stoppard, the playwright, said it very well. "When I started I wrote a play because I wished to be a playwright. Now I write plays because I am a playwright. It's not quite the same thing."

Similarly, I subject myself to my regime, not because I want to any more but because I have to. At the base of my mime technique is the self-exposure of the actor and the self-punishment of the dancer. The marriage, not without its arguments, is for life.

On nutrition

If the body is the instrument of the dancer and mime, and to a lesser extent, the actor, it should be axiomatic that such a body demands very special attention. It is, therefore, very surprising how many would-be artists in these fields not only ignore but prematurely destroy their instruments in a way they would never think of doing to a violin or piano.

The poison one self administers in the way of junk food can be gotten away with in the late teens and early twenties for the mirror on the wall records only the remnants of acne and a blemish or two. If the mirror, however, could reflect the lining of the lungs or arteries, the viewer might well be aghast. The next time you are in a supermarket look at the trolley of the woman in front of you. Denatured foods filled with synthetic colourings, emulsifiers, additives, preservatives, softeners, bleaches, artificial flavours, hydrogenated fats and sundry other random chemicals, these are the ingredients that line, year in and year out, the stomachs of the unaware consumer. No wonder while the manufacturers fill their coffers, we fill our coffins!

A steady dosage of carcinogenic cigarettes, white bread and white sugar, confectionery palming itself off as quick snacks washed down with beer and sister alcoholic drinks, this kind of quickly masticated rot soon takes its toll. With imitation fuel, one's endurance and stamina quickly go the way of all flesh.

If the actor wants his body to be his friend rather than his enemy, if he wants to have a career in the years of his carefully nurtured experience, then he must make wise eating as much a part of his regime as his exercises.

The question of balanced diet is for the purpose of functioning well and for a very long time to come. There are any number of people who will counter sage advice on eating with the statement that they'd rather enjoy their poisons now and keel over whenever that may happen. What the eat, drink and be merry contingent don't take into account is the strong possibility that they may not keel over, but instead live on indefinitely once stricken, incapacitated. Isn't it better, as it were, to eat your vegetables than to end up as one? And while on the subject of vegetables, let us briefly touch upon that emotive subject of vegetarianism.

Training is total; it isn't only how you exercise but also what you eat, those you love, what you read, who you help, the compass of one's compassion. Is one's sustenance derived from the killing of God's other sentient creatures, animals who cannot fend for themselves with petitions and committees? Does one enforce one's place in the sun by poisoning the fish and by infecting the planet with insecticides, pesticides and other chemicals which serve only to extend the shelf life of the product while shortening the life of the consumer?

Regarding vegetarianism and the actor's instrument, it is an established fact that an excess of animal protein in the body contributes towards the degenerative diseases so rife in western man. Many people eat meat three times a day, bacon for breakfast, ham sandwiches for lunch and steak for dinner. The human frame, not designed for such absorption, rebels in premature diseases—heart trouble, high blood pressure and cancer among others. Arthritis and rheumatism take their toll in the joints and fingers of people who contaminated their digestive organs with a surfeit of meat throughout a lifetime.

So we have the danger of excess animal protein and, to boot, profit-making antibiotics, fed to the hapless animals in order to fatten them with less food.

And now we arrive at the most important reason for vegetarianism, the sacredness of the lives of our so-called lesser brethren. Animals have as much right to a good life and peaceful death as we humans.

How man relates to animals is a measure of his spiritual development. In the western world, vegetarianism was advocated by Greek philosophers such as Pythagoras, Plato, Socrates, Ovid and Plutarch. In more recent years, other respected names have been added to the list—the greatest universal genius of all time, Leonardo da Vinci as well as Milton, Tolstoy, Sir Isaac Newton, George Bernard Shaw, Mahatma Gandhi and many, many more.

For health reasons alone, there is sufficient justification for becoming vegetarian. For humanitarian considerations alone, there is ample justification. With both reasons combined, there is no murky fork in the road, but a clear avenue of light for the actor who takes seriously his spirit and body, the single instrument of unobstructed transmission.

ON STAGE

On being neither too close nor too far away

When performing a solo, don't remain at the very back of the stage nor at the extreme front. Hiding oneself at the back robs the scene of its immediacy and urgency. Staying too close to the front robs the scene of its frame and perspective. Move about to be sure, but don't get stuck at either extremity.

Playing two characters in one item

Never arbitrarily finish one characterization then casually walk into another. The suture from one character to another must be swift and invisible. The in-between must not be a glass window partition for the audience to view the operation. Never dismember a scene without the anaesthetic of instant transition.

Among the many solos I created for the late and grievously missed Nathaniel were *Newsreel: 1920–1929* and *The Drag Queen*. In each of these items he portrayed some half dozen characters, switching from one to the other with the speed and dexterity of a magician.

To watch him playing so many people, jumping from a few seconds of one to a quarter minute of another, with absolutely no visible transition, was an object lesson in virtuosity. I can only agree with Kazimir Kolesnik when he recalls Nathaniel as a comic artist on a level no less than that of Laurel and Hardy and Buster Keaton.

Leaving a stage empty

For a solo performer to leave the stage empty while he goes off to change costume is the equivalent of requesting the audience to go home. Many do, of course, or go out for refreshments and don't return. On a mountainous road, a good driver will not release his hands from the wheel. Neither will a good performer release his audience for one moment. The mind wanders very easily. Permitting the public to mentally twiddle their thumbs is to encourage the return of the audience's pressures and problems which they have momentarily discarded in order to be with you, the actor.

Grunting and gasping audibly

Why announce to those out front the fact that you're working hard? It is terribly distracting to watch interesting body movement accompanied by the occasional gasp. Effort isn't interesting. Result is.

The gymnast flies, the skater skims, the dancer floats, the mime emotes—all creatures of unremitting non-stop effort. The inadvertent and sharp exhalation of air, a gasp, succeeds in destroying for the viewer the quality of ease which he has a right to expect. It can estrange his sympathies if he feels the performer is straining to please.

Of all performers, dancers and mimes must beware the pitfalls of audible breathing at best, panting at worst.

Beginning and ending a performance

Don't keep an audience waiting more than seven or eight minutes past the announced starting time. I, personally, don't like to begin exactly on time in order to allow latecomers leeway in which to arrange themselves, thereby not distracting other members of the audience and myself.

To begin too late, however, is to overpass the public's point of anticipation. The resultant restlessness that sets in is another obstacle for the on stage artist.

When the lights fade to black at the end of an item or at the end of the performance, sustain the final pose for some five seconds for despite the blackout the eye perceives, immediately after bright light, a moving figure. Too often we see otherwise experienced actors exiting too soon from a fade to black.

When entering the wings, keep moving until completely out of the audience's sight line. How often have we, sitting at the extreme right or left of an auditorium, seen an exiting dancer flop out of a poised *arabesque* into a disgruntled waddle into the wings?

Relationships within an item

A playwright can delve deeply into the complex relationship between a sister-in-law and her second cousin removed. In the more visual world of movement, this isn't possible unless one wants recourse to copious programme notes.

What is clear in the mind of the creator is often a very long distance from the comprehension of the spectator. To be simple and safe, stay away from the adopted brother-in-law's niece. There are many other relationships under the sun which lend themselves more easily to the choreographer's narrative.

Audience expectation

Few people wanted to buy a ticket to hear Dame Nellie Melba sing *Home Sweet Home*, not when her formidable reputation had been built on the fireworks of Italian grand opera. Not too long ago, that most amazing of all male dancers, Mikhail Baryshnikov, disappointed a Chicago audience when for his sole appearance he did a *pas de deux* choreographed with flexed feet, distorted hips and arch expression. This type of pert-precious movement, so popular with American avant-garde choreographers, proves only that the dancer in question is attempting to stretch himself.

In every performance there will be members of the public who are seeing an artist for the very first time and also for the last. Experiments should not be performed in public, certainly not by stars of stellar magnitude. The ideal balance, when performing a new role, is to include on the same programme a tour de force item which has earned the artist his reputation.

Audience assimilation

Be careful not to crowd ideas one on top of the other. The audience needs time to digest and assimilate both images and concepts. Allow sufficient time for visual imprint and dramatic registration. This subtle knowledge arrives only after much trial and error. In the hands of the experienced it emerges as instinct.

Working with marionettes and puppets

In the west we tend to think of puppet shows as children's entertainment. In many parts of the world, marionette theatre is taken quite seriously by the adult population. In Indonesia, for example, the shadow puppets form a large proportion of that country's entertainment. The *wayang golek* is a three dimensional puppet; the *wayang kulit* or shadow puppet, is two dimensional and is worked from behind a screen lit by a special light.

When I was performing in the Indonesian islands of Java and Sumatra, my red, white and black make-up reminded some members of the audience of their own indigenous puppets, the puppets' faces being painted the same colours as mine. "Wayang golek, wayang golek," some of them called out to me.

I was as real to them as the puppets or, perhaps, the puppets were as real to them as me. And in that equation lies the secret of working with puppet theatre. The puppeteer must believe in the humanity of his inanimate objects. They must not be props merely to be jerked by strings or stretched by fingers.

They must be as human as flesh and blood partners. Two actors must take over the stage, not one cleverly manipulating a mechanism.

In my item *The Village Idiot* I believe implicitly in the actuality of the ragdoll. On no other prop have I ever shed so many tears. When, after the performance is over, I pack my suitcase, the clown hat, telephone, Thai nails, tragedy mask and other props are carefully placed so as to avoid crushing. But the ragdoll is put away with a word or two (silently or otherwise) of fond farewell, as one does with a beloved dog when having to leave it alone for some hours.

For a scene to come alive with a doll, marionette or puppet, the actor must not make believe. He has to, he must only, *believe*.

On adjusting the performance to the theatre's size

One must always work with strength but the degree of strength must depend on the distance between the front of the stage and the last row of the theatre. To work with an excess of power in an intimate theatre is to disturb the balance between the performer and the public. To call upon a minimum of energy in a huge theatre is never to arrive in the minds of the cheapest ticket holders.

How can one arrive at this indefinable degree, the student may well ask? Instinct is the answer, the instinct which is the product of cumulative experience. In the enormous Alhambra Theatre (now demolished) in Cape Town, South Africa, I enlarged. In the theatre in Brazilia, the capital of Brazil, the orchestra pit was not only very large, thus acutely separating me from the first row, but the auditorium seats were set at a sunken level. This peculiar architectural lay-out distanced me from the audience so I had to employ a more embracing force.

The examples just cited point out the necessity of adjusting the level of one's performance, of never only repeating the performance of the previous theatre. Always keep in mind the importance of adjusting the energy level, the angle and the scope of one's audience embrace.

False endings

There are certain moments in some items that lead the audience to believe that the piece has concluded when, in actual fact, it hasn't. What the audience thinks is a conclusion could be the performer's absolute stillness of movement accompanied by a complete fading of the sound to silence.

This sense of false finale must be avoided so as not to mislead the viewer. If, on stage, there is a physical immobility and/or a diminishing of the lights, the mental motor of the performer must be kept running so the audience doesn't sense a complete withdrawal. The running of the mental motor is sensed by the public who are then aware of the performance's continuity.

To prevent the viewer from misconstruing my intentions, I keep at least one part of my body operative, however minuscule and subtle the movement. This prevents premature applause which, if it takes place, cuts the meticulously cultivated mood. On the occasions when the audience insists on applauding anyway, I ignore it as if it never happened. Quickly the public realize the error of their enthusiasm. They stop. I continue. When the item actually does end, the audience then applaud with the security that they are now on cue.

On what to do when the lips dry during a performance

Wait until your back is to the audience and then lick them quickly. To do this in front of the audience is to announce the fact of either discomfort or nervousness.

Stage mishaps

Until now I've managed to keep to a minimum the number of accidents that have befallen me during performances. This is, perhaps, because I at least double and sometimes triple check every detail before starting time. I never trust to luck and certainly not to strange stage crews.

Costumes must be checked to be sure a seam isn't coming undone. Props must be checked to be certain that they're in good working order. The floor, if there is no floor cloth, must be checked for splinters, rough edges, metal fittings, holes and other traps which can break a toe or otherwise incapacitate a performer. If strips of linoleum or carpets are being used to cover the floor, the masking tape joins must be checked for tautness. The tape recorder, of course, must be checked with the performance tapes clearly marked so as to differentiate the first and second acts.

Despite all the precautions one is to a great degree dependent on the know-how and good will of the local technicians. In retrospect I have sometimes danced where angels fear to tread. The grandchildren of headhunters in Sumatra do not constitute the most predictable of audiences.

The funniest stage accident I know of never happened to me nor did I even witness it. But opera buffs recall the moment when Tosca throws herself off the battlements of the castle prison. Ordinarily, she cries out her piercing final utterance then throws herself off, landing on a mattress some four feet below. In this instance, however, the rather ample young American lady singing Tosca landed not on a mattress but on a trampoline, reappearing 15 times, sometimes the right way up, sometimes upside down, sometimes giggling with glee, other times fuming with fury.

That evening, not only did the protagonists expire, the audience must have died laughing as well.

On tradition

When Olga Preobrajenska corrected me in that now long ago Parisian summer of 1952, I knew that she had been corrected in turn by Christian Johannsen, partner of Marie Taglioni, reigning goddess of the Romantic Ballet during the 1830's. When Bronislava Nijinska was teaching me in that now distant California spring of 1958, I was aware every moment of her legendary lineage. (In the early 1970's we meet again during the interval of the Kirov Ballet at the Royal Festival Hall. I kiss the hand of Nijinsky's sister. With her is Nijinsky's wife Romola whose raucous laugh is the counter-traction of taunting hell in whose fiery walls she has lived through half a lifetime with her stricken genius.)

Tradition is the tingling awareness of continuity from its inspiring source.

... Having just taught a mime class for the Royal Danish Ballet at the Royal Theatre in Copenhagen, I am doing a barre in the studio in which August Bournonville rehearsed his last ballet shortly before his death and soon after the completion of the present theatre. Bournonville was an exact contemporary of his good friend Hans Christian Andersen, both of them having been born in 1805. Oil paintings of the great Danish choreographer and of Vincenzo Galeotti, earlier ballet master of the company, hang on the walls, guardians of yesterday's glory as the matchstick of tomorrow's flame.

Bournonville had a lifelong ability as a mime during the span of his own performing days, an ability which was revealed in his own ballets. He believed that mime could encompass "all the feelings of the soul" whereas the dance "is essentially an expression of joy, a desire to follow the rhythms of the music."

... I am in the London Museum holding the make-up tray of Anna Pavlova. Having been trained by her partners, protégées and colleagues, living near her Ivy House in London, having performed in her native St. Petersburg/Leningrad, the connection is very close.

I hold her threaded needle, knotted for emergency use, open her powder box whose puff emits a small cloud of dust, its perfume having long vanished in the interim of runaway time. Lifting up her pink satined cape from *Christmas*, then the heavily jewelled costume from her *Russian Dance*, I feel the blue flame of her self immolating life.

While holding Pavlova's last *Dying Swan* costume, a white feather from the left breast releases itself from the bodice and spirals towards the floor. The museum trustee, sensing my affinity, offers me the feather/relic.

Tradition, for the revolutionary, is a springboard of departure, its defiant acrobat leaping netless from the familiar tenets; tradition, for the conservative, offers the grounded acceptance of the tried and tested past. For the mid-way liberal, the best of two worlds can be drawn upon—the security of proven yesterday and the risk of tentative tomorrow.

On will power beyond belief

"I don't think my grandmother will be dancing *Swan Lake* tonight." So spoke Ivan Monreal at the Gran Teatro Garcia Lorca in Havana. In the entire history of ballet, no 23-year-old ballet company member has ever been able to make such a statement. In his backstage conversation with me, November 8th, 1982, Ivan was referring to his grandmother, prima ballerina assoluta Alicia Alonso.

The occasion was the closing night of Alonso's 8th International Ballet Festival in Cuba. Participating were stars of the Bolshoi Ballet, Kirov Ballet, Paris Opera Ballet, Vienna Opera Ballet, Royal Swedish Ballet, American Ballet Theatre, Teatro Colon in Buenos Aires, National Ballet of Cuba as well as Kazimir Kolesnik and myself.

Two days earlier Alonso had sprained her foot, an injury which deprived her public of seeing her dance the *Swan Lake* Act 2 *pas de deux* with the magnificent *premier danseur* Jorge Eskivel, himself, the finest Albrecht and Apollo I've ever seen.

Alicia Alonso, born December 21st, 1921, fighting intermittent blindness throughout her life, has triumphed to create her own illustrious career and the brilliant National Ballet of Cuba of which she is both director and star. When the boys in her corps de ballet can each do at least seven *pirouettes*, the so-called technical level of other ranking companies surely comes into question. There is also her flourishing school from which emerge the present and future dancers.

As Fidel Castro is the President of the country, Alicia Alonso is Cuba's untitled queen. No other artistic celebrity in any other land occupies a parallel position. To see public gatherings rise as one at her entrance, to view her heroic profile on postage stamps, to hear the average person in the street refer to her as Alicia, is to understand the depth of reverence that has been accorded her.

Impeccably groomed down to her long and lacquered fingernails, she is the supreme mistress of her every off stage role. When she is practicing, she is actually studying, a look of acute discontent occasionally crossing her features as she exerts herself to maintain a step which has caused hoarseness the night before in wildly bravoing audiences.

When she is listening to a toast in her honour or the presentation of an award, she is truly listening, her upright neck projecting her mental participation. When she is administrating she is a general plotting out the future moves of her dancing battalions. When she is being spoken to she is, without any doubt, listening with absorptive energy to the speaker. And when she, herself, makes an impromptu speech, we hear the eloquent Spanish prose, the poetry of a woman who sees all art in its function as higher guide to mankind.

It is early morning in Havana. On the way to my own practice session, I see her at the barre, working from flawless fifth positions, being coached by her devoted daughter, Laura Alonso. The years have reversed the pedagogic procedure. It is now the daughter who is instructing the mother.

Later that night we see Alicia gliding magisterially through the *Nutcracker* adage, interspersed with the multiplicity of sparkling supported *pirouettes.* On another evening we see her, the very essence of ethereal romanticism, in her most luminous role, *Giselle.* As we, in grateful astonishment, watch her perch on pointe in perfect *arabesques* or skim with meteoric speed through the *entrechat quatre*, *passé* variation in Act 2, we may well ask if we have not accidentally stepped backwards in a time machine.

Then we accept the fact that we are, indeed, very much in 1982 but that what is happening is the fact of our witnessing nothing short of a miracle, for this remarkable woman has taken on, singlehandedly, the plague of faulted vision and consumptive time. Nothing, apparently, calls a halt to her art and artistry.

Alicia Alonso, marathon dancer of our earthly race, la divina of life's unfinished dance, we who have been replenished by the example of your life, bow down deeply, humbled and inspired.

OFF STAGE

On not leaving valuables in the dressing room

Everywhere we go we seem to be potential victims of blatant as well as sophisticated robbery. It is not uncommon for waiters to return to their customers someone else's expired or stolen Diners Club card. Not everyone checks that carefully what the waiter returns. Chambermaids have been known to steal three or four cheques in the middle of a book of travellers' cheques, thus escaping detection since few people look at sequential numbers during a purchase.

For the performer, the time for him to beware and be aware is during the performance itself, especially if it's a solo performance. The pickings are almost as inviting during the performance of a large company if the entire cast is on stage simultaneously.

I never leave my passport, cheque card, Diners Club card, keys, money, watch, jewellery or any other valuables (not to mention my appointment book with its essential and assorted information) in a dressing room unless I can have a key to that room. If there is no key or I think the dressing room window is accessible from the street, then I give these valuables to my impresario to keep for me until the performance is over.

I'm not advocating suspicion as a constant companion but, believe me, it is no fun to be fundless or bereft of passport in the middle of nowhere.

On being classified

The person with restricted ability often has fewer problems than people with more than one string on their bow. The multi-faceted person diverts his energy and shoots concurrently at many targets. The person with one goal usually remains on his single if repetitive track.

The by-product of versatility is the bugaboo called classification, category or encapsulation. The public are lazy. They wish for and demand an immediate label. Agents and other marketing men insist on name tags.

Though in my own career I'm identified as a mime artist, I am, as well, a dancer, choreographer, teacher and writer. But if I were to attach all those descriptions to my name, my credibility would be questioned. The flesh peddlars and media manipulators, for the sake of quick convenience (like frozen food), demand their comfortable little boxes.

At least initially, don't fight City Hall. When one is sufficiently established in one area, it is then safe to spread one's wings to full expansion. Play the human puppeteers at their own game until such time as it is practical to cut the strings.

In any case, a label is merely a name. And a name is just a hanger. What rests on that hanger is our true identity.

On writing letters

In the western world it's necessary to know how to promote oneself, as it were, in addition to cultivating the actual talent. Would that we could concentrate on only the art, as do our eastern European brothers, but such is not the case. If our world is far from perfect, neither, as we well know, is theirs.

The words *viable* and *bankable* grate my sensibilities, defining, as they do, an artist's work solely on an economic basis. That, unhappily, is usually the gauge by which impresarios, producers and agents size up a potential client/package/product. Like it or not, the theatre is a business so for people who free lance it is imperative that fire is fought with fire.

The free lance performer as a salesman, an unpalatable thought but preferable to the extinct species of once was actor. The first step in this style of salesmanship is to master the job of letter writing.

All business letters should be typewritten. Few people care to decipher the heiroglyphics of sloppy penmanship. Handwritten letters tend to remain at the bottom of the unanswered pile. The difficulty of handwritten letters is compounded when writing to or receiving mail from foreign lands. Add illegible script to a less than perfect command of a language and we have loss of interest added to eye strain.

Always keep a carbon copy of your letters for future reference. Though you may think you'll remember what you wrote, many months and letters later, you won't.

It's enough of a feat, face to face, convincing strangers of your merits. Think of the far greater difficulty in reaching out to someone who doesn't see, hear or feel your presence. With this considerable obstacle in mind, enclose telling photographs (having had copies made from the original) along with your well constructed letter. And don't be discouraged when most of the letters go unanswered. By writing a prodigious amount, the chances increase that at least one of them will hit the mark.

Be succinct and always to the point. Be correct without being cold, polite without being subservient. If there is an absence of response or only negative replies, forget them and think only of the next letters to be written.

On travelling with as few suitcases as possible

Once I arrived in Cape Town, South Africa, with some 14 pieces of luggage and boxes of souvenirs. After counting seven or eight valises it is extremely difficult to count the remainder quickly and not lose track. There in the middle of the Cape Town air terminal I was trying to keep count of the hoped for total when a local man insisted on assisting me in the absence of an available porter.

When I arrived at the hotel I discovered the theft of my typewriter. The moral of this story is not to travel with more than an airline bag and two pieces of luggage if it is at all possible. Aside from the impossibility of keeping count thereby exposing oneself to loss or theft, it must also be kept in mind that porters are not always at hand. Often, as well, a trolley is nowhere to be found. Two arms in no way can manage 10 valises.

On posing for photographs

There is no difference in posing for a photographer than in appearing before an audience. One is giving a performance in both cases. Inexperienced people tend to withdraw when facing a photographer's camera instead of lighting up from within as they would try to do in a theatre. The tendency to curtail one's energy must be resisted, for the camera is the equivalent of a thousand eyes.

As in a performance there must be preparation. In my case it's during the time of making-up. As I put aside one face replacing it with another, my sense of high-strung alertness has been awakened. Just before the photographs are actually taken, one must plug in all the wires, in a manner of speaking. In being electric a short cut is a short circuit.

When the photographer clicks his shutter, the subject must be caught at maximum energy. It's too late to reach that peak during the click of the camera. That high point must be arrived at beforehand and then held when the photograph is taken. During the hold, the inner volume must be lifted. This raising of the emotional decibel level makes the difference between a living and a lifeless photograph.

It has often been stated that the camera loved Marilyn Monroe. I believe it was the other way around. It was *she* who loved the camera. That being the case she responded to it as the beloved does to the caresses of the lover.

On flamboyant publicity and subsequent repercussions

Newspapers have creative memories, inventing when the truth is tepid. The tabloids, especially the cheaper variety, ignore the positive news and constantly revive scandal, semi-truths and falsehood. *The Sunday Times* is no better than *The News of the World*, the difference being that the former's stories go back further in time with the furtive lovers being titled. Sometimes, as moral punishment, they're stripped of their titles. In *The News of the World* they're simply stripped.

Just before appearing at the May Fair Theatre in London in 1980, the *Daily Mail* reported that one of my productions was once banned in Edinburgh and that on another occasion during a press conference of bored journalists, I had taken off all my clothes. Neither statement is accurate.

First of all, I was never banned in Edinburgh.

Between 1968 and 1970 I wrote, choreographed and directed three productions, the Japanese styled *Narcolepsy* and *Vultures* as well as the audacious *Umbilical* (in each case using an author's pseudonym) in which the unadorned human figure figured prominently. By pushing back the barriers of theatrical acceptability, I tried and succeeded in attracting attention. I had to. Without expensive promotion and elaborate machinery, London's bridges were not exactly falling down since my arrival in the city almost two years earlier. Considered by the then managements as precariously uncommercial and alarmingly different, I was in the unenviable position of having two strikes against me. Impatient in the bleachers, I was determined to remain in the stadium. So I struck back.

My three startling productions were highly praised in many quarters, no more naked nor erotic than Rodin's *The Kiss*. The publicity was another matter. Playing the media at their own game, I held, in London, "the world's first nude press conference" in which the principal performers, Flora Gatha and Nathaniel, carefully lit and covertly posed, answered questions from a rather hot under the collar bevy of journalists. I, myself, as is my custom with strangers, was fully dressed.

At this press conference, a rehearsal of the play *Narcolepsy* was staged, preceded by my doing three items from my repertoire, one of them being *Audition Time, Broadway*. It was in this item that I, as a desperate actor at an audition, removed my clothes and cowered bare, from the back only, for a few seconds.

The coverage for this press conference was enormous but it backfired somewhat in that its publicity trailed me into the future as a candle that refuses to blow out.

That this distorted bit of fabrication should surface again in the *Daily Mail* is typical of our newspapers' disproportionate coverage. Why don't they write about my charity performance for discarded children in Madagascar or for deaf mutes in the Philippines? Perhaps because good deeds help Boy Scouts, not Fleet Street circulation.

On keeping clear records for income tax purposes

All free lance performers should keep records of income earned. Not to do so is to invite problems from the income tax authorities. Though you may think you will remember your engagements and fees earned, one year later they tend to blur together and for the life of you, you cannot recall the difference in salaries between Eastbourne and Essex.

In my own case the problem is multiplied considerably by fees earned in the currency of many countries. To avoid the Tower of fiscal Babel that would surely ensue, I keep a chart, an excerpt of which is shown on p. 73.

This is a sampling I, myself, keep to ensure accuracy of recall. I also note television appearances which in the following middle eastern tour took place in all the countries except Afghanistan. Weekly receipts of everything spent should be kept as well in a special book, including rent and telephone bills if part of one's flat is used as an office.

One's accountant should be versed in the intricacies of taxable and non-taxable expense incurred by people in the theatre.

If the performer is also teaching, lecturing or writing, that income should also be recorded.

Income tax authorities (and custom officials) have a way of making the

PERFORMANCES, 1976

THEATRE	CITY	COUNTRY	DATE	REPERTOIRE	FEE
USIS Theatre	Kabul	Afghanistan	March 8th, 9th	Same as Iran	$...
Al Kabbani Theatre	Damascus	Syria	March 11th, 13th	Same as Iran	$...
New Theatre, American University	Cairo	Egypt	March 22nd, 23rd	Same as Iran	$...
Opera House	Istanbul	Turkey	March 26th	Same as Iran	$...

interrogated feel as if they are covering up a crime, in all likelihood, they didn't commit. To stay clear of this most unwelcome inquisition, it is worth the expense of an expert accountant. Remember that the more disorganized the client is, the longer it will take the accountant to sort out his affairs. The accountant's bill, accordingly, will be larger.

So be supremely organized; keep a performance list. There is enough chaos to be encountered in our lives without contributing to the confusion.

On being interviewed by the press

An interview with a journalist, as a session with a photographer, is akin to a performance on stage in that in both cases, the consciousness of the public is being penetrated. Before the journalist's arrival, know which kind of readership his paper reaches. Theatrical devotees, health enthusiasts, the post-graduate generation, senior citizens or general?

Relate on a person to person level with the interviewer for often he is apprehensive or even nervous. By putting him at his ease you will come out in a more sympathetic light. If the interviewer doesn't like his subject, he can, quite easily, taint a saint. All that's needed are a few well-barbed adjectives. Chat with him as he sets up his cassette or readies his pen and paper but don't get into the crux of your story until the reporter is actually ready. By starting ahead of time, the journalist will scramble your facts in his less than total recall.

For those of you whose words trip too lightly off your tongue, be very careful. Never relate any information to a newspaperman you don't wish to be printed. No asides such as, "Just between you and me, this is not for publication, so and so's a crook!" For it's just those choice tidbits of aggressive gossip that the reporter is hungry to devour, knowing that it will earn for him a pat on the head from his editor. That you will, once the paper comes out, half die from embarrassment, does not enter his scheme of things.

I begin an interview feeding the journalist statistical information then proceed from there, sticking with topics that will whet the reader's appetite to see the performance (if that is why the interview is taking place). If I were to wait only for the reporter's questions, the emphasis of the article may turn out lopsided. If and when I trust the journalist implicitly, I just answer whatever questions he throws at me.

Have prepared answers for questions you consider too personal for public consumption. Not every performer cares to wash his private linens in public. Some of us have mothers, fathers or families not quite as emancipated as ourselves. Though you may have the courage of your convictions, are your nearest and dearest impervious to the fall-out of such publicity?

Regarding accuracy, there is little insurance. If the journalist has brought a cassette, at least your words will be recorded verbatim, but that is still no guarantee that the actual words will be published in the article. If the journalist is taking notes, the chance for accuracy is even more reduced. If he is merely listening, you can be almost certain that the next day's edition will feature a fictional variation of your supposed utterances. How often have I had words literally put into my mouth, even, to my dismay, opinions.

Sometimes the journalist is outstanding, his story is accurate but a world leader has been shot, an event of far greater significance than your opening tomorrow night. Your one-hour conversation is condensed into five paltry lines.

Worse than having an interview condensed is when the editor's scissors snip out most of the topics discussed, leaving usually the most insignificant bit of information to represent you, the subject.

At the interview's conclusion, thank the journalist for his story to be. If, by some stroke of luck, you find that you like the article—and this does happen once in a blue moon—then send him a thank you note. He will appreciate your gratitude as you do the audience's applause.

On minimizing jet lag

Scientific tests have been carried out which prove that jet lag is minimized when liquids are consumed before, during and after a flight. Drinking water seems to counteract the dehydration caused by the pressurized cabins.

On protecting the stomach while on tour

Never sample native dishes the day before or the day of the performance. Your stomach may well rebel with abdominal pains as the result of the invasion. For new food is often just that, an invasion, as far as the digestive tract is concerned.

Never, of course, eat food bought from a street vendor. With unsanitary conditions, low prices sometimes include high temperatures.

On greeting unusual visitors after a performance

Some three hours before one of the performances during my 1980 May Fair Theatre season in London, I was sitting in the stalls with Marita Phillips (with whom I shared that season), testing the decibel levels of the tapes. There had been some static the night before.

Suddenly, a small posse of men entered with a Labrador dog which, at once, began racing methodically up and down each and every aisle. This was a bomb detecting dog checking out the theatre before the arrival, that evening, of Prince Charles.

As the dog approached my aisle I thought it prudent to vacate, for its speed was such that had I blocked its path ... The thought wasn't even completed when I found myself in the more secure proximity of the royal detectives. The clever dog then pounced onto the stage all over my newspaper placards, into the wings, through the props, such was the mission of man's most faithful friend. The night before when Prince Charles had attended a performance at the Royal Opera House, two dogs had sniffed out 3,000 seats during which time the theatre was closed for two hours.

Some hours later as *Hearts and Flowers* concluded the performance, I waited, as the jack-in-the-box within my oversized box, for Marita's character to expiate her sin of insensitivity, thus bringing that item and the evening to a close.

After the performance, in the dressing room, I found Prince Charles, accompanied by his equerry, to be a genuine and activated listener. Few people fool me with the pretence of listening. Most people, when left in the dark as to an artist's intentions, merely remain quiet, pretending to have received the message. Prince Charles had the brave humility to admit his puzzlement of some of the repertoire.

"This is the first mime performance I've ever seen," he stated.

His sense of humour was marked, a consciously cultivated shield with which he counterbalanced the gravity of his environment. Always there were the specialized dogs, the unending formality, the guards and detectives, the historical restrictions, the bowing and scraping of others which too often must surely deteriorate into obsequiousness.

Pointing to the programme he remarked that he found the following sequential titles rather entertaining, reading them to me as a run-on sentence; *The Father Who Searched For His Long Lost Son While In The Bathtub.*

"Was that Maria Callas?," he asked, referring to *The Cripple and the Madonna.*

"Yes," I answered.

"Which opera?," he queried.

"*Don Carlos*," I responded.

"Last night I heard one of your countrymen singing in *Simon Boccanegra*," he reported.

"Who was that?" I questioned.

"Sherill Milnes. I was moved to tears," related the heir to the last of the great western monarchies, unafraid of not only parachute jumping but also of revealing his sensitivity.

"I enjoyed *The Lovers*," he ventured to continue, imitating my undulating hands, not too successfully, I may add! As he intertwined his rather stocky fingers in attempted imitation of mine, I was very amused, unlike his great-great-great grandmother Queen Victoria who, as we are not allowed to forget, was *not* amused.

"I like your robe," he told me, noting the silver and white kimono from China which I had bought in Singapore.

"Is that a wig you're wearing?," he questioned, observing the Chinese hair from Hong Kong.

After explaining the mechanics of covering my own curly hair, he commented on my crossed and anguished feet during the death section of *Claustrophobia.*

"That's what I feel I'm doing, getting my feet in a twist, when I make a gaffe in public." To the end, self-deprecating, to the end, interested and considerate.

"I'd better let you take your make-up off," he said in preparation for his exit.

As we shook hands, I recalled that earlier, when addressing Marita, he had informed her that his favourite item of her repertoire was *Secret Idols: Dalilah, Cleopatra, Salomé.* Did Prince Charles identify with the Walter Mitty daydreams of the frustrated librarian who imagined herself as those early forerunners of women's lib? Would the prince, on occasion, prefer to be the pauper?

With one detective sitting two rows behind him during the performance and another detective stationed outside the door of the theatre, it was clear that we all have our special cages, even when the bars are made of gold.

On the young mime finding work

Assuming that the aspiring mime has had sufficient training to give him the right to appear before the general public, there are a number of pathways possible. Every one of these approaches requires enormous perseverance and an extravagant portion of good luck.

To begin with, the young mime must try and amass experience, preferably with a group of like-minded people. If such a troupe doesn't exist, then it can be formed by the communal force of everyone's will. If local funding (from an arts council or grant) isn't forthcoming, then the group must pool their resources and find financial short cuts to obtain rehearsal halls, tapes and costumes. Eventually they must persuade some local community centre to present them. Such a single performance can lead to another performance and if the pattern extends itself, the nucleus of a company has been created.

I would advise very few people, if any, to begin their careers with solo performances for such a presentation is not the first rung of the ladder but, clearly, the apogee of a life in art. I, myself, had some 15 years of experience in ballet companies, television and musicals before embarking on my subsequent solo mime career.

Where there is a will, usually there is a way. Sometimes performances are secured for the young mime by friends and personal contacts, associates not necessarily working within the arts but who, nonetheless, have helpful connections.

There are many art centres in Britain or their equivalent abroad, organizations which present experimental and avant-garde theatre, modern dance and mime. Many young groups appear under their auspices. These organizations are a very good frame for the young mime seeking experience.

All kinds of festivals take place in Britain and abroad, many of which present only stellar attractions, but there are others that offer opportunities to newer groups in their fringe category. There are any number of theatre departments in universities which occasionally present mime among their series of weekly attractions for the student body.

Not to be overlooked are governmental sources of presentation. The artist as cultural envoy is a mighty propaganda weapon for the government which sees its artists as prestigious theatrical exports.

To secure an agent who believes in you is an aim more easily wished for than achieved. Too often agents give the impression that they are, indeed, working for you. Six or more months later, there is often a discovery but not the kind devoutly wished for. The discovery is the fact that the agent has done nothing.

As it happens, most agents will only handle people for whom there is already an existing market. Generally speaking, the mime does not fall into this category. Though finding an agent is difficult enough, finding an impresario is even harder. An agent can secure separate engagements but an impresario can organize a national or international tour.

Television, needless to point out, is vast exposure but the obtaining of such engagements most often requires an agent, impresario or other highly influential intermediaries.

Sometimes there is the possibility of patronage such as was found in Renaissance Italy. Patrons of the arts do exist who for reasons of pure devotion, love of the limelight or tax exemption, will make possible performances otherwise out of the question.

Lastly, there is the element of luck, that golden dragon belching provocative fire at us, the omnipotent croupier of life's roulette.

So we see that there are many avenues. Few of them, though, are on the map. All of them are hard to find. If and when located, however, one's destination is to be found.

From the poetic to the practical, the question arises; can a young mime earn a living in today's inflationary world? Though many people in many walks of life are struggling with current runaway prices, for the artist who offers his soul freely (and too often for free), economic survival is usually harder.

The young mime, not yet established, can teach or in the time honoured tradition of other actors, hold down a part-time job. The important factor is not to give up and not to equate success with steady income. If it is any consolation, the greatest artists throughout history have been poverty's steady escorts. Naturally, one would prefer to be the consort of consumer success.

For few people is life a royal wedding cake. Most people have to struggle for their basic bread, the artist included. This fact, sobering as it is, does not deter the true artist to the role born. He will survive and flourish within his own uncommon kingdom.

2. The Method

THE LOVERS

I want to follow you like a child.
Feel you in each wave,
unable to deny the insomnia
of your hands in my hair.
To drown the city
in the phrases which form
the poetry of your name.

José Luis Naranjo Ferrer

In this chapter, I will alternately address you as either students, actors, mimes, dancers, singers or *teachers, assuming that these are the principal divisions of the readership.*

A few words about teaching are in order at this point before beginning the actual chapter on the method.

A good teacher never lets the reins slip during a class. He can ride from a gallop to a trot but the horse never comes to a halt.

Each student must have the feeling that the teacher is aware of him and that, at any moment, he, the student, may be called upon to demonstrate a point or answer a question.

An occasional clapping together of the teacher's hands will jolt the student into a vertical attentiveness, the percussive sound of handclaps tending to increase the group's adrenalin.

The teacher's explanations should be long enough to clarify the next exercise but not so long that the students' energy subsides while waiting.

After an exercise of maximum emotional or physical output, the teacher's following demands should be of a more lyrical nature, consequently permitting the students time to refurbish their forces.

As a good performer keeps the audience guessing as to what he will do next, so should the good teacher. Following by rote every day a prepared syllabus quickly deadens an otherwise creative atmosphere. The teacher of experience should often do variations on a theme, the variations being short trips abroad before returning to the home port of call or prepared lesson. The students tend to relax if they are too certain of the lesson's structure.

The students' comments, opinions and questions are not to be allowed, with only the rarest exceptions being made. Firstly, the student has entered the course to benefit from the teacher's assimilated knowledge, not to listen to the undeveloped thoughts of his equally unschooled classmates. Secondly, a dozen or so steady interruptions break into the flow and rhythm of the lesson, cutting the concentration and allowing the muscles to get cold, thus inviting serious injury.

Always, the teacher must dominate by the sheer force of his presence and personality. He is the high tide in the sea, the student the tentative swimmer who, once in, has no choice but to go with the current.

As the student develops technique, he must be aware of his gains in order to consolidate them. That is why I am unstinting in my praise of accomplishment. If the student is unaware of his momentary excellence, the newly acquired virtue may never return to him. He or she must know how or why it happened and then cling to the recently discovered knowledge.

On the other hand, of course, if the student is doing the exercise incorrectly, that person's error must be rectified at once.

The teacher must relate to his group with humanity but, by the same token, never be mistaken for a doormat. Insolence is fashionable in today's social climate but totally unacceptable within the true and timeless framework of learning.

A student may be fat, skinny, too short, too tall or even untalented. None of these setbacks alter his right to have the opportunity of learning, at least, under my supervision. There is one character trait, however, that can negate his right to study, that is, within my circumference. This most undesirable trait is public combativeness. If and when this situation occurs, that student is out, for revolutions, as far as I'm concerned, are to be fought in the streets, never in the classroom. Unlike a political dissident, the student is free to leave any time he chooses.

One hopes, though, for this kind of behaviour to be the rare exception, for a period of chosen study expands the mental wingspread. By that means, one stays longer, aloft.

Inflation/deflation

Breathing is the mainspring support of life and in a parallel way the mainstay support of great movement. The breathing in and breathing out process must be translated into total body movement so that even the fingers and toes seem to inhale and exhale.

To watch an entire body breathe gives life, organic life, to the movements that person is executing. Like a glider, the movement takes off when we breathe in and like a glider the movement completes its landing when we breathe out. To hold the breath, to sustain it, gives the movement a coasting quality, the impression of staying air-borne.

So, in essence, as we breathe in and out to sustain life, so do we *inflate* and *deflate*, the very basis of movement support.

We breathe, while performing, through slightly parted lips rather than through clenched teeth for to lock the lips and breathe only through the nose is to invite a snorting sound. The slightly open mouth approach ensures silence, contributing to the atmosphere of effortlessness.

1a

The student sits cross-legged with the spine and head collapsed. When the teacher says *preparation*, the student gathers his mental forces, concentrating on the exercise about to begin. (ill. 1a)

The *inflation* begins with an impetus in the stomach, almost as if someone has slapped you in the solar plexus. This is the initiation, the inauguration of the movement which then travels up the torso, sequentially, progressing upwards through the ribs, armpits, upper arms into the fingers and then beyond.

Movement is never finite. It passes successive boundary lines reaching towards infinitude. (Ill. 1b)

At the highest point of upward reach (with shoulders down at all times), the descent begins lead by the stomach with the chest, head and arms following (Ill. 1c). In this, the deflation, there is a rippling effect, the head lingering last before it too, follows the rest of the torso in descent.

1b

1c

At the lowest point of the deflation the movement continues back into the inflation. At the highest point of the inflation, the deflation then begins. Thus, the motor, once switched on, is never switched off.

1d

When the exercise has ended, remain there, framing the previous effort in reverberating silence. Stay with definition. No twitching or adjusting brassière straps or dance belts. No looking around. A concentrated composure. (Ill. 1d)

It should be remembered that during the inflation, the torso begins to rise and the arms subsequently follow. The arms have no choice but to follow the torso. They do not move independently of the torso.

Each time the inflation begins, there must be an impulse emanating from the stomach. This triggers the movement, propelling the energy upwards. The inflation is executed with anticipation while the deflation has an air about it of reluctance.

We climb the mountains of our lives with eagerness while the inevitable descent is tinged with resistance.

When the arms are lifted, let the fingers breathe; avoid the sewn together look. At the conclusion of the deflation, you cannot, physically, go down any further. At this point, a mental shade is pulled down over the mind, so that the body, now having stopped, is followed by the mind retreating into a state of nothingness. This total completion finalizes the movement for the audience.

Relate to the musical phrasing so that you are at one with the sound and not in opposition to it.

Regarding the duration of *inflation/deflation* and all the other exercises to follow, this is a discretionary judgment to be made by the teacher. Generally speaking, a time span anywhere from one to three minutes is a good length. Always, the knowledgability and stamina of the students must be taken into account. For beginners, each exercise should be done briefly, stopped and corrected, then repeated.

Facial exercises

Again, preparation. Remember that the preparation is the assemblage and clarification of one's thought prior to the actual exercise. The mind is cleared and left free to respond to the stimuli of the theme, music and movement. A cluttered mind muddies the transparent waters of thought.

Focus your attention on self. As you develop technically, you must become a transmitter of ordered emotion in motion. No tug-of-war with the music. Don't resist. Surrender. Acquiesce.

With the preparation now in order, we are ready to do the facial exercises. This is not an expressive exercise. It is designed to stretch and isolate the facial muscles.

Lift the eyebrows slowly, twice, then quickly three times. Following this, stretch the mouth into a maximum smile with the same count, one, two, then quickly, one, two, three.

After each lift of the eyebrows and stretch of the mouth (showing all the teeth), release the muscles so that the eyebrows and mouth return at once to their starting position. Like a released rubber band.

These exercises can be varied with four counts of fluttering of the eyelashes, then another four counts of keeping the eyes wide open or combining them with the eyebrow lifts and mouth stretches. A constant assortment of daily exercises are always introduced so that the student cannot predict the pattern of the teacher. The element of surprise and unexpectedness keeps the student, literally and figuratively, on his toes.

During the exercises, the eyes do not wander. They remain at a fixed point. Care should be taken that during the stretching of the mouth exercise, only the mouth and cheek muscles are called into play, not the chords of the neck as well. If the chords of the neck are used, the function of the exercise is negated. The purpose of this exercise is, I repeat, to isolate independently the muscles of the face. Facile facial muscles answer immediately to insistent thought.

When doing these exercises, there must be a crisp, sharp attack. No blurring or overlapping. No dripping water colours. Each shade must be absolutely clear.

Hand exercises

Flexible hands are like pronounced insteps. You have them, as it happens, or you don't. Nevertheless, stiff hands can be worked so that they are more pliable than originally.

This exercise is one of the few that I, physically, demonstrate. In virtually all of the other exercises, I encourage the student's creativity by permitting a wide latitude, improvisationally. However, in the hand exercises, the student must copy my movements as closely as he can.

Shaking, twisting, rotating, undulating and stretching the hands backwards to previously untried angles, the student finishes the exercise with a tingling, blood racing sensation. Never before have the hands been pushed through such unexplored terrain. So the student will feel after the first attempt.

Hands can speak volumes. Soaring fingers can write poetry in space. When doing the following hand exercises, the student should take pains to shoot the fingers out like antennae. Every thrust and ripple is maximum.

We will now begin a few exercises designed to make more flexible and expressive those most potentially eloquent extremities, the hands. Each of the exercises should be done rhythmically and in multiples of either 16 or 32, depending on one's degree of developing stamina.

a) *Shake the hands*: Keep shaking them as fast as possible until they seem to blur. Rings, watches and bracelets should not be worn as the weight impedes the desired quickness.

b) *Fists and open*: Clench the hands into the tightest fists and then open with the fingers splayed as far as possible. The emphasis is on the opening of the fingers. Each of the fingers must feel as if an arrow is being shot through it, escaping through each finger's end.

c) *Rotating wrists*: With elbows locked, rotate the wrists in an inward circle, then reverse by rotating them in an outward circle. The arms are held to the side.

d) *Stretching the knuckles*: Lock the left elbow with the arm parallel to the floor and the palm facing upwards. Then, with your right hand, grab the left hand by the four fingers (leaving out the thumb) and pull the fingers downwards. Each time you pull the fingers downwards, stretch them a little further. Change to the other side.

e) *Stretching fingers from the prayer position*: With the hands in front of one's chest as if in prayer, begin to open the hands towards a horizontal position, making sure that the fingers stay locked all the time. Some people's hands, stiffer than others, will be able to open only to an acute angle rather than to a horizontal straight line. Whichever the case may be, the fingers, from the base, must remain firmly glued together. If the fingers release, then the desired stretch is nullified.

   So as not to be discouraged, I must mention that very few people, indeed, are capable of a horizontal stretch of the hands with the fingers remaining pressed together from the base upwards to the finger tips.

f) *Rippling the hands*: With clenched hands at chest level, move the arms outwards in front of yourself, quickly locking the elbows. Without pause, then snap the wrists (palm downwards), then snap the knuckles, then push the fingers, joint by joint, until the energy flow has released itself through the ends of the finger tips.

   Elbows, wrists, knuckles and finger joints must be worked separately in a staccato rhythm and sequentially as just listed. Then the exercise is done in one continuous flowing movement so that a ripple of the arms seems to be taking place.

One of the most rewarding discoveries for any student is to unearth his own unknown capabilities. As strange as it may seem to those who see *my* hands as a focal point of my own performance, I was oblivious of their future potential until one particular performance in the holy city of Assisi in Italy. After that performance for a few thousand members of the Vatican, an Italian composer approached me and suggested that one day I create an item solely for my hands. Though I listened to his words, the seed he planted didn't sprout until a year later. The bloom was *The Lovers* in which two creatures of mankind meet and merge in the ecstasis of spiritual and physical union. In the blurring hands can be seen the eyes of Tristan and Isolde, the lips of Hadrian and Antinous and passion's countless other joyful slaves.

Tension/relaxation

For four counts the body strikes a pose of total tension, the intensity pervading every muscle from the crown of the head to the tip of the toe. (Ill. 2a)

In the next four counts—relaxation—the entire body completely collapses, instantaneously, as a marionette at once cut off from its strings. (Ill. 2b)

Each pose of tension and relaxation is different so that there is no repetitiveness. Avoid predictability. A continuously repeated pattern encourages

2a

2b

the audience to think they know what will follow. Without the element of surprise and unexpectedness, the audience tends to cut off. Their eyes may well be on the stage but their brains are elsewhere.

Be precise in the change from tension to relaxation. Musical precision is a must. If the change from tension to relaxation is intended for the fifth count, then it must happen on that count, not on count 5½. There must be a perfect fusion between sight and sound. Anticipating the count or lagging behind it jars the vision of the viewer. They can't actually put their finger on the cause of the disharmony, but they are aware of it. Once distracted, forever lost.

In striking the positions during the tension section, don't only execute contracted poses. Stretch out, elongate as an El Greco or Modigliani painting.

Don't be conservative. Be radical and take a risk. Strike poses that dare.

As the course progresses, all tension poses are done on one foot, the relaxation on two.

In the tension, the foot is either flexed or pointed, not in between. Don't take all day to point the toe. Have your brain send your foot an emergency cable, not a greetings telegram. We must not see the foot in transition during this exercise. Only the immediate result.

Be certain to participate fully in both the tension and relaxation sections. In other words, every part of the instrument must be operative. A relaxed right arm in tension tends to make a liar out of the rest of the body.

Traction/withdrawal

In this exercise, the student stretches his arms oppositionally, always in a straight line. The arms, after having reached the maximum stretch, are always in either a horizontal, vertical or oblique line. Never are they parallel.

With a central impetus (as if being slapped in the stomach), the arms move outwards for four counts until they reach the maximum stretch through the fingertips (Ill. 3a). Then, on the withdrawal, they return to the starting point, also for four counts.

At the peak moment of the movement, the upper back has opened, expanding the chest as a result (Ill. 3b).

3a 3b

During the withdrawal of the arms, care should be taken that the arms are not in "relaxation." The current must still continue to flow.

Be careful to have both arms open at the same time, not one arriving before the other. This is a common failing since most students find even this simple coordination difficult. *Traction/withdrawal* is always done with *inflation/deflation*. In other words, as you do traction, you simultaneously inflate. As you do withdrawal, you simultaneously deflate. Unaccompanied by this breathing support, the exercise deteriorates into ordinary gymnastics. The inflation and deflation colour the entire movement, imbuing it with a living, pulsating quality.

The exercise can be given with two counts in each direction. In its more advanced form, it is given lying on the floor with the legs opening during the inflation and closing during the deflation. It can also be given, at a later date, with a *developpé* or unfolding of the leg, exactly at the same time as the arms are executing the traction.

For the most advanced student there is a detail which, when utilized, lends added excitement to the movement. That is, on the fourth count of the traction, when the arms are at their most stretched, before returning in the withdrawal the student stretches even further, going beyond what was thought of as his maximum. This is count $4\frac{1}{2}$.

This peak upon peak could be seen as a symbol of man's mountain climbing mentality. A snow-capped peak cutting through diamond-white clouds is not merely a heavenly decoration. It is a challenge and test of man's audacity. So it is with the count $4\frac{1}{2}$ of traction. Upon arriving at the furthest point of the traction stretch, the student dares to reach just that much further before the inevitable return to the starting point, the ground base of aspiration.

In this exercise as well as in all the others, the student must, when counting, do it silently and invisibly, never mouthing.

Sequential movement

Good movement begins centrally and radiates outwards. This exercise, one of the most valuable for the beginning student, leads him away from the kind of peripheral movement favoured by beginners.

The student gets on his knees with his hands clasped behind his back. Imagining he has been struck lightly in the stomach he begins to move his torso in various directions. The clasped hands behind the back ensure that he is moving only the torso, not the arms. The kneeling position eliminates the legs from participating (Ill. 4a).

4a

4b

Rotate the torso, undulate, sway, reverse directions, ripple, but always keep it moving.

Then release the clasped arms and let the arms follow the moving torso. I repeat. Let the arms follow the torso, not the other way around. The torso is leading, the arms are following. This is the proper sequence (Ill. 4b).

Then stand up. The legs can now participate as well but they must follow the leadership of the torso. So remember—the torso leads, the arms, legs and head follow. This, then, is the sequence, hence the term *sequential movement.*

When kneeling, don't bunch up the insteps. Keep the feet flat against the floor, not turned in or sickled. A sickled foot (when the heel is behind the pointed toe) destroys the line.

A sickled foot is acceptable and even necessary if it is deliberately used for dramatic purposes such as the characters of cripples, addicts or mental institution inmates.

Most people are comfortable with bunched, sickled feet in kneeling positions. But comfort cannot be the gauge. Correctness is the yardstick.

When I teach sequential movement, I am always on the lookout for illogical movement, movement that begins on the edges and works its way inwards. Sequential movement, correctly executed, makes a habit of moving from a central impetus, the energy distributing itself outwards through the extremities of the body.

Stillness/activity

When you strike a position of stillness, it must not be frozen or dehydrated. It must be living and though anchored to the ground, teeming with life and energy. The way to achieve a living stillness is to do an instant inflation at the moment of striking the pose. This ensures the alive quality of the exercise instead of allowing it to be static.

Assume a position of generous proportions. Don't be stingy and introverted in movement. Be giving and philanthropic. The stillness must have definition. Avoid the hazy outline. One's script must be set out in the clearest typeface, never employing a smudged or running alphabet.

When in a precarious position, don't give in to the beckoning forces of gravity. Resist and oppose the negative pull. In other words, pull up! Even in a contracted position, particularly in a contracted position, pull up. This reverse pulling away will counterbalance the body, enabling it to sustain a pose otherwise dangerous. For example, if you are tilting to the left (precariously), pull up and feel as if you're reaching towards the right.

Don't show tension in the fingers unless deliberate. Let the fingers breathe.

During the opposite part of the exercise, the activity, begin it with an impetus in the solar plexus. The body must then cut patterns through the

Stillness

Activity

air, the torso reaching out of itself, moving towards some new direction. Don't meander. Don't wander. Move towards some chosen location in space.

The activity must take the form of fire. Once lit, the flame can be lowered, the movement can simmer, but never permit the light to be extinguished.

As the course progresses, stillness is done on one foot. Here inexperience makes itself most apparent in dangling and hanging feet. Energy must not terminate at the ankles or either at the wrists. Nothing mars line faster than an inarticulate foot. Intensive, unending ballet training guarantees the awareness of a pointed, turned out foot that at once answers to the brain's command.

The stillness must connect with the activity. This results from an inner impulse which overlaps the two sections. *Relevé* (rise on the ball of the foot) on the fourth count of the stillness and then *tombé* (fall) into the activity. This rise from the stillness into the fall of the activity helps join the two halves of the exercise.

Each movement must always be initiated or inaugurated, never just casually begun. One begins with definition and ends conclusively. There must be no question marks in the viewer's mind as to whether a movement phrase has begun or ended.

The stillness must be bursting with the life force. It is not inanimate. Avoid the temptation of making it so. One can be racing about a stage and still be dull while conversely be motionless and thrilling.

Ribs/armpit

Ribs have been talked about since the biblical days of Adam whereas armpits have not, at least in polite society. This fact notwithstanding, the armpits and the muscles surrounding them are potentially one of the most expressive areas of the body.

This exercise produces exceptional results. Hitherto unused parts of the anatomy are brought into play, increasing noticeably the plasticity of the mime actor.

"Ribs," I call out and the consciousness is at once distributed to the ribs, causing the torso to undulate with new found nuances.

"Armpits!" As the order is snapped out, the student body discover the interplay of muscles in that region that has previously lain dormant.

When ribs and armpits are called upon simultaneously, the torso sings a song, danced for the first time.

Expansiveness of gesture

With the feet in a stationary position, reach through space, passing through your usual comfortable periphery. Stretch from the base of the spine, escape from the waist.

Immerse yourself thematically in this exercise which is to colonize space. Take over with an imperial grandeur. The reaching to the side must be as maximum as the stretching above or the reaching downwards. In every direction the movement must be aggressively explorative; circularly, vertically up, diagonally down, horizontally left and so on.

You are now doing a *pas de deux* with space. Space is your partner. Don't stand outside yourself and observe the results. This type of detachment is felt by the audience, thereby divorcing them from your performance.

So though the meek may inherit the earth (according to orthodox theology), they do not inherit the space surrounding it. The student must stake his claim, his right to inhabit it.

This exercise helps make habitual an assertive and emphatic upper body. Note. I did not say assertive and emphatic arms, for exciting arms begin at the waist, not in the armpits. When the gesture begins in the waist, it carries along with it the companion torso.

When teaching this exercise I specify, at first, in which direction I want the movement. Later, the student is free to make his own patterns but always remembering to escape from the captive waist.

Preparation/activity/echo

Preparation means exactly that. Get ready. Clear the mind of extraneous thoughts. Settle down with the body. Erase the mental blackboard of previously written exercises. Clear the slate.

Don't adjust underclothing. This habit, unless nipped in the bud, tends to become a nervous reaction preceding every exercise. A fidgety student irritates the teacher. A nervous performer isolates the audience by making them apprehensive.

A good preparation is not only a clearing of the mental stage. It is also the entrance into the particular precinct of the exercise. Who are you becoming? Where are you coming from? Where are you going? Why do you want to get there? How necessary is it for you to arrive? All this is part of your preparation.

Go into the mind in order to come out of the body. Flexing muscles without the brain as conscious pilot is to fly blind. Everything begins with the brain. Empires, inventions, masterpieces to massacres, all begin with a mental concept. The brain is the habitat of all thought and feeling.

Your preparation is a focussing of the brain.

The activity is the scene or exercise as devised by you or the teacher. Your preparation has propelled you. Now let its momentum thrust you full speed ahead. Let one thought feed another. Allow one idea to nourish the next. Don't be a policeman directing your own traffic. To do so results in an atmosphere of self-consciousness, the arch enemy of the actor. Make the effort to express yourself. It is your right as a human being and your duty as a potential artist, the ultimate destination.

When the activity concludes, stay. Remain physically motionless. This is the echo section, the reverberation of your preceding efforts. Don't cut off and amputate your earlier result. If it was good, it deserves the decrescendo of a clean conclusion. If it was not so good, a fine ending can somewhat compensate. Only rank beginners arbitrarily terminate.

An echo can be as visual as it is aural. Hold the final pose. Though the body is stilled, the brain is still activated, demanding attention until the final fade to black. The echo is the imprint, the registration, the giver's final gift.

Distribution of energy

Everyone lies down on their backs with the feet facing the teacher. Whichever part of the body is called out, that is the section which must move and dominate without the participation of the rest of the instrument. The feeling, for the student, must be that of having a 2,000 watt follow spotlight centred on that particular section of the anatomy.

I may call *chest* so the chest must begin to move with a domination that rivets the attention of the viewer. Some ¼ minute or ½ minute later, I may call out *feet*, then *wrists*, *elbows*, *armpits*, *ribs*, *stomachs*, *shoulders*, *throats*, *hips*, *thighs*, *knees*, *heads*, *hands* and *faces*. Each time that part of the body is called, it asserts itself with an arresting authority.

In western society the teacher will observe a certain reticence when asking the students, especially girls, to assert the pelvic area. The hips, of course, are bound up with our Christian-Judaic legacy of shame. When I gave this exercise in African countries such as Cameroon, Sierre Leone and Madagascar, the hip rotations were immediate and full out, the pelvis being as pivotal to their dance culture as pull-up is to classical ballet.

Back to our own more self-conscious culture. The students are still lying down, having exercised every required area. Finally, they are called upon to stand up and move all sections of the body, no longer in isolation, but concurrently. Their new found freedom is quite striking.

Flowing/fragmented movement

The uninitiated in movement fragment everything. Few arrive with flow. The student body is told to begin flowing movements. As must become their custom, the movement begins with a central impetus, begun in the solar plexus. Without respite the student must feed his consciousness to keep the movement flowing from head to toe. Jerks, seams, stops and starts are to be avoided. The flow permeates the entire body, crisscrossing in every direction.

The most common failing is to see an arm become disengaged from the otherwise total flow. Since a locked elbow encourages rigidity, the students must remember to keep the elbows bending as they would the knees. A bent elbow absorbs the shock of a staccato landing. A stiff elbow accentuates it.

In the fragmented section, the student must deliberately chop up the movements with an attack that leaves no doubt in the onlookers' thoughts as to the abrasive quality of the movement. The fragmentation must begin in the spine, not in the appendages, the arms and legs. Begin the fragmented, staccato movements with the spine which takes with it the torso which will, in turn, bring in the arms. This is sequential movement, working from the centre going outwards.

As in all exercises, the duration varies between the opposite requirements (flowing and fragmented) so that *flowing* may be one minute while *fragmented* may be ¼ minute or vice versa. For a change, both may be of equal duration.

As the course progresses into the second month, I pair up partners who loosely link arms during the exercise. One person begins with the *flowing* while the other begins, at the same time, with *fragmented*. When I give the order to change, the person doing *flowing* immediately does *fragmented* and the person doing *fragmented* conversely does the *flowing*. If the arms release, the couple must imperceptibly re-connect.

By pairing opposites, the extra demand of concentration is called upon, for it is very disconcerting to have another body touching yours while doing the reverse. The gain in strengthened concentration is worth the added obstacle.

Energy/lethargy

Many very young people overflow with energy privately but lose most, if not all of it, under the theatrical spotlight. To be the life of the party is no guarantee that one can rise and shine at any hour in any emotional weather. Inhibition, shyness and fear of failure all tend to dilute the source of energy which is at the very base of the actor's equipment. Energy, it must be understood, has little to do with talent. But talent will not flower without energy.

Energy must be cultivated so that it is automatic. Energy must become so habitual that it is ever present without effort. It is simply there. Energy in the performer is like a magnet, drawing and arresting the eye and mind of the people. Intermittent energy is more annoying than no energy at all for we who watch are aware of how close the student is to the target. So near and yet so far.

In giving the *energy/lethargy* exercise, the student soon arrives at an awareness of the difference, the contrast between the two. They must be as clearly marked as black and white, light and dark.

In the actual improvisation of the *energy* section, the student creates movement which strikes out forcefully as a bolt of lightning. Sharp leg extensions, sudden twists of the body, dynamic arm thrusts, sweeping runs, decisive lunges, incisive jumps, these and whatever other kinetic patterns conceived by the student, must all come into play.

In the *lethargy* counterpart of the exercise, the student devises movement which is the extreme reverse; fatigued and depleted. Virtually dragging himself about, he goes through the same movement he invented in the *energy* section, the difference being in the lethargic or drowsy heaviness of the previous steps.

By working with polarities (*tension/relaxation*, *traction/withdrawal* and *energy/lethargy*), the student can comfortably find his middle. The centre between the outer edges then becomes relatively simple, the student having already arrived at the contrasting extremes.

During my recent appearances in Japan with Kazimir Kolesnik, the performances we saw of the Kabuki Theatre in Tokyo were a perfect example of polarities in action. Strutting figures postured continuously and threateningly around a barely moving seated and central figure, yet the stilled and pivotal figure was as much if not equally in evidence as the contiguously thrusting figures. As observed in this Kabuki production, the more passive section of the polarity was not less, only opposite.

The leading actor in this central and passive role, 25-year-old Kyonosuke Nakamura, employed a subtle energy at the very root of his characterization which gave counteraction to his otherwise muted portrayal.

When we visited him backstage just before the performance began, we realized that he was about to do this role for the first time. "Look upon me with kindness," he humbly requested. As it happened, his performance was such that we could only look upon him with admiration.

Impetus/improvisation/conclusion

Every movement must begin specifically. This is the *impetus*, the physical impulse which initiates an exercise in class, a variation on the stage.

The *impetus* command is given. The student responds as if he has been slapped in the stomach, contracting the muscles in that area. He then freezes that reaction. The movement that follows the *impetus* must logically result from that imagined slap in the stomach. If the student were to pursue movement that is completely unrelated to the *impetus*, he would be negating the purpose of this part of the exercise.

When the next order is given (*improvisation*), the student logically follows the direction of the *impetus*. This means he devises an *improvisation* inaugurated by the *impetus* begun in the stomach. The *improvisation* must not be comfortable. The student must not play it safe, instead, risking, daring and challenging himself.

When I say *conclusion*, the students, again logically, bring to a finish the improvisational movement they have been doing. The *conclusion* must follow inevitably from what has preceded it. It must not be superimposed or tacked on. That is to say that if a student is doing movement close to the floor, he would not conclude his efforts with a reach towards the ceiling.

As the *impetus* has clarity, the *improvisation*, creativity, so the *conclusion* must have true finality. If you begin well, you take the audience with you. If you end well, that is, conclusively, you leave them fulfilled.

Avoid, if you can, frustrating the onlookers. They have enough of that in their lives before they arrive at the theatre.

Dynamics in movement: three levels—breeze, wind, tornado

Dynamics implies the use of fluctuating energy, the reaction to forces producing changing levels. When listening to a good speaker, one is aware of vocal dynamics, the variation of pitch and other nuances of voice production which keep the listener concentrated.

All experienced practitioners of the movement arts employ dynamics, the subtle use of energy changes as manifested through the body. An excess of even a good quality tends to deaden the senses of the spectator. Non-stop lyricism or unending attack soon alienate even interested viewers. Balance and variety are essential if one is to keep the public genuinely involved.

By asking the students to move as a *breeze* (the lowest level of dynamics), they learn to call upon a minimum of kinetic power. Next requesting them to move like the *wind*, they graduate to a stronger force. Finally, when commanding them to move as a *tornado*, they well understand the zenith energy to be called upon.

As is usual, the entire body must participate, not just the extremities. The body cannot be divided up into participant and observer. Everything joins in.

Then, not in ascending sequence, the student is asked to move as a *tornado*, a *breeze*, the *wind*, a *breeze*, the *wind*, *tornado*, the varying levels of dynamics out of sequence so they are unable to anticipate the request.

The most obviously difficult section is the *tornado* or maximum force. Most young students simply do not have the strength to sustain such power for more than a few seconds at a time. Their energy tends to come and go rather than be kept up at a uniformly high plane.

The other weakness is the *breeze* or lowest level of dynamics. At the point of incipient energy, the beginning student tends to let slip the subtle hold of power, the result being a sloppy form of *relaxation*.

The manipulation of the life force through the body is as vital to the mime actor as the ability of the pianist to range from *pianissimo* to *fortissimo*.

Articulate extremities

All the students sit on the floor with their legs stretched out in front of them.

"Heads!" And the collective heads of the class snap to attention as if some light from within has suddenly turned on. Their heads are in close-up, centre stage. So must everyone feel as their suddenly positioned heads take over.

"Change!" And the heads assume another position or angle, always coming alive as if lit by some roving, revealing light.

"Hands!" And the energy shoots through the arms towards the finger tips, causing the hands to become the focal point of the body. "Change!" The hands abruptly switch positions, again dominating the attention.

"Feet!" The brain sends an immediate signal to the feet which either twist, point, flex, overlap or anything else they choose to do as long as they take over as powerfully as did the hands and feet earlier. "Change feet!" And the feet snap to attention in yet another position.

"Heads, hands, feet!" With that triple command, the extremities all participate, each equal in speed and intensity. So sharp is the combined effect of heads, hands and feet razor edging into the pose, that the rest of the body becomes equally electric.

This exercise gives definition and frame to movement that might otherwise blur at the edges.

Contained balance/expanded balance

Hold a position on one leg, a position that is contained (4 counts), then begin to expand that position, extending the working leg (count 5 and 6). *Relevé* or rise on the ball of the foot during the 7th count then *tombé* or fall on the 8th count.

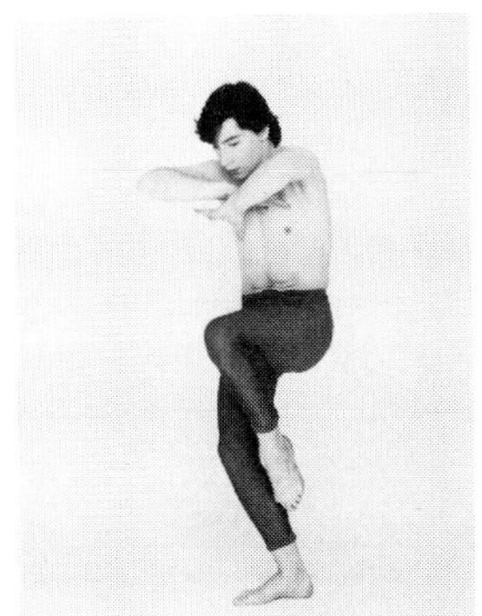

Count 1–4

Count 5–7

Count 8

Change legs and repeat to the other side in a completely different pose.

Never think of a *développé* or leg extension as merely a movement of the leg. The extension begins in the torso then infiltrates itself into the leg. In this way the entire body participates in the movement, not just the extremities.

If, in this exercise, you inadvertently hop, don't let it throw you. Use the hop as if it were deliberate. Learn to master the accident, major or minor, rather than the other way around.

Don't let the fingers or toes wiggle or scratch at the air. This unconscious nervous twitching is decidedly distracting to the viewer who has his own state of nervousness to escape from. He did not buy a ticket to witness yours. Move your fingers and toes when you wish to, not unknowingly.

The exercise *contained balance/expanded balance* places in perspective for the student when a movement is locked in and when it is released, when the movement is imprisoned and when it is freed. Contrast.

The body must be used as a musical instrument, capable of the most sombre (contained) and brilliant (expanded) tones.

Impose/recede

The student assumes a near stationary pose facing front with the feet slightly apart. Though this exercise barely moves an inch in any direction, it is one of the most fatiguing. This is due to the fact that because its gathering energy doesn't quite release itself (fomenting just beneath the surface), the student feels a physical fatigue from the holding back of his agitated mood. The ignition of force without its combustion is depleting.

The student works at a high mental pitch, using a powerful inner monologue. "Look at me! Look at me!," he insists. His imagined viewer, though, is obstinate and refuses. "I said 'Look at me, damn you, here I am! See me!' " So goes his running inner monologue. The element of resistance from an imagined person is essential for it triggers the desired conflict in this, the *impose* section.

The student must choose a situation that has an urgent significance for him. Is it an audition? Why does he need to be so noticed at that given moment? If it is solely to have his new shoes admired, such an insignificant need will not propel the exercise off the ground. There must be an urgency and immediacy.

The longer the student is ignored in his insistent demands, the more demanding he must become with his emotional stance. Good manners must be thrown to the winds. All of us have been brought up with a sense of politeness and reticence, qualities that make exercises such as this all the more difficult.

These exercises are designed to offset the restrictive conditioning of all our earlier lives. But they are for theatrical and artistic purposes, to be called upon when one wills it. This is technique, this is professional theatre as differentiated from personal therapy. This type of technique requires great freedom with an equal amount of control.

I have just explained the *impose* section of the exercise. To be able to do it well cultivates the assertiveness of the young mime actor. Its by-product is a stronger stage presence. When doing *impose*, the mind must be fed continuously with a thought to be followed at once with other thoughts. Don't work in spurts. One thought must feed the next in a continuous chain of belligerent images.

The opposite end of the exercise, *recede*, means just that. Mentally disappear. "Don't look at me. I'm not here. I've disappeared." So goes the inner monologue. This situation of mental escape is familiar to everyone. Who has not undergone the feeling of acute embarrassment when one fervently wished to go through the floor as a result of being in the midst of a discomforting situation?

As in every exercise, the teacher's instinct must determine the length of each of the sections. At the beginning, *impose/recede* is split up evenly as far as length of time is concerned. Then each section is shortened unevenly, the student going back and forth between the two opposing moods, perhaps $\frac{1}{4}$ minute for *impose* and five seconds for *recede*, then 10 seconds for *impose* and four seconds for *recede*, the irregularity of alternation developing an emotional agility.

Once in Darwin, the capital of the Northern Territory in Australia, the sound didn't begin as anticipated before *King Of The Silent Screen: Before The Talkies Hit Hollywood.* As the seconds dragged on and I realized a technical mishap had occurred, I thought with recurring intensity, "I'm not here. Don't look at me. I've gone." With that protective thought I disappeared off the stage until the sound system was repaired.

After the performance, one member of the audience told me that during that escape action of mine, the audience turned away from me to see what was wrong with the audio engineer's equipment. When they returned their gaze to the stage, I had disappeared. Calculation or coincidence, it worked!

Circular/angular

The entire body participates in the circular movements, not just the arms and legs. The periphery of the circles varies, from circumscribed to voluminous. During the *circular*, the body reverses direction and speed. Rotating and undulating, rippling and encircling, the mime actor makes patterns in the space around him, always curved and rounded. The lower body also joins in with extended arcs and *attitudes*, extensions of the upper body's circles.

When executing the *angular*, the movements are again begun from a central spasm. The navel, as if struck, precipitates the angularity, inciting the rest of the body with a robot-like rigidity and jerkiness. The energy comes in spurts, jolting the body into acute and obtuse angles in every position. The spasmodic quality of the movement is more difficult than it looks, requiring speed and strength to sustain the frenetic pace.

As in so many of my exercises, *circular/angular* calls upon a diametrically opposed approach. The student who feels sympathy with the *circular* does not always feel comfortable with its opposite and vice versa. Since everyone has weaknesses in direct proximity to his strongest points, the weaknesses must be worked on that much harder.

For example, if one's right foot is stronger in a *relevé*, then the *relevé* of the left foot should be worked on twice as much to equalize it.

Before a class begins, incidentally and fundamentally, never make virtuosic demands on one's self. *It takes one second to be injured and many, many months to heal.*

For variety, *circular/angular* can be done with the class sitting on the floor, this position limiting the freedom of torso movement possible when standing. The legs, therefore, are called into greater play, now able to cut their own smooth or sharp patterns in the air indefinitely, the backside serving as a stabilizing base.

Run with activity/freeze lifelessly; reverse run lifelessly/freeze with activity

Everything in life is motivated. In everything we do there is a reason behind it even when we, ourselves, are unaware of the reason. On stage the interpreter must be abundantly clear of his intentions if his role is to be comprehended by the audience. What might be a subconscious motivation for the character must be a very conscious one for the actor.

As the student advances, his movement becomes wedded to dramatic necessity. This is a key difference between mime and modern dance in that in the latter the movement may be its own reason for being whereas in mime, the movement must convey a thought, a mood or a feeling.

The class is asked to *run with activity*, to run for a reason. They must be in a hurry to arrive somewhere. They mustn't be late. They truly want to get there. Hurry. Hurry. So they *run with activity*, a motivated run.

'Freeze lifelessly!," they are told. And they suddenly stop, caught in their tracks, inanimate. Deprived of intention, they freeze as devoid of heartbeat as the girl from Pompeii, her death by Vesuvius still to be seen by history's tourists.

The students remain in their frozen and lifeless positions until they hear the repeat order to resume their runs with activity, again to cease suddenly and freeze lifelessly upon hearing that specific order.

Then the exercise is reversed. The students now *run lifelessly* with the appropriate thought in mind that would precipitate such aimless running. Perhaps one is a shell-shocked bomb survivor, running, running, he knows not where. The class, in this state, or with another thought that will achieve the same results, runs lifelessly.

"*Freeze with activity!*"

An instant awareness grips the ensemble of actors. A burst of adrenalin has relocated them. Frozen to the spot, they are in the state of poised awareness and instant readiness common to runners seconds before a race.

Subsequently, the four instructions—*run with activity/freeze lifelessly* and *run lifelessly/freeze with activity* are mixed at random. The group's mental dexterity is thus tested. They have begun to employ the why of moving.

Shifts in balance: strike a balance then while still balancing, shift axis

The students strike a vertical balance on one leg, conscious of a perfectly north to south (vertical) axis (Ill. 7 a).

"Shift balance," they are told. The angle of that balance is then changed, the group doing their best to sustain the balance while remaining on the one supporting leg without tottering (Ill. 7b).

7a 7b

When a balance is shifted from, let us say, a vertical position to a horizontal one, the student must avoid succumbing to the beckoning forces of gravity. To avoid hopping and stuttering with the feet, he must pull away, oppositionally, from the source of danger, namely, the floor.

The arms should be spread out as the wing span of a plane, one arm reaching in one direction, the other arm reaching in the opposite direction. Do not let the second arm hang as mere decoration. The novice tends to work with only one side of the body instead of using both sides in a form of oppositional traction. The opposing pull gives the student stability and surety. Its absence pushes him over the precipice of precarious stance.

The further you reach in one direction, the further you must reach in the other direction.

"Change!" The student now balances vertically on the other leg. "Shift balance!" Again he moves his body off the vertical axis without having altered the original position. The more daring his shift, the more he must pull up, the more he must reach oppositionally to avoid collapsing in the torso.

The length of time from the striking of the balance to the shift of the balance will vary as it does in all the exercises. Let the head reach out of the neck and let the arms reach out of the waist (not the armpits), particularly as the tempo accelerates from the vertical to the off the vertical balance.

Spatial patterns

Using the body as a giant paint brush and space as a huge canvas, paint a huge mural. Make patterns that employ the diagonals, figure eights, horizontals, verticals, circular, zig-zag and any other designs that come to mind. Like a kaleidoscope, the pictures one can draw are limitless. Don't remain in two or three grooves of increasing similarity. Be unpredictable. Make it a surprise journey for the public instead of a route they travel blind.

Many years ago when I grew up in New York City, the subway riders never looked up from their newspapers when the train crossed the East River. Only children and visitors stared out at the phalanx of colossal edifices, 24 hour a day guards of New York's glistening black jungle. Don't let your efforts, whether in a classroom exercise or on stage, deteriorate into a route travelled without curiosity. Keep your audience interested. Force them to look out of the window and view the river of unexpected vistas.

When doing the exercise *spatial patterns*, the student must remember that he has staked his claim to the environment and must fascinate us by his exploration of it. He must not walk around with the prosaic approach seen in supermarket aisles. The audience, even if they are hungry, do not want another can of beans. The theatre is a restaurant of the spirit. Nourish them.

So move with zest. Reveal the life force in full. Use space, writing a love poem with your body as the paint brush. Or even a hate poem, graffiti, if you must. But do say something on that blank space. And say it with force.

When I studied acting with Shelley Winters in Hollywood during the mid 1950s, she once referred to Bette Davis saying, "Right or wrong, she goes!"

Conducting an orchestra

It is an established fact that conductors, as a group, generally live to a ripe old age. This laudable durability, I am convinced, is due to the incessant exercise of the profession. I recall one evening backstage at the Israel National Opera in Tel-Aviv, the veteran conductor returning to the dressing room, his black tail-coat drenched in sweat.

Some time after when living in Haifa, I used to coach a prize-winning woman conductor. She had been having problems with male orchestras not taking her seriously due to her gender. If she wore something feminine, she believed she would be distracting them. If she wore a tailored suit, she thought she would be confirming their implied prejudice. The answer, I told her, was in the authority she wielded over them, not in her apparel.

I made her conduct an imaginary orchestra lying on her back, on her knees, on her stomach, on her hip and on a revolving piano stool. With such fatiguing obstacles, by the time she stood up to conduct on two feet, it was mere child's play. She needed half her energy to impose her musical will while obtaining double the results.

To conduct Debussy required a different approach than Wagner, the first more filigree, the latter more monumental.

The power she exerted had to reach two targets, the orchestra in front of her and the audience behind. Each group of people had to be mesmerized into submission.

Out of that experience evolved the exercise *conducting an orchestra*, an exercise which cultivates stage authority and release, two irreplaceable ingredients in the chemistry of a powerful performance.

So, repeating the instructions first given to the Israeli conductor, conduct an orchestra standing up, then sitting down, kneeling, on one hip then the other hip, on the stomach, on the back, while pivoting on the backside then finally, again on two feet. And remember that all arm movements emanate from the pit of the stomach.

The musical accompaniment should be Verdi, Rossini or any other bravura and rhythmic composer of that era.

Duality of concentration

The mime artist has to work on a multi-dimensional level, concentrating both emotionally and physically at the same moment. When either aspect is absent, incompleteness results.

In the following exercise the students become puppets, expressing a variety of emotions. To begin with, they bounce around to an allegro rhythm provided by the pianist, keeping the rhythm without any tempo alteration. Once they succeed in sustaining a rhythmic regularity in their movements to the music, an emotion is added without changing the tempo.

Happiness. The mime artist communicates joy, all the while keeping the rhythm established earlier.

Apathy. Care must be taken that the student doesn't slow up, for this mood encourages a retardation in tempo.

Anger. Always calling upon a genuine source of remembrance or the honest projection into fantasy, the mime actor expresses anger while staying with the rhythm.

Yearning. The student craves and longs for some unrealized goal, still clinging to the puppet rhythm.

So there we have the exercise *duality of concentration*. The rhythm of the puppet hasn't been sacrificed for the addition of the emotion. The student now begins to appreciate that acting while moving to music is not as simple as it looks.

Motivation exercise

As a wordless actor, the mime must at all times know why he is doing what. If the reason is unclear to the mime artist, how can it possibly be clear to an audience? Clarity begins at home, in this case, the mind of the interpreter.

The actor always has an "action" or purpose, intention or objective. Call it a goal, if you will. He also has an "attitude" that colours that action. By understanding the character's need, we further comprehend what makes him tick, his reason for behaving as he does, his motivation.

The character might not understand why he behaves as he does, but the actor playing him must. The motivation exercise helps bring to the forefront of the actor's consciousness, the reason the character behaves as he does.

The members of the class are divided into two groups. Each group will run from one end of the studio to the opposite end then without stopping return, still running, to the starting point. The first group begins the run after a specific emotion is called out. (The second group waits its turn.)

Anger. The student runs contaminated by that eruptive state of mind. Quickly he must understand the reason he is running while so angry. Has someone picked his pocket or tried to rob him?

Compassion. Someone in the street has had an accident. Run as quickly as you can to help.

Fear. Imagine (without difficulty for a big city dweller) you are walking home very late at night and a group of unruly looking teenaged boys are trailing you. They start to accelerate their pace. Run, for you are very frightened.

Denial. Run denying the accusation that you have committed a theft.

In these previous runs, the student must borrow from the generous fund of his own experience. If the given incident lies outside of his actual knowledge, then he must call upon his imagination.

Once in a while a student will justify his inability to do a scene because he, himself, has never known the experience. As it happens, few of us have ever strangled our beloved so how do we cast *Othello*?

One's religion, sexuality or ideology cannot be the deciding factor in being or not being the dramatist's creation. An actor, whether mime, dancer or singer, should not be an exhibitionist. If the so-called actor is unfortunate enough to fall into that lamentable category of show-off, then he would have a valid excuse for being unable to act outside the sphere of his own familiarity.

The true actor transcends the barricades of passports, passion and politics. He can be anywhere for fantasy succeeds where facts have failed.

Tautness in lower body/plasticity in upper body: reverse

Everyone lies on his back with feet towards the teacher. At the signal to commence, the student makes the lower body rigid (from the waist down) while moving the upper body with as much plasticity as possible. The student feels peculiar dividing the body into two such opposing camps. He wants to move with either head to toe rigidity or head to toe plasticity.

When the word *reverse* is heard, the student moves the lower body with extreme plasticity while keeping the upper body rigid.

Doing this exercise in oppositional isolation leads to a fuller control of one's instrument.

Compensation

There are dreaded periods in the movement artist's life when an injury has occurred either before the day of a performance or even during. On the occasions when a replacement is out of the question, compensatory technique must be called upon as the emergency 999 on the telephone.

Once on Liberian television I pulled a muscle in my groin preventing me, the next night in Sierra Leone, from lifting my leg more than a few inches off the ground. To compensate I used my upper body with accelerated intensity so as to distract the eye from my earthbound legs. The compensation worked. My injury was not in evidence despite my being aware of it every second.

Another time, on opening night in Jakarta, Java, the adjoining building "stole" some of the volume from my sound system. (Another performance was taking place in this theatre complex.) I could barely discern the telephone rings in *While In The Bathtub*. Calling upon even more frantic antics, I tried to be more comic in what was for me a very unfunny situation. I compensated. What other option is open? To hold up the white flag of surrender?

Let us now do the *compensation exercise*. The lower body is to be incapacitated. Don't move it. Work only with the upper body.

Conversely, the upper body is, after a minute or so, to be incapacitated while the lower body compensates with much movement.

This exercise can be extended by sitting on the floor with the hands held behind the back and the feet pressed together. Now convey the desire to break the invisible bonds by escaping through the torso and unhampered face. Again, we have compensated.

When a problem presents itself, the experienced performer will, intuitively, employ compensation. The novice will advertise his predicament. Remember that one never apologizes on stage. Obliterate the error by increased excellence. Redeem yourself by brilliance.

Inflate/run

Firstly, these runs are to be stylized, not actual. No racing to catch a bus. No one needs to be taught how to run down the street. That you already know. The stylized run about to be learned can be called upon in a time-stilled sequence such as a reverie or daydream.

In the preparatory *inflate*, the feet are placed together. Rise on *demi-pointes* (the balls of the feet) while inflating, the inhalation inflating the entire body through the fingertips and crown of the head. The torso goes forward but the arms go slightly behind the shoulder line, the arms placed at the side. The torso wants to go forward, the arms think differently. Again, opposition. But the body will win and the arms will have no choice but to follow.

This is conflict in movement. Whether we like it or not, conflict is part of our lives from the moment we resist our entry into the world (who would wish to leave such absolute security as we once knew in the womb?) to the ultimate moment on earth. Conflict is the very weave of great theatrical fabric.

As we prepare to run, conflict has already made its presence felt. The reluctant arms follow the more insistent torso. The run has begun. The runner remains on *demi-pointes*, the heels thus remaining off the ground. The toes touch the ground first which is the opposite from the usual walk in which the heel precedes the toe.

The arms are held lightly to the side with bent elbows. If the elbows are locked during the run, the arms will jerk with each reverberation. Bent elbows take the jolt of the journey as surely as a Rolls-Royce rides smoother than a second-hand jalopy.

Don't look at the floor when you run. By looking at the ground, the attention of the audience is drawn to the floor, thereby anchoring their focus to base level.

To avoid repetitiveness, the runner can alter the rhythm of the steps; long step, long step, short, short, short step, for example.

While running, lift out of the waist. Don't be a turtle retreating into its shell.

To run beautifully brings pleasure to the eye of the beholder for people vicariously identify with effortless transit.

Body stops/thought continues

With a particular thought in mind such as *fear*, *begging*, *encouraging* and *refusal*, the students start running around the studio. Then, at the command, they stop running, freezing on spot. Though the body is frozen, the thought continues. The brain does not cut off.

Fear. Immediately the student finds the emotion so familiar to everyone in some degree. Who has not known fear? When one sees a student who is faking that emotion, it is generally due to the fact that he or she is afraid to confront the memory or the imagined reality. There can be no moral cowardice if you want to be an artist. The genuine actor has to have the courage to strip himself psychically, unafraid of exposing the sentiments within himself.

The student runs afraid. Stop! The body immobilizes but the thought still registers in the body and face for the brain continues to clock its ticking terror.

Begging. The class runs around the studio while begging. Wait. Let's begin again. What and why are you begging? For a cup of tea? For a biscuit? If you select a trivial image, there will be no immediacy or urgency. Choose a thought that will trigger you into maximum action. Find for yourself a do or die mental picture. If you settle for an optional image, the begging run will not ring true. A genuine beggar is at the end of his tether.

I, myself, have the most horrific memories of leprous beggars in the West African country of Mali and of a boy without a nose in Kabul, Afghanistan.

You can't fool me and more importantly you cannot fool yourself.

Encouraging. Run encouraging someone. Is your friend trying to complete a marathon race? Is someone you care for attempting to complete a swim across the Channel? Find your image and hang on to it. Stop! The body freezes while the encouraging thoughts continue in full force.

Refusal. The group begin to run, each person having selected the image which will initiate the exercise. Once again the choice of thought must be strong and constant. No intermittent images. Find the thought. Feed it. Nourish it. Don't let it die on the vine.

Stop! The group is rooted but their believability is as potent as when they were running in adamant refusal.

Whether the body is motionless or moving, the mind never goes on holiday under the piercing light of public penetration.

Singing with the torso

The class, en masse, sing a song such as the Russian *Dark Eyes*, moving their bodies in accompaniment. Then they stop the actual singing, transferring the sound of the song into the still moving torso. The torso is, consequently, enriched by the transference of the previously heard but now visualized melody.

People tend to become encased by a cylindrical rigidity of the torso. The body tends to become imprisoned by the enveloping walls of one's own timidity. A breakthrough is called for. The torso must more than speak out; it must sing with such eloquence that we have no choice but to listen.

To begin the exercise, the students sing while moving the torso. At the command, the students stop singing, redistributing the song into the body.

This exercise helps the student achieve awareness of his torso as a musical instrument, capable of soaring melodic line.

Hand-held mask exercise

When a hand held mask is used well, it becomes an extension of the mime actor's arm. It is not a prop that he is clinging to, but a part and parcel of his being.

The moment the actor touches the handle of the mask, he is transformed into the character of that particular visage. If the mask is grotesque, his body becomes contorted. If the mask is that of a deity, he becomes god-like and omnipotent. The mask assumes a strength of its own, permeating the actor's mind, thereby colouring his absorbent body. The mask becomes the master, the actor, his servant.

In the exercise, the group becomes professional mourners at a funeral, the kind still to be found in certain parts of southern Italy. With the mask held in place, flat against the face, the mourner writhes and insinuates himself among the genuine throng. Then the mask is removed. The mourner becomes oblivious of his surroundings, untouched by one iota of grief. Suddenly, awareness returns and the mask, abruptly, is placed against the face. The lamentation continues, the mask becoming the focal point of synthetic sorrow.

I repeat. The hand held mask is not an appendage. The mask is the arm elongated, the hand extended.

Walking/trotting/running

Everyone begins walking in any direction around the studio. At the command each person accelerates to trotting. With the final order, each person graduates to running. The divisions between the *walking/trotting/running* must be imperceptible.

Once everyone understands the necessity of smooth links between the sections, the students are divided into three groups. The first group begins with walking, the second group commences with trotting and the third group starts with running. When the teacher claps his hands shouting, "Change!," each group moves into the next division.

For example, those who begin walking now trot. Those who begin trotting now run. And those who begin running now walk. When the teacher again claps his hands, the groups move into the next division. And so it continues with the teacher clapping his hands at unexpected time lengths.

The effect of these concurrent groups accelerating at different speeds create an air of unreality, tearaway pages from Kafka-like intimidation to Sartre-style confinement. There is no exit for the perpetual runners.

Inflate, run, stop and deflate

The inflation is the equivalent of the warming up of a plane's propellers. The run is the flight, the stop is the landing and the deflation is the coming to a halt of the airborne apparatus.

The inflation is the anticipation of the run. The run, itself, is sustained by wings of flexible elbows and breathing fingers. This is followed by the deflation, the termination. The body has ceased to move though the exhalation takes a few more seconds to complete itself. The deflation achieves a lingering and pacifying effect which contrasts with the preceding and energetic movement.

Cause and effect balance

The student runs and abruptly stops in an off the centre balance, a balance so precarious it cannot but falter. The student then falls in a position dictated by the previous and "risky" pose. The runs, cliff hanging balances and plunges, are continued, each time with a new and always bravado balance.

The fall from the precarious balance must be a logical one, a natural culmination from the position which precipitated it. If one strikes a balance that tilts to the right, the fall must be to the right, not to the left. If one strikes a balance which inclines to the front, the fall must sequentially continue to the front. To fall backwards in the latter case would be a reversal of the natural impulse, a result counter to the purpose of this exercise.

After the fall, the next run is resumed without cutting off the energy flow. This means that the student falls and keeps the motor on during his held position before the next run begins.

The precarious balance is the protest, the cause. But the student failing, falls. This is the effect. The lost balance is thus the cause, the resultant fall, the effect.

Walking past each other with and without contact

This exercise makes no technical demands but calls upon the emotional resources of the student.

The students walk past each other, coming and going in every direction, disassembling, reassembling, caught up in the human web of the milling crowd. The physical proximity is such that bodies touch as quickly as they pass each other but there is no emotional contact. The heat of the throng does not melt the wall of ice encasing each individual. Strangers. Coming and going. Hands brush past each other's bodies but without one whit of emotional warmth.

Change. Now walk past each other *with* intense mental and emotional contact. In this instance, however, there is no physical meeting, no touching whatsoever.

Keep moving throughout the entire scene. Despite the temptation to stop when aware of a particularly attractive person, you must never stop walking, continuing to move until that person disappears. The eyes linger but the body keeps going until the next desirable person comes into view.

The beautiful being that attracts you is the person in the opposite aisle of the plane, on the train or just passed by in the street, never seen before and never to be seen again.

To restate: The students walk past each other touching each other lightly and briefly but without emotional contact.

Reverse.

The students then walk past each other without touching each other at all but establishing brief and intense emotional rapport.

The strength of the mind's intention is of uppermost importance in this exercise; touching when feeling nothing and not touching when feeling everything.

One minute solo in three speeds: slow, medium, fast

The same choreography executed in different speeds will take on a different look with each tempo. By repeating the same solo in a slow tempo, then medium and finally fast, the apprentice choreographer will begin to realize the important part varying degrees of speed playing in colouring movement.

To walk with excessive slowness is to create a surreal ambience. When, in the cinema, the camera records in slow motion, the movie goer is transported to a world seen only in a dream.

To walk in an ordinary tempo is to endorse our known reality, the every day speed recognizable in our own as well as other bodies.

To walk with exaggerated speed is to flirt with farce. Double time speed makes us laugh for the outrageous antics of the buffoon are recalled, from among other sources, the quickened jerkiness of the silent screen.

The apprentice choreographer/performer first creates his one minute solo. Having memorized it, he dances it with an exceedingly slow control. The solo is then danced at a midway speed. Finally, the solo is danced double time.

The variations of speed are one of the principal flavours in the recipe of great performances, the other ingredients including technical virtuosity, dramatic truth, musical affinity and spiritual aura.

Elbows and knees coordination exercise

Sitting on their backsides, the students draw in their legs and arms, bending them to the maximum. With this position as their starting point, they proceed to straighten both arms and legs at exactly the same time. The knees and elbows will now lock simultaneously (Ill. 8a, Ill. 8b).

8a

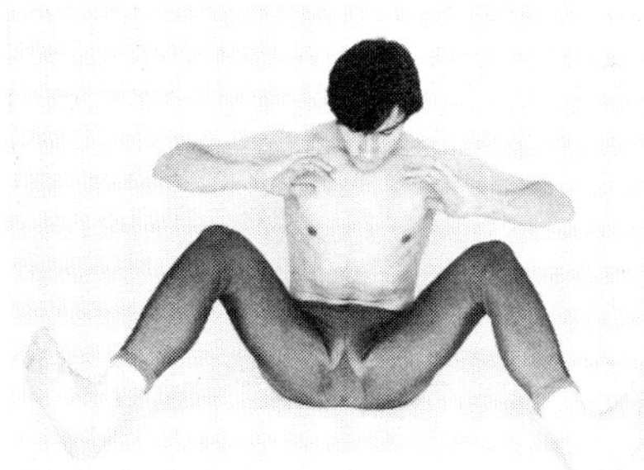

8b

The straightening and bending of both elbows and knees go on for a rhythmic 32 bars.

The tendency is for the student to lock the knees before the elbows or the reverse. This must be avoided for the point of the exercise is to develop a precise coordination between those most worked joints of the body, the elbows (the knees of the arms) and the knees (the elbows of the legs).

The stretching of the spine is also brought in, a third coordination factor. On the *and* count, the spine is collapsed while the arms and legs are in their maximum bent position. On the *1* count, the elbows and knees straighten while the spine pulls out of its sunken position into a fully stretched vertical.

To recapitulate: The knees and elbows are bent while the spine is collapsed. Then everything straightens jointly; elbows, knees and spine. From this moment on, the sinking/stretching rhythm is continuous.

Continuity of movement

Continuity of movement is the hallmark of the finest movement exponents. The seamless, endless, infinite quality of movement is a joy to behold (for the viewer) and for the student, the rainbow at the end of his troubled skies.

The body, consisting as it does of so many bits and pieces, tends to work partially. The moment awareness is not distributed equitably throughout the body, jerkiness rears its uninvited head. Head to toe consciousness must prevail, a consciousness that enables the dancing actor, the expressive mime and the moving singer to move cohesively, to move with flow and fluency.

Firstly, the body must be sufficiently strong and cultivated so that every muscle answers at once to every command. No hesitation. No resistance and never rebellion. Secondly, as one begins to move, the propelling thought must contain a total picture of the entire body in motion. If, therefore, the right leg is dominating, one mustn't lose sight of the other limbs contributing to the overall picture. As a further example, if the chest is the focal point of the movement, do not forget the left hip, right foot and so forth. Never concentrate on one part of the body to the exclusion of another part.

Think of the body as a total unit.

Jerkiness and fragmentation tend to take place, in particular, when the movement becomes difficult such as lowering the leg from a high extension, the descent from a balance or the coming up from a backbend. No matter how complex the series of movements, there must be no stops, no discordant interruptions.

There must also be a cause and effect relationship between the arms so that a dominating right arm does not put into the shade the progress of the left. Nor does a dominant left arm mean that the right arm must be inert. Be aware that though either arm can be relatively passive, it is still participating.

During the student's improvisation, special attention must be paid to the uninterrupted flow so that the end of one movement blends into the beginning of the next. From the crown of the head to the tip of the toe, there must be a non-stop motion. Not one part of the body can be static for even a moment. Even when apparently still, there is undercurrent.

Symmetrical body line exercise

The right side of the body must always relate to the left. What happens to one side always causes a reaction to the other. An instantaneous interreaction between the two halves of the body is not instinctive. Harmony between the two halves must be cultivated, otherwise a state of civil war will exist between the north and south, the east and west of the body.

To begin the exercise, the student strikes straight line poses with the arms. Whatever the right arm does (in a straight line) is paralleled by the left arm (also in a straight line). If the right arm reached straight up, the left arm might reach straight down. If the left arm reaches horizontally to the left, the right arm reaches horizontally to the right. And so forth. With each new straight arm position, there is a complimentary relationship between both straight lines. The position of one straight arm automatically sets the supplementary position of the other.

These straight arm positions are the simplest in the *symmetrical body line exercise*. We now graduate to the more difficult curved symmetrical lines.

The principle remains identical, the difference being that now one arm strikes a curved position to be counterbalanced by a curve of the other arm. The torso does not observe rigidly but joins in with a tilt or inclination appropriate to the newly struck design. The torso is the moving mediator between the curve of the left arm and the curve of the right arm.

We now arrive at the most complex section of the *symmetrical body line exercise*, the angular position. Again, the principle of an equal relationship continues. With this third attempt, the arm (always starting from the torso) strikes an angular line. Both elbow and wrist bend in any direction decided upon by the student. The other arm, as before, follows instantaneously with reverse angles or, perhaps, identical angles.

When giving this exercise, I break the progression by mixing them (angular, straight, curved or straight, angular, curved, etc), so that the class cannot anticipate the command, varying also the duration of each of the sections.

This exercise, which helps develop instant relationship between two halves of the body, brings to mind a ballet world tale of two halves of a piece of fruit.

The eminent ballet teacher Cecchetti once stated, "There was an apple in the world. One half was Pavlova and the other Spessivtzeva." Then, in a magazine interview, Diaghilev added, "But the sun shone towards Spessivtzeva," perhaps resenting Pavlova's defection from his company after their first Paris season together. The swan, it can be added, never forgave the chinchilla for that remark.[1]

High voltage/low voltage

The electrical analogy is deliberate. The high voltage is great inner intensity releasing itself in highly charged muscular gestures. The low voltage is a lowered inner intensity releasing itself in more subdued muscular gestures.

To do the exercise, each student goes on his knees and with palms to the chest pushes forward with high voltage. The high voltage gesture of the arms begins in the stomach, extends through the pectoral muscles and releases itself through the arms.

Having gestured out with great intensity, one returns to the palms to chest position with a much lowered intensity or low voltage. Low voltage is not to be confused with relaxation. The arms do not become limp; they only reduce their intensity from a high to a lower voltage.

Now the students must reverse the procedure by gesturing outwards with *low* voltage and returning to their chests with *high* voltage.

A more complex variation on this exercise would be to have the students gesture out with high voltage which suddenly lessens into low voltage as the movement completes itself. In the reversal, the low voltage gesture inwards concludes with high voltage. In other words, the voltage changes within the same gesture.

A singer, whose gesture fluctuates in intensity, is much more interesting visually than a singer who remains on one note physically. One plane of energy, no matter how exciting, soon loses its impact. The mime/actor/dancer/singer must play a scale of many octaves on his variable instrument, the body.

Small gesture/low voltage; large gesture/high voltage: reverse

Do a small gesture with low voltage. Stop. Now do a large gesture with high voltage. So far there is no problem for what I have asked you to do has registered in your mind as logical.

[1] Diaghilev was nicknamed "chinchilla" because of the prominent white streak seen through his black head of hair.

Now think carefully and correctly do the following.

Do small gestures with *high* voltage. Continue doing this until these movements become second nature. Vary the small gestures, drawing designs in the air around you, remembering, however, that high voltage permeates the exercise.

Now change to large gestures with *low* voltage. Keep painting patterns in space, always retaining the minimal voltage within the large movement.

The student can then be allowed to change the gestures and voltages at will: small gesture with low voltage, small gesture with high voltage, large gesture with high voltage and large gesture with low voltage. This exercise helps the student to develop a chameleon-like ability to produce body tones and colours, from the subdued to electric.

Punctuation in movement

Write a love letter. Why do you seem so surprised? Everyone in this room, I would venture to say, has at least once put down on paper passionate feelings distilled into near poetic form. Love, the great narcotic of the soul, when let loose happily into the veins, permits us to fly without wings.

The air about you is the paper. You are the pen. Put your most eloquent thoughts to paper as you write a letter of love to someone past or present. When I, the teacher, name the specific punctuation, you, the student, interpret that punctuation in movement.

Dear, whomever you are addressing your letter to. Write that person's name with your body movement.

First paragraph. Write this paragraph with improvisational movement, expressing your deepest affection to the addressee.

Question mark. Do you really love me?

New paragraph. The student continues "writing" until I may say, "full stop" or "period." His body then assumes a completion stance.

The student resumes again until I say "comma," suggesting a slight separation. His body indicates that pause.

Continue until the word "ellipsis" is spoken, an ellipsis in printing being the ... which signifies omissions. Do you remember that night on the deck of the ship.... ? The student conveys the left out reflections in movement.

Final paragraph. Sum up the essence of all your loving thoughts, composure now having given way to exposure.

Yours devotedly. Then sign your name.

This étude (exercise sounds rather prosaic for a letter of love) makes few demands on the technical knowledge of the student. It does, though, call upon the contribution of the actor's aide-de-camp, fantasy. The student must translate, without hesitation, the writer's punctuation into imaginative movement.

Weight and weightlessness in characterization

This exercise has nothing to do with actual quantity of heaviness. One can be physically thin yet, emotionally speaking, heavy. On the other hand, one can be plump yet, in a personality sense, light. So, as can be seen, the weight I'm referring to is emotional, not physical.

You, yourself, can begin the day heavy with the pedestrian cares of unpaid bills and other domestic distractions then later in the day receive a good news phone call that lightens the earlier mood. Similarly, a theatrical character can begin with one weight then fluctuate according to the circumstances.

When I played Puck in the first Swedish production of Benjamin Britten's opera, *A Midsummer Night's Dream*, the springy lightness of my character's movement quality almost taunted the ground. It was as if by touching upon the earth I was doing it a momentary favour since my natural habitat was air. Puck, of course, was domiciled in dreams and as such could flit and float beyond the scope of fleeting man.

We're now going to do a "light" characterization, that of a conductor conducting frothy and ebullient music such as Rossini or von Suppé. With the imagined baton in hand, each student creates a lightweight maestro.

Stay. Now change into a "heavy" soprano singing, possibly, Mahler or Wagner.

Reverse. Now be a "heavy" conductor, conducting, perhaps, Sibelius or Richard Strauss.

Stay. Now be a "light" soprano singing the other Strauss, Johann.

Other characters from heavy to light can be asylum inmates, alcoholics and on a less burdened level, tightrope walkers and circus strongmen.

The physical images must permeate the muscles so that the "light" characters are weightless while the "heavy" characters are weighted. Additional characters to be given to the class can be clowns, lightweight in performance and heavyweight behind the scenes and professional mourners, heavyweight with masks on and lightweight with masks off.

The ability to weight a character with accuracy lends credibility to the creation, assisting the audience in their belief of the stage image. Only in rare circumstances when an actor feels an instinctive affinity with a character, can he, without analysis, attack the role. Generally, he must build, bit by bit, the character, using at all rehearsals, every means of understanding at his disposal.

Greek tragedy and comedy masks

In this exercise the main concentration is in the face with the rest of the body contributing in a subsidiary way.

To begin with, all the students bring to life the image of a Greek tragedy mask, emphasizing the mournful mouth. The pose is framed by a body racked in grief.

Next the students recreate the image of a Greek comedy mask, the body again framing the overstretched laughing face.

Finally the students instantaneously etch the portrait of a wailing scream, the mouth contorted in an elongated O. This primeval cry is bordered by gesture frozen in archaic anguish.

The three poses (tragedy mask, comedy mask and screaming mask) are alternated, not in succession, and with different time lengths.

Then the class is divided into three groups of the three masks just mentioned. Moving at will about the studio, the tragedy mask group will verbalize in a made up language, the comedy mask people will laugh continuously while the screaming mask group will wail with a muted scream.

At the signal, each group moves to the next division so that the tragedy mask people become the comedy mask group, the comedy mask people become the screaming mask group and the screaming mask people become the tragedy mask group. Change! Each group again moves on to the next.

Now, the three groups will all interrelate to each other on a physical and emotional level with the invented language group (the tragedy masks) being the most audibly conspicuous. This exercise, when done by knowledgable students, transcends the limits of the classroom, reviving the great open air theatres of antiquity.

Musical phrasing

To be truly musical goes far beyond mere metronomic obedience. The most minimal aspect of musicality is keeping to the beat. Any dancing teenager, dizzied by disco lighting and deafened by rock rhythms, can keep a steady tempo.

A person who is musically masterful reflects the spirit of the composition, mirroring its very essence, capturing its soul, so to speak.

Response to music is, I believe, inborn. Sensitivity to Chopin cannot really be taught. In a way, a great teacher brings out what the student subliminally knows.

The sound of Bartok calls forth its movement counterpart as the sound of Bach calls forth another. If someone whispers lovingly into your ear to awaken you from a long night's slumber, you react one way. If that same person were to shout at you suddenly, you'd wake up with a start. There has to be a difference in reaction as there must be when you move to Debussy as differentiated from Dvořák.

With a waltz as an accompaniment, have the class kneel on both knees and gesture outwards with the right arm (1,2,3), left arm (2,2,3) and right arm (3,2,3,4,2,3). Note that the final gesture of the right arm has extended to two phrases.

Repeat the exercise to the left. After the class has learned the exercise with this phrasing, they can then do a variation of it with any phrasing of their own choice.

The arm movement should not begin at the shoulder but, as always, from the navel area of the stomach. If the movement doesn't begin from this central base, we have flailing appendages from immovable trunks.

This exercise, taught at a fundamental level, is designed to develop the rhythmic response of the student, helping him to move *with* the sound and not against it. To play with the phrases, taking subtle liberties, comes at a later date. To *be* the music is, of course, the ultimate rung of the ladder.

Running forward, backward, sideway, circularly

Opposition must be introduced in all of the above categories. When running forward the feeling is not only towards the destination but also straight up, this imagined axis from the head to the ceiling, insuring the verticality of the run.

When running backward, an awkward feeling at the best of times, one must have the sensation of being pulled front. This counterbalances the tendency to land on one's backside! As one runs backward, reach front with the arms. This pulled front gesture offsets the inclination to topple backwards.

When running sideway, again feel a pull from the opposite side in order to prevent falling.

Lastly, when running circularly, so as to minimize dizziness, spot. To spot means keeping the head as long as possible at one point, then at the very last moment whipping the head around back to that original point as quickly as possible.

Running in movement theatre requires the same degree of stylization as talking does in the theatre of Shakespeare.

Sustained inner motor

Everyone in the class moves about the studio in a very slow and stylized manner (the feet pointing and the walk controlled), physically and emotionally relating to various objects as he or she passes by them. Perhaps the student touches a wall or window or gently caresses a pillar or chair as it crosses his slow moving path. Whatever object it is that he relates to, he keeps his inner motor turned on. The engine can accelerate or retard. Never, though, does it switch off.

The experienced artist can remain motionless on a stage and have no difficulty in retaining the interest of the public. The newcomer tends to take rest periods when not working full out. In moments of seeming inactivity, he often turns off his motor, consequently cutting his performance in two.

Once the motor is turned on in the wings, it is never turned off until returning to the wings. The motor, that inner source of energy which instigates the body into action, does not cut off.

Whether the exercise lasts for two minutes or five, this sense of heightened awareness must be sustained. Occasional good moments will not suffice. The level of excitement must be unbroken.

The student's inner motor is as much in evidence when he stops to touch a wall as when he moves from one part of the studio to another. Whether kneeling, looking, touching or stationary, the inner motor, that organic aliveness, is switched on, on stage, at all times.

Attraction/repulsion

Each person selects a partner and when the go-ahead is given, responds with the attraction he feels for that person. Do not equate attraction with only physical appeal for the word embraces other desirable qualities as well. Intellect, for example. Artistic admiration. There are many kinds of attraction other than sexuality though if that aspect is chosen, it is perfectly valid.

During the *attraction* section of the improvisation, each person responds to the other, reciprocally expressing his or her interest.

The opposite, *repulsion*, follows. The disgust expressed need not be for only a physical deformity though this response springs quickly to mind. The repulsion can be severely negative reaction to the person's character, the viciousness of their disposition. You select what you will but convey what you must. If your partner is particularly charming and personable, the repulsion section is dependent on a well secured image of distaste.

Now, we do the improvisation so that one person feels attraction while the other person, concurrently, feels repulsion. Change! The person feeling attraction switches to a feeling of repulsion while the partner who felt repulsion now changes to a mood of attraction.

The thought must be all powerful so that the body answers, without hesitation, to the given situation.

Communication through face only

First of all, let me make clear what I feel about the facial expressions of too many mimes. They grimace and pull faces, thereby ruining whatever other virtues they may possess. Mugging is for street mimes and has no more relationship to the theatre than begging in the street has to Margot Fonteyn launching a charitable appeal on television.

All the students now sit on the floor with the legs crossed and hands behind the backs. At the given signal the following emotion is to be expressed through the face only.

Begging. Some 45 seconds later, *anger*. After a similar amount of time elapses, *compassion*. With each of the emotions being kept to a corresponding duration, the next is *enthusiasm*, then *disapproval* and finally *exasperation*.

The emotion must be channeled primarily through the face. There will be, inevitably, an emotional overlap into the body but effort must be made for the face to be the main outlet of the required state of mind. The temptation is ever present but try not to let the thought disperse itself indiscriminately throughout the body. Keep the thought on the track, that very short track from the brain to the face itself.

Don't mouth. Never mouth when miming unless it's deliberate such as a silent screen portrayal. Encourage the thought to escape through every feature of the face, not through the lips as if talking.

Allow one thought wave to spill over into the next. You are the transmitter of your thought waves, radioed through the features of your potentially expressive face.

Communication through hands only

Still sitting on the floor in a cross-legged position again convey the emotions of *begging*, *anger*, *compassion*, *enthusiasm*, *disapproval* and finally *exasperation*, but in this exercise, only through the hands. The principle of directing the thought into a particular part of the body remains intact.

The face is now in the shadows while the hands are in the emotional spotlight. If the face is the mirror of the soul, then the hands are the handle of that reflection.

When Mediterranean people use their hands, it is usually an expressive extension of their thought but when Anglo-Saxons use theirs to embellish speech, it is often distracting and even ugly. I, for one, do not relish a politician's index finger menacingly pointed into my eye or his chubby, laced together fingers slicing the air while accentuating each and every word.

For the mime artist, hands can and do speak volumes in the absence of words. To paraphrase Thomas Wolfe, the artist is the tongue of his unuttered brothers.

Communication through feet only

This exercise, compared to the face only and hands only exercises, is the one that seems most unnatural, for feet, for most people, are for walking, not talking. Nevertheless, feet can, indeed, communicate.

I've been told that my toes curl independently of each other when I contort in *The Addict*. I assume the observation is accurate though I couldn't swear to it since I don't watch myself in a mirror when rehearsing. Nor can I, it goes without saying, see myself during a performance.

As in the previous exercise, the students sit on the floor. Again, the thought takes root in the mind and travels, express, to the feet. Instead of aiming the message into the face or hands, extend the message to the feet then release that thought through the insteps and toes. The thought process is the same as in the hands and feet exercises, the difference being in the greater distance the mental image must travel.

Articulate feet are a necessity, feet that point, that don't sickle but turn out, that shoot through space with the swiftness of an arrow, that descend to the ground with the controlled lightness of a balloon, such feet are the result of unending ballet training. Feet either work automatically or they cannot be considered as working at all. If you have to think about what your feet are doing, it's too late. The ugly line or the dramatic lie have already been perpetrated.

Automatic feet are capable of expressing the many seasons of experience. Scales must be played to perfection before the melody can lull us into willing captivity. Attention, therefore, must be paid to unending feet exercises.

Having separately done the communication through face only, through hands only and through feet only, the student now combines the three during the course of one exercise. Each of the emotions is expressed through everything, the face, the hands and the feet, concurrently. The rest of the body has no choice but to join in when the extremities are such full participants.

Begging. Anger. Compassion. Enthusiasm. Disapproval. Exasperation. Each of these emotions is now expressed totally.

The resultant electricity gives vibrancy to the outer edges of the body, framing brilliantly the picture within. The end product can be a moving work of art.

Out of focus/in focus line

Strike a pose *out of focus*, that is to say, a blurred pose as if taken by a middling photographer with an inexpensive camera. Hold that *out of focus* position. Now, without actually changing the position, switch to *in focus*.

The image is now sharp and crystal clear. Henri Cartier-Bresson has taken the photograph, a master photographer with a perfect subject.

Out of focus

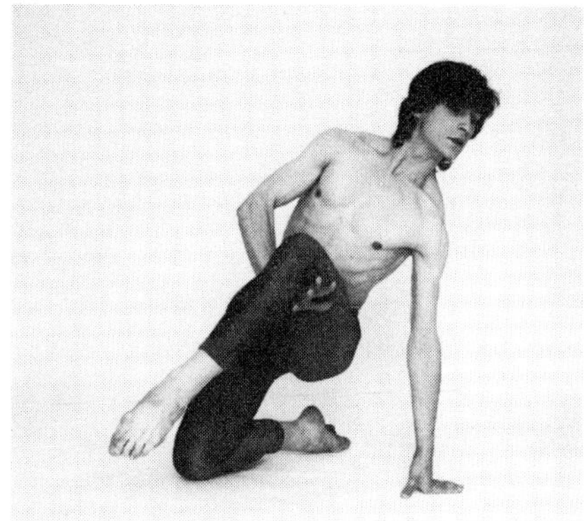

In focus

To achieve the *in focus* definition we must inflate, lighting up from within. Externally, the body hasn't changed perceptibly from the *out of focus* pose, but one's inner awareness has escalated so that the person's personality leaps out from its earlier inert position.

Out of focus equals lacklustre. *In focus* equals lust for life.

The position during *in focus* remains unaltered but the inner light turns up from dim to dazzling. The *out of focus/in focus* images alternate from quickly changed to long held positions.

Magnetism and radiance are the ultimate pedigree of the great actor, qualities that are rare even among the most skilled technicians. Like buried treasure, however, they are, on occasion, to be found. This exercise is that necessary map.

Lifting/lowering upper arms with resistance

The world loves to watch a winner. If the contest is won too quickly, the spectator feels cheated. He wants his money's worth, the feeling that the spoils of victory were not handed to the victor on a silver platter, that the winner waged war and won.

The parallel must be seen in the mime and dancer's domination of the stage, a domination earned.

Movement that gives the impression of effortlessness has at its foundations some element of resistance, of opposition. Not strain, I hasten to add, but opposition.

Everyone sits on the floor with the legs crossed. With the spines collapsed and the heads drooped over, each person starts to inflate, the arms, of course, being lifted at the same time. On the descent, the deflation, the arms, as always, lower.

Attention must be paid to the subtle effort of the arms to rise and their subtle reluctance to descend. The arms do not go up with total ease nor do they, with total ease, come down. We are now, as the name of the exercise implies, *lifting/lowering the upper arms with resistance.*

Imagine a weight on the upper arms as they are lifted. Despite the obstacle, the arms attain their maximum reach. Then the torso begins its return to the collapsed position, but the arms, enjoying the view from the heights, are in no hurry to join the descending torso. There can be no choice but to obey, though, for the torso is in command and the arms, accepting the reality, acquiesce.

So the arms, though fractionally behind, do follow the descending torso.

Do remember when the torso goes up, the arms, with slight resistance, follow a split second later and when the torso comes down, the arms, with slight resistance, come down, also a split second later.

Always bear in mind that the lifted arms do not work independently of the torso, that the torso lifts and, as a result, the arms connected to the torso, follow. On the reverse, when the torso descends, again the arms follow suit. This is the logical sequence of organic movement.

The element of opposition, the introduction of resistance, lend texture to an otherwise overly smooth fabric.

Medieval stained glass windows

Above all else, an actor must be believable. Technical capability adds up to nothing if the sum total is untruthful. In order to ring the bell of emotional accuracy, the actor must have an affinity with the different epochs of history. He must be able to wear a costume of 500 years earlier with the same ease as if he were sporting the blue jeans and T-shirts of today.

To absorb the spirit of an era requires regular trips through time reversed; visiting the antiquities of foreign lands, reading books, losing oneself in great paintings and works of sculpture, walking down the hallowed aisles of sacrosanct religious buildings, to name but a few ways of steeping oneself in the bygone mentality of earlier life.

The exercise of *medieval stained glass windows* is one of the few that I, myself, demonstrate. Technically, there is little to it but few students ever achieve its accuracy at the outset. Standing in the *contraposto* position (the S curve seen in Greek statues where the weight rests on one hip, the head inclined in that direction) is a very foreign line for most students (Ill. 11a).

To visually imitate someone else doing it helps translate the image into one's own body. As I strike each of the stained glass window poses, I see in my mind's eye the saints, madonnas, martyrs and priests who populate the magnificently coloured windows of the great cathedrals. The sanctity and devotional approach of these holy figures must be seen by the brain and then disseminated through the body (Ill. 11b).

11a

11b

Unlike many of the other exercises in which the student's creativity and originality is encouraged, the success of this particular exercise depends on its replica accuracy. So I repeat: Absorb, through illustrations and observation in churches the special tilt of the head, the open palms over drooped wrists, the fingers breathing as in their marble and painted counterparts, the sitting on the hip, the downward stance of abject humility and the upward gaze of pious aspiration.

Once the external line has been reproduced, the most important quality of all must then be found – the immaculate selflessness of the figures themselves.

Elasticity/control

This exercise encompasses the alpha and omega of physical extremes; utmost elasticity at one end of the pole with consummate control at the other end. In between lies an endless range of movement fluctuating between the two polarities.

To be only elastic is to be floppy while, conversely, an excess of control can border on rigidity.

Elasticity, it must be understood, does have control at its base, while control, at its best, conceals an invisible elasticity.

A well-trained physical performer has, in his daily workout, exercises that achieve both suppleness and strength, leading to both elasticity and control.

The students now begin the exercise of *elasticity/control*, starting with *elasticity*. The improvisation calls upon every part of the body to be as yielding and flexible as possible. The movement patterns employ a maximum looseness through every conscious joint of the body.

Change. *Control*. The students now strike poses of long held positions for *control* implies lingering images. However, *control* does not entail a uniform intensity throughout the body. For example, a knee may be locked while an elbow is bent, the feet may be tensed while pointing though the fingers are relaxed and so forth.

To control is to keep the body in a position as commanded. The intensity may vary in different parts of the body but that body does not waver and flounder. A controlled body gives the impression of effortlessness, hiding, in fact, a great reserve of strength.

The *elasticity/control* exercise now hops back and forth between the two so that the adjustment between the two polarities is made instantaneously.

Embracing space

Reaching out and drawing in the air around him, the student envelops and embraces intangible space. The improvisation calls upon the class to embrace space continuously as if the surrounding air was uninterruptedly escaping.

At the beginning, the students' efforts are usually tentative. Young people seem apologetic when asserting themselves as individuals rather than the simpler way of finding strength within the group. This reticence is a remnant of our repressed conditioning.

As the exercise progresses, the class must be encouraged to reach out further, to bring in the air with more involvement, to stretch out in new directions, to embrace more space with more possessiveness. To do all this necessitates sustained energy, a commodity in short supply with neophytes.

For newcomers, comfort, unconsciously, is the gauge. Beginners don't intend to let up insofar as energy is concerned, but they do tend to throw in the towel when discomfort makes its presence felt. For the seasoned performer, comfort plays little or no part in doing or not doing; only the result is important. That result is often manufactured with exhaustion, exhaustion manipulated and reversed to power.

While we're on the topic of amateur to professional, one of the differences between the two is that the amateur fluctuates between something wonderful and nothing at all while the professional's variable in performance level is so slight as to be almost invisible to the majority eye.

Responsiveness to sound/reaction to silence: Pierrot taking curtain calls

I'm about to explain to you a great subtlety to be found within the panoramic arc of powerful performance. When silence abruptly follows music or sound, there must be a reaction to that silence.

Let us say the music is building to a climax and then stops suddenly. A few seconds silence ensues to be followed by a continuation of the music. During that silence the mind, thus the body as well, must increase in heightened awareness so as to counterbalance the absence of sound.

To exactly parallel the silence by diminishing one's repercussive authority is to ensure a decrease in the audience's interest. Though the sound has disappeared, the performer does not have to do likewise. Instead, he must offset the aural stillness with an increased inner volume of assertiveness.

In *Claustrophobia: Birth, Life, Death*, a sudden silence follows the sound of screaming in the birth section. During that dramatic silence which follows, my intensity accelerates rather than decreases. When the sound of factory machinery is heard in the next section, I instantaneously react to the sound, the jolted recipient of yet another shock.

One can, of course, react in a neutral manner to the absence of sound. In the long run the reaction depends on the intention of the choreographer or director. Nevertheless, in a dramatic work, it is intriguing to see an emotional build-up concurrently with the cessation of sound or music. The contrast can be one of striking impact.

The students, in the following exercise, will portray the melancholic Pierrot. Suddenly, without warning, the music ends. In the immediate silence that follows, Pierrot searches here and there, everywhere, trying to locate his lost accompaniment. As abruptly as the music ended, it comes back and in those opening bars of welcome, Pierrot responds in gratitude for the return of his missing melody.

And so the exercise continues, the music stopping then re-starting, all the while Pierrot becoming lost when the music ceases and joyously found upon its return.

The demarcation line must be clear between the responsiveness to the sound and the reaction to the silence. Every cause creates its own effect. The sound of music camouflages the imprisoning solitude of Pierrot while the silence reinforces his abject loneliness. The difference must be well delineated by the student.

Walk of inevitability

This walk is almost a personal signature, an individual motif which embroiders its red-threaded way through my performance.

If I'm about to turn over my placards, I see, in my mind's eye, the placards before I actually turn my head to look at them. This inner image is the motor, the motivation, that turns my head. Then, my head having turned, I start to walk towards the placards, my feet pointing as slow motion arrows directing me towards the next objective. The arms are down at the sides of the body, the palms facing in the direction one is moving. In this case the direction is towards the placards.

The walk is not one of complete volition. There is a sense of some resistance, some miniscule reluctance which keeps the walk at a post-dream, pre-awakening tempo. One moves inevitably but reticence prevails, a conflict between caution and fulfilment.

The students are asked to do the walk of inevitability all around the studio, in any direction they please. The chest must be placed just over the pelvic bones, pulled up and perfectly aligned, a very vertical axis. The student tends to sway back when doing this walk.

Each foot barely leaves the floor as it moves into the leading position. The quality is one of almost gliding.

The head is slightly inclined to the right, a touch which adds to the feeling of submissiveness. In this particular walk, one is drawn towards the destination, seemingly, by some hidden force, hence its inevitability and therefore the name of the exercise.

Controlling breathlessness

The most extreme case of panting I ever heard took place backstage, in the wings, during the debut performance of a 21 year old English dancer as Odette/Odile in the full length production of *Swan Lake*. This was in Mona Inglesby's International Ballet in 1953. (I had just completed the Spanish Dance in that same Black Swan act.) The young lady in question was heaving and huffing with such audibility that the middle-aged stagehand solicitously standing by her side must have thought that this swan queen was going to die in the wings rather than in the water.

At the risk of seeming immodest, I am therefore obliged to tell you that three decades later, not a sound is heard from my own lips, even after a two hour solo performance. This silence is maintained even at the close proximity of a few feet. Regime plays its part as does another factor; that is, leaving the mouth slightly open and exhaling through it.

This is not a partial exhalation but a complete one as if a balloon was totally deflating. Most people, after strenuous exercise, hold on to the exhalation, meaning, they try to prevent the logical conclusion of the air going out. By doing so they ensure that terrible gasping sound, synonymous with severe athletic exertion.

The students must rid themselves of the habit of huffing and puffing each time they finish a mere two or three minute exercise. Once the exercise is completed, the mouth remains slightly open, allowing the air to escape completely, not partially. By completing an exhalation until there is no more air to expel, silence is guaranteed.

The students will now move about the studio doing very strenuous movements. After two minutes or so, the exercise is abruptly terminated. Everyone must be very aware of permitting the breath to escape with *one long deflation*, the air emitted through a slightly open mouth.

To audibly heave after an item or solo is to call attention to the effort rather than the result. It is distracting for the public and, as well, extremely uncomfortable for them. Many of the audience equate huffing with a heart in acute distress. Even profuse perspiration upsets many people (though that cannot be controlled to the same degree).

Gasping is an acute distress signal for the majority. Instead of identifying with your creation, they proffer sympathy. It is far better to let the audience feel sadness for your Pierrot, rather than to feel sorry for you personally.

Tension in one arm/relaxation in the other/relaxation in both

When children begin to study ballet and you ask them to straighten their knees, they often straighten the elbows as well. Few people, even adults, can independently operate different parts of the body at the same time. This exercise calls upon concurrent control of separate parts of the body, not an easy task but essential for supremacy over one's own instrument.

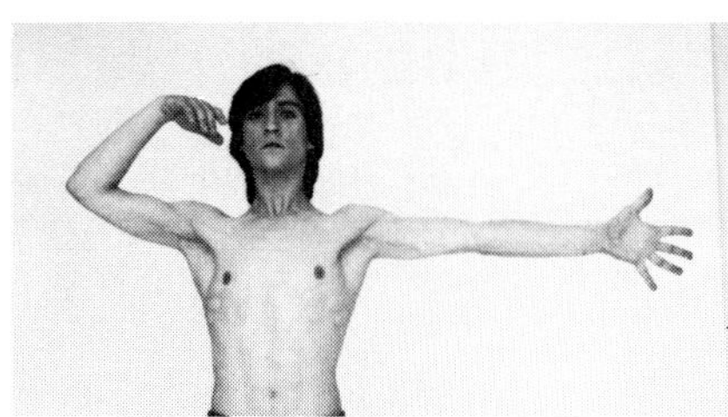

The student tenses one arm while, exactly at the same time, completely relaxing the other. Reverse. The reversal must be instant and simultaneous. Finally, the student goes limp in both arms, the relaxation section of the exercise.

Begin all over again.

Reaching out from a central impetus

The group sits on the floor with legs comfortably outstretched. Then, with a localized energy emanating from the solar plexus, the inner current continues to reach out, released through the crown of the head, the fingertips and the tips of the toes. This charged current is continuous with no respite at the peak of release.

Good movement must begin centrally, never commencing from the outer edges. This exercise brings home to the student the muscular origin of his movement, the physical source of his energy.

As the student continues to reach out from his central impetus, he is not allowed to reach a finite point. Instead, he must, non-stop, continue to reach and reach and reach. The maximum point of one stretch propels him into the next and so on. There is no rest for the weary nor for people aspiring towards organic, flowing movement.

On a more poetic level, the student seems to be aiming for horizons always slightly out of reach. As he returns to the central impetus of his stomach, he is renewing himself, finding further fuel for the journey that knows no arrival.

Terrestrial/celestial Movement

We're now going to move as gravity bound and grounded creatures who are familiar with no other home but mother earth. Terrestrial movement.

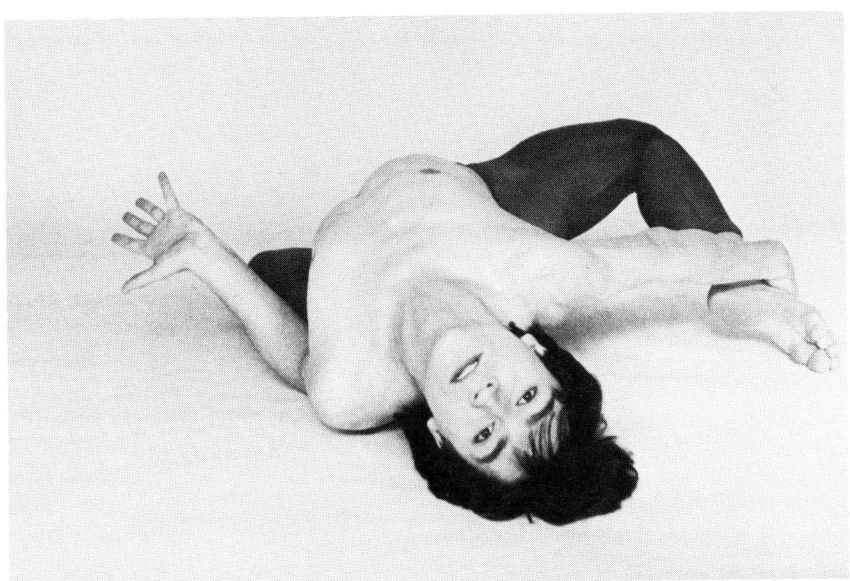

Move at floor level with terra firma as the partner in constant attendance. Roll, twist, kneel, lie down, rise but return always to the magnetizing force that keeps us ground bound.

Introduce the oppositional quality of striving for the air but, inevitably, surrendering to earth.

Change to *celestial*. Your natural habitat is now the air. In order to create a believable image, inflate while moving, feel the air under the upper arms and armpits (an air lift); resist the descent from a high *demi-pointe* or ball of the foot.

A quick rise and a slower descent give the impression of floating. Arms that descend after the torso has already "landed" help consolidate the impression of being airborne. Think high for a stolid mind makes for a solid body.

Alternate between terrestrial and celestial movement. The sudden changes between the two develop the students' ability to work at the opposite levels of height and depth, to live in equal peace with the binding element of earth and the bounding element of air.

Magnet exercise

This exercise is designed to help the actor bring the audience to him rather than he going out to them. In the American show business vernacular, the entertainer "sells;" he very definitely goes out to the audience. For me, comedians border on the pathetic when they plead with the public for acceptance. The please-laugh-at-my-joke syndrome is both demeaning and unnecessary.

The actor, comic or otherwise, must develop his mental strength to the point where he can magnetize an audience into the workings of his own mind. This means, bring the audience to you!

To begin the exercise, the students face front, standing up. Speaking to an imagined person, they implore, demand, cajole, insist, "Come to me, come to me. I said come here, not later, right now, this very moment. Come, come to me this very second."

With a variation on this thought, the student extemporizes, continuing, without break, his entreaty. While he is talking, he beckons, using magnetic gestures which reinforce his spoken plea.

The student must bear in mind that the person he is speaking to is not interested in what he is saying. This is the reason for the insistent quality of the monologue, an insistence which escalates into aggressiveness.

Having discovered the truthfulness of the situation by talking, the actor then eliminates the spoken monologue, replacing the words with a silent monologue, an inner and solo conversation. The thoughts while miming are the same as they were when speaking, to force the imagined person to obey.

"Come to me, come to me," the need has not altered. The actor is still trying to force the person to come to him, as a pin to a magnet, but without words. The gesture has taken over, driven by the unabated inner monologue of "Come to me."

Much physical energy is required for the actor's arms to draw in, to himself, the resistant person. This exercise of emotional insistence cultivates a magnetic quality, the ability to bring the public to you rather than the other way round.

Waltz: happy, fatigued, distracted, pompous

The student is taught to waltz, ballroom style, with the accent up, up, down, up, up, down, the first step musically emphasized and on *demi-pointe*. Once the actual step is under control, it would be overly optimistic to say "mastered," the student must then waltz in varying moods.

Now, the problems of the dramatic dancer begin to be appreciated. Acting while dancing appears easy. Such is not the case as the student will soon find out when he has either lost the rhythm of the waltz or the mood of the characterization or both!

As in every dramatic situation, the selected mental image must be sharply in focus. No blurred or overlapping pictures, diffusing into a generalization. Only the most experienced movement artist can generate truth from a generalized base rather than a specific one. If someone asked me to waltz in a fatigued or distracted fashion, I could do either with emotional accuracy because I can command the memories of those feelings to serve me instantaneously, having had such long experience in doing so. I can, as well, waltz automatically.

Subsconsiously, I can borrow upon the interest from my extensive emotional balance. The very young actor, starting out, does not yet have savings. He must first deposit.

To ensure dramatic accuracy, the student must locate a single image, cling to it and realize it through that chosen character who, incidentally, is waltzing.

Do you wish to play yourself? To coin Cole Porter, anything goes, providing you can truly enter into the moods of the four waltzes; *happy*, *fatigued*, *distracted* and *pompous*. If you do believe in what you are doing, there is every chance that the audience may well believe it too. Your own belief is not insurance, merely the first step in the long journey over the footlights to expiate the sin of cynicism with which many of the audiences are guilty. It is not their fault. They wish to be pardoned. Do so.

Allegro music: move quickly, move slowly
Adagio music: move slowly, move quickly

This exercise helps the student avoid the predictable when moving either to music or text. Allegro music is played and the student responds obviously by doing an improvisation that is equally allegro. This would be a natural reaction just as moving or gesticulating quickly would be when rapidly delivering lines.

The student, having done the obvious, is now asked to do something more demanding. He must move *slowly* to the allegro music. This opposite reaction, this reversal of the obvious, creates a subtle dramatic tension, just as moving very slowly would do when speaking non-stop and quickly.

Now adagio music is played and the student interprets its legato quality with slow and expansive movement, flowing and flowering. Again, this is a natural reaction for slow music calls upon a slow movement parallel. Then, abruptly, the call for quick movement is given.

The student now moves *rapidly* to the adagio music. The verbal counterpart would be for the actor to move *quickly* while *slowly* speaking.

The unexpectedness of the juxtaposed rhythms, slow against fast, and fast against slow, contribute to the audience's continuing curiosity for the performer has introduced the completely unexpected. Choreographically, there is increased interest as well for the dancer or mime becomes less slavishly obedient to the form. And everyone, as well we know, is intrigued by incipient rebellion.

Changes of mood

Sitting on the floor, the class members shift from one emotional extreme to its opposite. The transition is not immediate but, rather, progressive as a pianist moving up and down the keyboard, note by note.

The emotional polarities will be *happiness to sadness*, followed by *irritation to patience*, followed by *courage to fear* and finally by *giddiness to sobriety.*

The student must not be allowed to indicate, that is, put on the emotion as one would an article of clothing. The source of the expression must be from within. Just as one relaxes one's physical muscles with a masseur or osteopath, the student must relax his mind, letting down his mental barriers so that the psyche can travel to remembered experience.

There is no poverty in memory. Everyone is a millionaire in recall, if one gives permission to reflectiveness.

Don't push a feeling. Don't force the emotion. Instead, surrender to it.

Don't wear a mood like a mask. Masks cover. What's required is exposure, indecent only if dishonest.

Dramatic counterpoint

Most actors, when the lights fade at the conclusion of a scene, tend to emotionally subside in a parallel way. In like manner the dancer or mime tends to diminish, at the end of a scene, when the sound fades to nothingness.

In this exercise, as the lights and sound fade together, the actor in his final pose accelerates emotionally. As the scene concludes with the diminution of the lights and sound, the actor does not likewise diminish. Instead, he holds his final pose with increasing intensity, thus achieving dramatic counterpoint.

This exercise heightens the climax of a scene or the conclusion of a theatre piece.

The students cup their hands to their mouths as if calling after someone. In the past I suggested, for their image, a lost child. There seemed to be little identification with this image, no doubt because few if any of them had as yet reproduced themselves. I then substituted a lost dog and the subsequent impact was very moving. Clearly, practically all of the students knew what it meant to love and be responsible for man's most devoted friend, a dog.

The students strike the final pose for frantic search, cupping their hands to their mouths as they call for their most trusting and adoring friend. The lights fade (to be imagined if not practical) and the final chord of the music continues to fade to inaudibility while the student, using dramatic counterpoint, builds his frantic call from urgency to dire emergency.

Expressive isolation: the back, the hips

In this exercise, we muscularly isolate in order to spotlight dramatically. The purpose of these physical isolations is to enhance the mime's expressiveness.

Each student becomes a conductor dominating an orchestra. The backs are to the teacher just as if we were in a theatre watching an actual concert. During the exercise the back must express the quality of the music being conducted. If Debussy is the composer, the back must be rippling, as impressionistic water colours blurring one into the other. If the music is Wagner, the movement must be monumental and heroic. If Tchaikowsky, a tragic grandeur and so forth. In each case the feeling is pinpointed into the back, transmitted from the receptor (the brain) to the receiver (the back).

The student's back, as well as interpreting the nature of the music, must also hold the attention of the public behind him while controlling the musicians in front of him. To hold both the audience and orchestra calls for inner strength transmitted through the back which in turn will charge the chest. The entire torso thus comes alive.

Now the hips will be expressively isolated. Everyone becomes Salomé enticing Herod. The biblical bitch, Oscar Wilde's wanton and Richard Strauss's harlot, comes menacingly alive in the perverse pulsations of the pelvis.

The isolation of the back and the hips are then alternated, switching quickly between the conductor and Salomé.

Expressive isolation is the equivalent of the screen director drawing our attention to whichever part of the body he wishes to focus on in close-up. When we watch a film we have no choice but to stare at an actor's eyes if that is the only part of the body being shown on the screen. Conversely, on the stage the audience has the latitude to look at everything or nothing depending on their inclination. However, when the performer has the magnetic faculty of making the audience look where he wishes them to, he has achieved the stage counterpart of the film close-up.

Inner monologue

Most mime artists grimace or turn their faces into masks of one and a half expressions. What a waste and what an insult to the expectations of the audience who are accustomed to actors whose faces reflect the inner workings of the mind.

To avoid posturing and the pulling of faces (it won't happen if one works honestly), everyone is taught to use an inner monologue which guarantees the production of thought. For if you're thinking something, your face will tell the tale. It's when the student doesn't think of what he's expressing that he then camouflages that emptiness with facial distortions.

In the following inner monologue exercise, the girls are Columbine and the boys are Pierrot. Columbine is pleading for forgiveness from Harlequin. Has a light-hearted dalliance become alliance? Has frivolity turned into fervour? Columbine speaks to Harlequin urging him to continue their relationship. She pleads with the obsessional need of one who lives in the black shadow of love's eclipse.

Pierrot pleads to his adored, yearning to be accepted. Is it Columbine or even Harlequin? For Pierrot is that stateless citizen, holder of a passport to nowhere, life's continuous drifter for whom the elixir of love is forever denied.

The student becomes his own playwright, creating his own lines and speaking loud enough to be heard as the teacher approaches. All the students speak at once, all of them audibly. At first the exercise is verbalized so that we actually hear the text. Afterwards, there is no sound, though the text continues as a vital and inner monologue, the continuing thoughts now permeating the entire body.

(Pierrot is one of my treasured incarnations. Together we have touched the pulse beat of people in the amber autumn of Estonia, the crystal spring of Sweden and the ebony summer of the Ivory Coast. I never worked at being Pierrot. I was. Part of me still is.)

There are never many bona fide Pierrots in any era. The difficulty of authentic casting need not deter us for, almost without exception, everyone has known to some degree the gnawing pain of unequal love. From this school of experience, many people, unhappily, never graduate.

Direction of energy

Energy cannot be tossed about indiscriminately. It must be aimed. When energy is directed, the recipient is struck. The performer must know in which direction, both emotionally and physically, he is headed. Energy that is everywhere equally quickly becomes irksome and fatiguing to the public.

In this group exercise, the student reaches out towards a specific spot in the studio. The reaching and stretching are continuous until another spot in the studio is designated. This constant release of energy, towards the requested area, results in a constant flow of gestures, remembering all the while that the arm movements begin at the waist and do not end even past the fingertips.

"To the ceiling!" And the class moves upwards, aiming to touch the rafters. "The floor!" And the group reaches downwards to the floor, so near yet so far away for however hard they try, the floor is unattainable. "To the wall!" The intensity of the stretching accelerates.

The commands change with rapid alternation. As soldiers responding to the drill sergeant, the students take aim. Each reach is a ricochet of bullets, each gesture a barrage of gunshots. The mime as marksman.

Direction of energy. Ready. Aim. Holy fire.

Serene/disturbed movement

In this exercise we work for a movement response to a mental state. Locate quickly and hold on to a serene image in the mind, an image as tranquil as a mountain lake at dusk. Now give vent to this mood of quietude in an improvisation reflecting your inner calm.

"Disturbed!" With an instant transition, arrive at a state of mental disturbance. There is no one in the studio who is a stranger to turmoil, minor tumult regularly and major tumult occasionally. Capture one of these jagged images that beset us in our private lives and then distribute the image throughout the body in an improvisation of acute disharmony.

Each time the brain commands and the body obeys. The exercise must not backslide into movement for movement's sake. The *serene/disturbed* exercise stems from a mood, its fountainhead being the mind which in turn activates the amenable body.

Melting/percussive movement

The objective of this exercise is clear from its title; melting movement to be followed by percussive ones.

When doing the *melting* section, keep in mind that to melt without opposition soon becomes boring. The oppositional quality is achieved by pulling up on the downward directed movements. For example, if you go from *demi-pointe* to *plié* on one leg, the torso lifts up as the ball of the foot descends to flat. The more the movement melts, the more one equally pulls up.

The *percussive* section is very robot-like in its mechanized jerkiness. The movement starts centrally, the spine the most active participant. Because the torso fragments the air, the arms and legs follow, having no choice, as usual, but to follow the leader.

As in so many of these exercises, *melting/percussive* works for mastery of opposites so that the middle is more easily achieved.

Connective movement (when reversing a run)

If you are doing a stylized run (rather than a literal one like catching a bus) in one direction then abruptly change course, the moment of reversal must be connected so there is no sense of termination. The momentum of the run subsides, but does not cut off, during the reversal of direction.

To avoid the danger of stopping and re-starting, there must be an awareness of energy still bursting to release itself through all the extremities. For a moment, during the reversal, the pivot foot is still rooted into the ground, but the propelling force that initiated the run is still surging through the body, escaping through the head, fingers and toes until, finally, the body moves in the new direction.

During the actual moment of reversal, if you step on the left *demi-pointe*, you twist to the right. When you step on the right *demi-pointe*, you then twist to the left.

Once on stage, never switch off, not when standing still, walking, running or, in the present exercise, when reversing the direction of a run. There can be no temporary blackouts or power failures during a performance. In this case I'm referring, not to the lighting equipment, but to our human apparatus.

Submissive/assertive

The body is the servant of the master and the master, as always, is the mind. The constant use of improvisation (stemming from the mind in a creative state) encourages the latent inventiveness to be found in everyone. With superbly trained ballet dancers, the order to improvise is generally feared owing to the fact that for so long they have been drilled into obedient copying. Not so with people who study this expressive mime technique since improvisation is an important ingredient in the over-all recipe.

In this exercise, the student becomes subservient as he imagines a dictatorial order. In effect, he becomes *submissive*. The student must know why and to whom he is submissive otherwise his effort will resemble a dumb show of feigned weakness. When the switch to *assertive* takes place, the student, without hesitation, demands and compels recognition. He declares, impatiently, his presence. As the students alternate between *submissive* and *assertive*, the passivity of the first must equal the force of the second.

What, you may well ask, is the difference between the exercise *impose/recede* and *submissive/assertive*? The answer is that they are partially related in that *impose* and *assertive* are blood brothers. *Recede* and *submissive*, however, are clearly different since *recede* implies withdrawal while *submissive* denotes remaining and giving in.

Impose/recede, it should be noted, is done almost without any physical activity, its expression primarily mental, while *submissive/assertive* finds its actuality in distinctly defined movement.

Adaptation to partner

Everyone enjoys this exercise for it allows the kind of creative liberty between two people which fortifies and frees the two participants. To work closely and creatively with another body is a satisfaction peculiar to movement artists. The sculptor's stone is inanimate. There is no reaction as he chips away at it. Likewise the canvas of the painter or the blank paper of the composer/author. But the choreographer, whether working with just one other person or a group, sees and senses the response of his every creative step. He is fed, so to speak, with the advent of each idea.

Each class member takes a partner. The exercise begins with one of the duo impovising a continuous dance, the other person following or mirroring his movements. The "follower" does not have to reproduce a photographic facsimile. He can mirror, if he chooses, in a distorted or surreal way. The quality of the mirror partner is more important than the movement by movement accuracy.

Change! The other person becomes the leader and the former leader becomes the adapting partner. This exercise leads the student away from the danger of self-centeredness into the shared responsibility of the duo, the dancing marriage. And, just as in a good relationship, it necessitates constant and instant adjustment to the partner's evolving needs.

Running: Changing tempo mid-stream

It is said that children have a low boredom threshold. So, as it happens, do audiences. To keep adult viewers happy, there must be surprises. Unexpectedness is a must. These thoughts are not only relevant to the structure of a theatrical work, they are also mandatory in movement.

The student is doing his stylized run around the studio, running on *demi-pointe* with arms that breathe at the elbows. During the course of his run, when the audience has grown accustomed to the established rhythm of his feet, he must suddenly change the tempo. He might take a long, slow step, another long, slow step then four quick short ones, repeating this series before reverting to his earlier continuous rhythm.

What will he do next, we wonder? The only way to find out is to continue to watch him. And isn't this a primary object of all our efforts, to hold the audience's attention so that they will receive our entrusted message?

Compressed/expressed gestures

Compressed, or inhibited gestures, are done with the thought that one would like to give out fully but can't. In other words, the movement is akin to a horse wishing to but unable to break out of a corral, restrained as he is by the enclosure.

When doing compressed gestures, the energy in the arms is en route but never quite arrives. To compress is to hold back. The compressed gesture, therefore, is repressed.

The expressed gesture, on the other hand, is the horse running free in the pasture. It is the energy in the arms arriving at its destination. It is uncensored thought unhampered through the body.

compressed gesture

expressed gesture

In *compressed gesture*, one imagines a strait jacket restricting the fulfilment of the movement; in *expressed gesture*, one luxuriates in the freedom of release.

Solo choreography: creating and memorizing phrase by phrase

Improvising in movement is spur of the moment imagery manifested through the body. It is giving immediate choreographic vent to pictures that flash through the mind. Brilliant though an improvisation may be, it is seldom that the mini-miracle repeats itself. Usually, the kaleidoscope of designs is replaced by a paucity of patchy patterns.

Choreography, on the other hand, usually implies set movement that is memorized and repeated verbatim. When creating movement, choreographers generally create phrase by phrase so that the passage can be learned by another dancer or group of dancers. Too long a section, at a given moment, will not be remembered by the choreographer as he transmits his ideas to the waiting dancer. Nor could the dancer absorb too lengthy a passage if such an extended section were to be thrown at him.

So the choreographer creates phrase by phrase as the dancer digests it at the same pace. In this measured way, a dance work progresses.

The aspiring mime artist must now begin to learn how to retain the freedom and scope of movement that he can call upon when improvising. If he is to create a repertoire, he must be assured of repeating himself at the same level of interest that resulted from his more exciting improvisations.

Within a set framework one can improvise details on stage. To totally improvise on stage, without a framework, is to invite disaster. What happens if one isn't inspired one evening and the ideas don't arrive? In such a situation there would be no performance. Set choreography assures an accurate physical reproduction even if the performer's adrenalin isn't flowing. Only rank amateurs have the audacity to walk on a stage with just their imaginations.

As the class exercise begins, the accompanist plays the first phrase of music as the student responds in movement. The accompanist repeats the same phrase as the student attempts to duplicate his initial effort. For the third time the accompanist plays the identical phrase and by this time the student, hopefully, is repeating his original choreographic response.

Then the accompanist goes on to the second phrase of music while the student choreographs the extension to his first phrase. With the second and third repeats by the accompanist, the student attempts to repeat his second phrase choreography.

The same procedure is followed into the accompanist's third and fourth phrases of music. Each time the student spontaneously improvises the visual parallel to the sound then tries to recapture that response with each subsequent repetition.

Now the accompanist plays all four sections without break. The student connects his own four sections so that they run into each other without hesitation. The student having now memorized his improvisation, phrase by phrase, has begun to learn the difficult job of choreographic retention as opposed to variable improvisation.

The ever present problem, always lurking in the sidelines, is the loss of spontaneity when slowing up to memorize movement. With practice and experience, creativity is not sacrificed at the expense of memorization.

Conflict in movement

Outstanding movement gives the viewer the belief of witnessing an obstacle effortlessly conquered. The first man to fly solo across the Atlantic and the first man on the moon were adulated because of the enormity of their achievements against the monumental forces of nature.

There must be a touch of resistance overcome in order for the audience to share the eventual triumph. Why is the tightrope walker applauded at the safe end of the high wire and the ballerina at the end of her 32 *fouettés* in *Swan Lake?* Because they have succeeded against very visible difficulties.

To a lesser and more subtle degree, there must be some concealed tension in some part of the body, always, though at the obedient end of the mime actor's will. This slightly oppositional quality adds texture to what otherwise could be bland movement.

The student, in slow motion, steps forward with his right leg accompanied by his left arm, also forward. Then, alternating continuously, he steps forward with his left leg, at the same time extending the right arm forward. This, then, is essentially an ordinarily walk but stylized and retarded to a slow motion tempo.

As the right leg steps forward with the left arm going forward concurrently (always in slow motion), the torso does a slight backbend. As the right foot secures itself into the ground with a *demi-plié* (half bend), the torso ripples up out of its backbend. Thus this stylized walk is imbued with an undulating quality.

While doing this walk (an exercise in *conflict in movement*), the student must feel a sense of resistance, beginning in the solar plexus and graduating to the extremities. Each forward step is achieved with the effort to win.

As the right foot alternates with the left foot, attention should be paid to the smooth transition connecting the steps. The arms mustn't jerk as they alternate, but instead keep a steady slow motion rhythm, for the student must never sever the flow of energy that makes a thousand steps seem one.

Run, stop and balance exercise: in plié, flat and on demi-pointe

When running, the impetus, or force, takes us forward. When stopping suddenly the force must be rerouted, *upwards*. This redirection locks the runner into a held position.

Teaching this exercise, I let the students run then suddenly say, "Balance in *plié!*" After the students balance for a few seconds, I give the command for them to run again only to call another halt and order them to balance on flat foot. Lastly, the instruction to run is given once more with the shout, "Balance on *demi-pointe!*"

So the first held position, after the run, is in *plié*, that is, the supporting leg is bent at the knee. The second held position is on the flat, that is, the supporting knee is locked with the entire foot touching the floor. Finally, the last held position is on *demi-pointe* or the ball of the foot. This is the most difficult to sustain as it requires a very secure balance.

Each of these above balances is executed, of course, on one leg. Always when striking a balance in any position, one must resist the forces of gravity and think upwards, even when the torso is bent over towards the floor.

Don't let the back collapse which, if it happens, causes a loss of balance. The further the torso is away from its invisible vertical axis, the more one must pull up, lifting the body out of the waist. In other words, the greater the risk, the more insurance one must take out in the form of increased pull up.

In all of these balances, the arms, beginning at the waist, must be stretched out oppositionally to support the precariously perched position. A good balance, like a good bargain, must be struck and then adhered to.

Postural alignment

The internal organs need space to function. How can they do their jobs if they're squashed and pushed in during the day and sagging well out of alignment on bad mattresses at night?

There was once a test taken in America proving that a group of unmarried mothers had an easier time in delivery than married ones. The unmarried ones, trying to keep the coming birth a secret, stood up straight and pulled in their stomach muscles, thereby concealing their developing bulges. The married women, with nothing to hide, relaxed into slumping postures even worse than before their pregnancies. When their babies were born, their muscles were not as equipped for the strain as the unmarried mothers.

The students now stand up, gripping the buttock muscles. Touching their own backsides, the students feel a hardened muscle tone. Now they must pull in the lower stomach muscles. With the pelvic area of the body gripped, each student pulls out of the waist. The sensation must be as if one is escaping from the waist.

The arms are very relaxed with the shoulders down. The tension is only in the pelvic area while the rest of the body is comparatively relaxed, though relaxed in an upwards direction.

The chest is fractionally in front of the pelvic bones, not, and I stress not, hanging backwards.

The neck is directly over the spine, not in front or in back of it, but an extension of it. The head, logically, is directly over the neck, not poking forwards or backwards.

From the well controlled base of the buttocks and hips, arises the very vertical torso and head. With this well placed alignment, the student walks around the studio, first slowly then quickly, never allowing the invisible axis of the body to deviate from its north south perpendicular.

A backside that sticks out like a pouch will prevent a beautiful line, flexibility of the spine, good balance, in short, technique. As mentioned earlier, bad postural alignment doesn't help mothers in the operating theatre as it doesn't help the actor's delivery in the legitimate theatre.

Oriental poses: tension focussed into hands and feet

The students are sitting on the floor and when the musical chord is heard, the hands and feet, in any position, light up as if struck by lightning. The frame (the hands and feet) thus become more dominant than the picture within.

Looking at, for example, Thai and Indonesian dancers, one sees and senses their energy extended not only *through* the hands and feet, but *particularly* in the hands and feet.

In order for a movement portrait to be polished, the aliveness of the artist must not fade out as the neck, wrists and ankles are approached. An Olympic runner does not call it quits just before the finish, nor does he even stop as he passes the finishing line. The force of his complete effort keeps him moving. The equivalent of the finishing line for the mime actor are his finger tips, toes and crown of the head.

There must also be an awareness of the sloping line of the nape of the neck, so indigenous to full length paintings of Japanese women. Also, when doing Japanese poses, remember the slightly turned in feet which one so often sees in the art of old Japan.

As the commands are given, the students change poses either sitting or standing. This exercise helps make habitual the necessity of working with every inch of the instrument.

Oriental pose

Accelerando/rallentando movement

This is movement that accelerates, or increases, but doesn't peak climactically, followed by movement that retards, or decreases, but doesn't stop completely.

The student must learn how to increase movement velocity as well as knowing how to decrease it. In the decreasing section there is the temptation to come to a near halt. This temptation must be resisted. Instead, we allow the speed to diminish but prevent the inner motor from being turned off.

When the word *accelerando* is heard by the student, he begins his improvisation which gradually increases in tempo. When the word *rallentando* is subsequently heard, the student slowly decreases his improvisation, careful not to allow his current to subside to nothingness.

This exercise assists the student in progressing his rhythmic intensity and conversely in declining it.

Relaxed/rigid balances

Though it may seem, on paper, quite obvious, many students cannot differentiate between relaxation or rigidity. When they are called upon to be relaxed, a part of them remains rigid. When they are asked to be rigid, some resistant part of the anatomy remains relaxed!

There is no more mutinous crew or rebellious platoon than the many muscles of the body. No wonder there is so much strife in the world at large when within our own minds and bodies there is so much impasse and revolution!

The student strikes a sculptural position on one leg, a balance which has about it a quality of relaxation. This balance, then, hangs loose without apparent strain, though there is sufficient pull up to prevent the person from falling down.

Then a rigid balance is at once demanded. The position of the balance doesn't change. It stays the same but the apparent quality of slack muscles metamorphoses into rigidity. The muscles tense from head to toe. The student is now becoming familiar with the gradations of muscular intensity.

The students now change legs before striking a new relaxed balance which will in turn lead to a rigid balance, all, of course, on one leg. When asked to do the next relaxed into rigid balance, change legs. This avoids overstraining of the muscles.

The mime artist of long experience can move up and down an endless number of steps between the extremes of relaxation and rigidity. The student is taught, to begin with, the black and white, without the midway colourful shadings, so that he familiarizes himself with the polarities. Once having been to the north and south poles, the movement explorer does not get lost in the more central latitudes.

Empathy exercises: nature, toys, animals, children

Children, as we have long since observed, have no trouble in identifying with nature, toys and animals. Adults, as it happens, find it embarrasingly difficult. The spontaneity and freedom of childhood is soon lost with the advent of so-called sophistication and maturity.

We do these empathy exercises so that we can identify with people and things well outside of our periphery. What came instinctively to us as children has to be rediscovered as adult actors. (We will forget about people who make a career of exhibiting themselves, exactly as they are off stage, and concentrate on the true actor who is a person of numberless guises.)

Let us leave the more calculated present and return to that earlier season of sunlit love when we could imitate a frog because not having been taught to feel superior, we could feel empathy. We were free of inhibitions.

In the first empathy exercise, the students identify with, successively, blades of grass, a drifting moon, an eclipsing sun, foam, a waterfall and a weeping willow tree. Imitation is not allowed. Pretense is forbidden, Mimicry is out. I want empathy identification.

In another lesson each student identifies with, successively, an elephant, a lion, a swan, a monkey, a cat, a peacock and a frog. Enter into the mentality and simple kingdom of those pure and uncluttered creatures who are our neighbours in this life but who are endlessly victimized by our exploitive savagery. As in the earlier empathy exercise, don't pretend. Be.

In a subsequent lesson, the girls become wind-up ballerina dolls and the boys, wooden soldiers, also wound up. What girl in the class didn't once relate to her doll as her most precious companion? And what boy in the class didn't once share the most heroic adventures with his small battalion of painted soldiers?

It is this lost sense of romance that must be retrieved, and can be, when the students become the toys in the buried attics of time over.

In this exercise, the students, as toy ballerinas and soldiers, begin wound up and then as the improvisation continues, unwind. They unwind with reluctance for even toys don't want their melody of life to be cut off mid-dance.

In yet another empathy exercise, each student is a child skipping and hopping. Dissolve resistance. Throw restrictions to the winds. Eliminate self-consciousness. No one is looking at you except the teacher if, indeed, he *is* looking at you. He may well be watching someone else who is doing it better, that student having conquered the actor's worst enemy, inhibition.

In the last of the empathy exercises, each student is a child playing with a kite. Telescope the cumulative years into an all but forgotten distant summer. Recall with the honest mind. Fly the kite and fly *with* that kite.

The empathy exercises are distributed throughout the syllabus, but for clarity's sake, are grouped together in this section. All of these inner identification exercises help stretch one's affinity towards creatures, great and small, play objects gone but now recalled and mother nature in whose powerful vise we are forever errant children.

Substitution exercise

An actor often finds himself in a scene or in a production in which the actual situation does not elicit from him the required response. For instance, he may have to shed tears when his stage grandmother is sent to an old person's home. The actor, never having been close to his real grandmother, feels merely an emptiness when the lines or movement require an acute feeling of sadness. In this case, the actor should call upon substitution.

Instead of thinking of his grandmother, he could think of someone close to him who has passed away. To call upon a memory, still raw with pain, is not comfortable. Many actors take protective steps to avoid it but, unfortunately, the cover-up shows. One has to be emotionally brave to be an actor. Psychological cowardice is a wall which obscures the actor's expression.

There are many powerful emotions required by the playwright or choreographer which elude the limited experience of the actor. Rather than capitulate when the response is not equal to the demand, the actor must substitute an image, an experience or a situation which will evoke the necessary emotional reaction.

One level of the actor's consciousness substitutes the replacement situation. Another level of the consciousness weaves this alternative into the over-all fabric of the scene.

Here is a scene that for many people would prove difficult. You are in a restaurant, having been kept waiting by the waiter a very long time. When he finally arrives, you become very angry at him and quite publicly give him his comeuppance.

There are many students for whom public anger is a completely alien experience. There are other students who, even in private, have never released that disturbing emotion. And then there are students who aren't strangers to the release of anger but who would never vent their spleen in a restaurant, having too much sympathy with the lot of the overworked waiter.

Because of the above difficulties we will now call upon substitution and instead of yelling at the waiter, in your mind replace the waiter with an intolerant mother beating her child or some young hoodlum pushing over a crippled old woman. You will find your anger very quickly.

Instead of inventing a situation to incur such anger, one can also borrow from the past or present reality of one's own experience. Ideally, the playwright's actual situation should invoke the desired emotional response. When it doesn't, then substitution should be used.

When I use substitution in my own repertoire, I sometimes have to call upon another source of imagery since the efficacy of the usual substitution has begun to wane due to overfamiliarity. Or, perhaps, with the passage of time, the source of pain I was using no longer has the power to hurt me. Unhappily for us, the reservoir of upset never seems to run dry though for the audience it ensures climactic dramatic moments.

Mobility on one leg

Each person stands on one leg.

Try not to hop around while permitting the rest of the body as much movement as possible. The tendency will be to lose one's balance and put the other foot down.

Change legs and repeat the improvisation. The result of this exercise will be a greater understanding of the maximum movement the body can manage while working from the base of one planted leg. After a while, more and more body freedom is developed with no stuttering at all of the anchored leg.

As the body makes its convolutions and gyrations on the one leg, emphasis must be placed on constantly pulling up. The more energetic the improvisation, the more pull up there must be in direct proportion. In this way the risks are reduced since the movement is supported.

The exercise, when done well, seems extremely free but underneath the liberty look lurks careful and cultivated control.

Relationship of feet to floor: suspicious, tender, confident, arrogant, resistant

Though we normally don't think that a relationship can exist between the floor and our feet, there is such a contact that varies according to our moods. If we're despondent, we tend to walk heavily and even drag our feet somewhat. When we're happy, we tread lightly and briskly on the ground.

Theatrically there are many other nuances which can be communicated between the feet and the floor. By discovering them, the student broadens his expressive range.

An improvisation begins in which the feet relate to the floor with the following emotions:

Suspicious. Tender. Confident. Arrogant. Resistant.

Each of these moods begins in the mind, as always, then carries through to the feet which, in turn, relate to the floor as a partner. The feet are quite capable of talking and in this exercise the student extends his expressive vocabulary by allowing them to do so.

Merging into the ensemble/emerging as soloist

The group stands in a large circle, facing inwards, their arms around each other's shoulders. Moving slowly to the right, they lose their individual identities, becoming absorbed by the slowly rotating mass. Faceless, not even a number, each person is part of the collective, swallowed up by the group syndrome.

The giant eraser called anonymity wipes clean all traces of the solo ego. As the students move heavily to the right in their submissive circle, they emit a droning sound reflecting their state of nothingness.

Then the order to emerge as soloists is snapped out and the students break loose from their circle of confinement, each one asserting himself as dynamically as possible. The sound of liberation accompanies the new found freedom and re-discovery of the self. When the order to merge back into the ensemble is heard, the class reluctantly (for who would willingly relinquish expression for suppression?) return to the restrictive circle resuming their earlier incarceration.

The length of time from ensemble restriction to soloist emergence is varied and uneven. Sometimes the merging goes on for a minute and the emergence lasts only 15 seconds. The time duration is never equal.

During the emergence section, the student does an improvisation revealing the joy of being captain of one's own ship. Most often, the student is initially hindered in this section by a reserve and hesitance. This reticence is the residue of an educational system which has stained us all with the dirt of doubt, a spot not easy to remove.

Spine/thighs

The spine is the fountain of youth. As people get older and eliminate the rotary movements that ensure its suppleness, the vertebral discs in the spine deteriorate, causing the spine to shorten slightly. But more important is the gradual weakening of the body muscles so that the spine is no longer held upright hence the apparent shrinking of very old people.

Aside from the anatomical importance of the spine, it is the base, along with the solar plexus, of the body's ability to move with plasticity. This exercise works away the rigidity that afflicts even the youngest of spines.

"Spine!" The students begin their improvisation varying the movements of the spine in as many directions as possible. They must concentrate on moving their spines laterally, forward, backward, circularly and diagonally. At times, the periphery of movement is contained, at other times freed to encompass a wider area of movement. As always in an improvisation, the rhythm and intensity must fluctuate.

When we think of the thighs, rarely do we attribute to them an expressive potential as we do, let us say, to the shoulders. Yet with conscious thought, the thighs by turning in, turning out, bending, rising and moving circularly, can contribute to the expressive sum total of the body.

"Thighs!" And everyone's thighs move in a multiplicity of patterns and levels.

Then the order *spine/thighs* is issued and the students alternate and/or combine the two, improvising with inventiveness and freedom.

Regarding the duration of this and other exercises, the knowledgeable teacher is aware that to do an exercise for too brief a period is to derive little benefit from it. To do an exercise for too long is to invite minor or even major injury.

Colour responsiveness

Colour, unconsciously, affects all our lives. Lightness on a sunny day buoys us up as the grey of an overcast morning tends to weight our dispositions. The pale green of a hospital operating room is easier on the eyes and minds of surgeons than would be savage red. Whether we are aware of it or not, we respond emotionally to the various colours of the spectrum. Colour therapy is now being used as an aid in certain ailments.

The students lie on their backs, their minds free and ready to receive the name of a colour to be announced. Their very first association with that colour will be revealed in movement response.

Red! The student may think of war or blood or a house of ill repute or whatever and move accordingly. The reaction, though, must be spontaneous. No hesitation for analysis.

White! The student's image may be one of religious affiliation or something more prosaic such as clean bed linens. In any case, the physical reaction must be instantaneous.

Black! Oppression, death or whichever picture comes to mind, that is the reaction to be communicated.

Gold! Purple! Pale green! Silver! Orange! Grey!

For each of the above colours there is a specific response channeled into movement. After each of the colours has been responded to, they are called out of sequence and in varying speeds so that *red* might follow *purple* only seconds later.

This exercise further extends the student's sensitivity to his environment, helping him in the process to become the maximum receptor of stimuli.

Feeling the centre of the light

The response to stage lighting should be a part of the student's knowledge, a weapon in his travelling arsenal.

Angle the spotlights of the studio so that each student, when called upon to improvise, finds the centre of the light and then proceeds to do the majority of that improvisation in its hottest point. By fluctuating from its centre, the blinding quality of the light will diminish. The student will soon know when he is outside the light's absolute centre. This awareness is essential if the student is not to accidentally play a scene in the peripheral shadows of a fixed light.

Once having found the mathematical centre of the light, the exercise will progress to demand emotional variation under changing colours.

Romantic pink! Melancholy blue! Passsionate red! Ominous green! Dazzling white! Mysterious mauve! Fade to black!

The student must react differently as each imagined light envelops him. To be bathed in *red* must elicit another response than would be called upon by *blue*, just as to be confronted on stage by an aggressive person would be a different experience than encountering a passive one.

Torso in constant motion while feet are rooted

A stationary lower half of the body tends to encourage immobility in the upper half as, for example, when the feet are firmly planted into the ground. Rigidity of the torso does not have to be the by-product of rigid legs. The lower half of the body can be very solidly rooted into the ground with oppositional plasticity on top.

With the feet anchored into the ground, keep the upper body moving in varying degrees of motion, from restrained to abandoned. The knees are allowed to bend, but the feet must not change their position.

To ensure the constant ripple of only the upper body, clasp the hands behind the head, thus localizing the concentration of the torso. After a while, release the hands and let them participate with the torso.

Exercises for the fluid torso are generally given with the feet freed of any restriction. To keep the torso moving with the feet stationary requires a degree of isolation, a result obtained with practice.

Enlarging, rather than exaggerating, exercise: a child, lost in a department store, searching for his mother

There is a world of difference between enlarging and exaggerating. When expanding movement for the stage, and one must, never exaggerate. Nothing kills truth quicker than phony amplitude. Exaggeration is for burlesque comedians leering, saucer-eyed, at enormous breasted chorines. Exaggeration is also acceptable in forms of theatre such as collegiate satire, men's club entertainment and army shows when the bombs are bursting just beyond the dressing rooms.

Exaggeration, in the process of ballooning, teeters on the bursting edge. Comes the blow-out and there is no more balloon. Similarly, there is no more characterization, merely oversized frantic antics.

The student, as a child, is lost in a department store and desperately begins searching for his mother.

In order to reach out to the furthest row of the highest balcony, the actor *enlarges* his feelings. He does not, note, falsify them. The emotional spark is kindled into a flame. That is enlarging.

To enlarge, one finds the mental image then releases it with a springboard force through the muscles, sinews and nerve endings.

Actors with a great power of communication more than release emotion, they catapult emotion.

So back to that department store in which, as a child, you were completely dependent on your mother to feed, guide and love you, that concluded chapter of our lives, that shoppers' thoroughfare of panic. Search for her!

With this re-enactment, you are touching upon a common denominator of experience that every child has undergone. Enlarge that long ago dilemma so that yesterday's quest is today's hurtful search. Let the entire audience participate in this experience.

The alphabet of joy to pain, when articulated with clarity and enlarged with the force of truth, adds up to words of universal understanding.

Marching/waltzing: same rhythm while changing moods—aggressive, sad, happy, tired

The students, en masse, march around the studio in an aggressive mood, then sad mood, followed by a happy mood and finally in a tired mood. The switches of mood are simple enough but not so simple is keeping the same rhythm during the different emotions. While marching aggressively, it is automatic to keep the allegro beat of the pianist, but when marching sadly, there is a tendency to slow down. The same tendency applies when marching tired, for one tends to slow down as all of us do when fatigued.

Keep the same rhythm despite the emotional turnabouts. Being capable of sustaining a quick tempo while communicating a "slow" emotion, helps the developing actor achieve an emotional-physical dexterity.

The same exercise is done while waltzing.

Kneeling without injury

The knees are one of the most complex mechanisms of the body. Don't abuse them for when they don't function (or when just one of them is injured) the rest of the body is barely operative insofar as full out expressive mime or dance is concerned. Never crash down on them for to do so is to invite damage of the worst order. I know whereof I speak. Between the ages of 19 and 21 I had recurring knee trouble that necessitated first the right leg then the left being put into thigh to ankle casts.

When dropping to the floor on both knees concurrently, let the torso tilt back obliquely so as to lighten the weight of the drop. As the knees drop to the floor, the torso holds back thereby retarding the fall. The actual contact of the knees to the ground is thus softened.

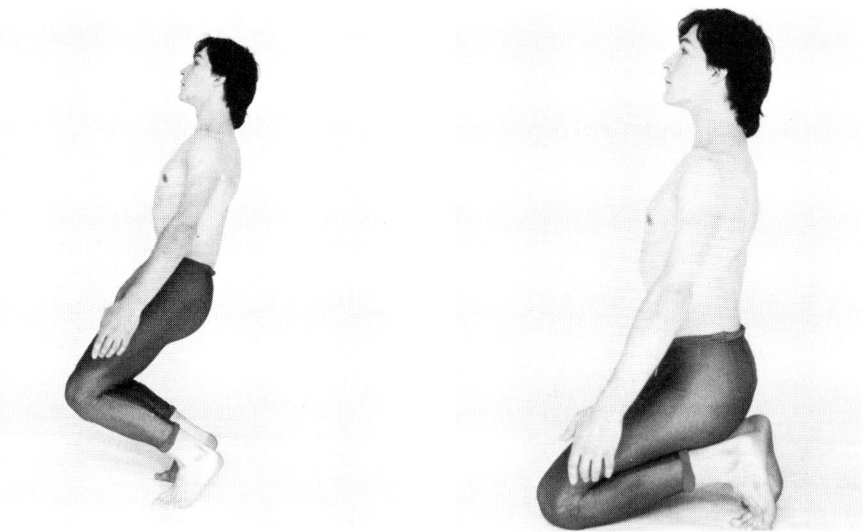

When rehearsing choreography which requires a lot of walking around on the knees, wear knee pads. In rehearsal one can repeat ten times what one does only once on the stage. Unprotected knees rebel with swelling and frightening stiffness.

When dancing the role of Otto Frank in my *Anne Frank Ballet*, most recently in Brazil and Ireland, I always wore knee pads under my trousers so that during the prayer sequence my emotional involvement was not diluted by the distraction of pained knee joints.

Never jump without being fully warmed up. Treat your knees with the utmost thoughtfulness for injured knees, at best, take ages to heal and, at worst, curtail careers. Injured knees also have the nasty habit of returning to the scene of the crime, that is, some months later the dancer/mime can again be similarly victimized.

Run and end climactically

The student runs and, when the pianist plays a final chord, terminates with a conclusive and sky reaching pose. This final pose is not static but growing, reaching upwards past earthbound boundaries.

Without an energy cut-off, the run is resumed and another climactic pose is struck, again stretching out beyond all confines.

This climactic pose is akin to an exclamation point in a sentence. It is nothing less than emphatic, demanding attention and receiving it. Make sure, though, that the movement impetus of the exclamation point leads directly into the next sentence. Movement, even when seemingly coming to a definitive stop, doesn't.

The student strikes any position he chooses as long as the pose is on *demi-pointe* (ball of the foot) and the torso and arms are in an outstretched line. The feet are rooted into the ground but the body continues to evolve in height.

Just before the pose is struck, the directional force (which has carried the runner forward) must be re-directed upwards to secure the held balance.

Height levels: low, medium, high

When choreographing a solo or a group work, or when directing an ensemble, variety must be achieved. The danger of repetitiveness and predictability has already been mentioned. One of the ways to avoid this double pitfall is to explore the different levels of height, in that way steering clear of the inclination to work on one level only.

The student begins his improvisation at the lowest height level. Working on the floor and close to the floor, he relates to the ground in an equal partnership.

Everyone now continues their improvisations on a medium height level. This level is, naturally, the most comfortable since it is the plane of daily familiarity.

Now the students progress towards the highest height level. Stretching upwards, reaching, rising, the feeling is that of climbing the most resistant mountain, of wanting something that is so near yet tantalizingly far.

The height levels are now called out with increasing rapidity and also out of sequence (high, low, medium etc.). The ascension and descension of the students' improvisations ensure interest in the future audience's otherwise wandering eye.

Attitude exercise: a person is lying on the floor in a coma with the onlookers registering puzzlement, disgust, amusement, compassion

Towards everyone and everything we have an attitude even if we're not conscious of that attitude. We relate to a husband, wife or lover in one way early in the morning then perhaps differently as the day wears on. We relate to the nurse in the hospital corridor in one manner and to the door to door salesman in another.

Though most people's attitudes are automatic and often unconscious, with the motives hidden even from themselves, the actor's attitude (regarding the character) must be completely clear otherwise it will come across as muddled to an audience who, once confused, will withdraw their attention. If the actor is vague in his intentions, how can the public possibly comprehend his role and his relationship to others in the production?

In the following *attitude exercise* a person is lying on the ground in a coma. The rest of the students are onlookers as we would find in a busy street if some unfortunate person keeled over.

Firstly, the onlookers register puzzlement. This is not difficult for, generally speaking, this would be the reaction of passersby when stopping to see a person prostrate on the pavement.

Next, the students register disgust. For this reaction, they must visualize the victim in a revolting state.

The next response will be one of amusement. Now, obviously, this is the most unnatural response to achieve since only someone viscious and twisted would find humour in a stricken and befallen creature. Therefore, the student must rid himself of self, leaving his own identity somewhere else to be retrieved later. Why are you gloating at the victim's misfortune? You select the answer that will ignite the appropriate response which is, as we know, amusement.

Finally, the reaction to the stricken person is one of compassion. This response should come naturally to all of us since there but for the grace of God goes anyone of us. Borrow from your experience, the constant companion of the actor, always in attendance.

Acting is reacting. Harry Cohen, the one time omnipotent head of Columbia Pictures, said to a screenwriter regarding the then reigning love goddess, Rita Hayworth, "Don't give her much dialogue. But lots of close-ups. She's a great reactor."

The actor must always understand his character's attitude. Without that understanding, he is piloting his creation while flying blind.

Heightened awareness: an improvisation in moving on a higher level of consciousness

The students do an improvisation which moves them throughout the studio, feeling as if they are on a stage illuminated by a thousand lights. The seats in the theatre are filled with people anticipating an extension of experience. You cannot excite an audience if you, yourself, are bored therefore boring. Deadened nerve endings are fine as you walk from your kitchen to the bedroom but they are inappropriate for a performance when your mind and body must tingle in unison.

Remember that the peripheral vision of the audience picks up many extraneous objects beside you, the limelit actor. You are in visual competition with everything else on that stage therefore your performing quality must be very marked. If it isn't, you will lose that competition, in effect, your audience. That audience owes you no allegiance so you must command their attention, unlike your fellow students who, no matter what you do, will offer you their moral support in a scene.

On a more practical note, the public has parted with their hard earned money on the supposition that you will deliver the goods. They cannot be sure, at the time of purchase, as they would be if they were to buy a scarf across the counter. So you must uphold your part of the bargain by *giving*.

In this improvisation the students walk, move and dance about the studio, touching and relating to passing objects such as walls, chairs, curtains, to name only a few. The objects may well be prosaic but your relationship with them is poetic. One must feel incandescent, alive from within, in full bloom internally, in a state of heightened awareness.

This acute mental alertness stimulates the nervous system which in turn triggers body reaction. The performer is now "psyched up," ready to move on a higher level of consciousness, more capable of flowing as a river rather than a stream.

What is the difference, I hear some student asking, between the *sustained inner motor* exercise and the *heightened awareness* exercise? The *sustained inner motor* exercise is the elementary version of the latter exercise which is more demanding, thus more advanced. The first calls upon the spark, the second, the flame.

Speeds (slow, medium, fast): person running after their loved one

Speed, in its varying velocity, distinctly affects the outcome of a scene. Changing tempi alter the impact of any given theatrical moment.

Imagine you are in a huge European railway station and your travelling companion, your loved one, is waiting for you on the train while you have momentarily left it to send a telegram. Panic sets in when you realize you can't remember which platform the train is at. Frantic fear takes over as you race up and down the station hoping to see his/her head leaning out of the window to guide you.

This awful situation did happen to me once though it resolved itself happily. I managed to jump on the right train just before it pulled out. Had I not, that would have been the end of my scheduled performance in Lanciano on the Adriatic coast of Italy.

For the improvisation, each student runs very slowly after someone he has once loved. When running in slow motion, the effect is surreal, as if in a dream.

Now, the student runs, still in pursuit of the beloved, at the usual tempo, the tempo familiar to us in our everyday lives.

Lastly, the student races double time. This pace, accelerated beyond the norm, achieves a comic quality bordering on farce. The accelerated projection of silent films has conditioned us to laugh at mile a minute speed which creates the effect of jerkiness.

Though the *outer* rhythm varies in the three speeds, the *inner* tempo remains constant. The *internal* emotional need does not change, only its *external* physical expression.

Interplay of movement

Many people, new to movement, when concentrating on using their right side, forget they also have another half, the left side. Or the reverse. If they do remember the equality of their bodies, they tend to minimize the area in between, the bridge that connects both halves.

In this exercise, the student must be very aware that movement must not get stuck in one part of the body at the stilled expense of another. There must be interplay, cause and effect energy that is always in evidence. We must not admire a participating torso at the cost of an inanimate left arm.

Bear in mind that the movement current shooting through the right arm must have immediate repercussions in the left arm. What happens in the east at once affects the west. The wind in the north blows quickly to the south. What one part of the body does causes an instantaneous reaction in another part. The left elbow does not remove itself from the workings of the right elbow.

As you sow with the right hand side of the body, so shall you, without hesitation, reap with the left hand side. Cause and effect in movement. Interplay.

Transition exercise: golden Buddhas

In Bangkok I once saw a roomful of Thai Buddhas, a male corps de ballet of golden statues. In great sculpture of the human body, we see movement trapped, seeing the statue in the "before" movement as well as the "after" movement if the sculpture could come alive. So, beautiful statues, though inanimate, are actually very animated. The life of that sculptured figure still lives, though arrested in time and space.

With golden Buddha images in mind, we are going to do a transition exercise. Now good transitions are difficult to achieve but not because they are technically demanding. The emphasis of many dance students is on the arrival only, not on the smoothness of the route necessary to get there. Such students are determined to achieve virtuosity and though the resultant *pirouette* may be multiple, the preparation and the finish leave much to be desired. And make no mistake about it, it is the finish that often registers longest in the viewer's memory, longer than even the blur of the many *pirouettes*.

In an *adagio*, the *passé* (the transition) is as important as the completed *écarté* (in this case the destination). If one gives value to the many bridges of movement, they will enhance the peak points of the choreography. If one devalues the links, the route travelled is bumpy, preventing the destination from being enjoyed.

Each student strikes a pose as a golden Buddha, holding the pose. He then does a smooth transition into another oriental pose and holds that pose as well. Another transition follows into yet another far eastern sculptural image. And so it continues.

The transition from one pose to another must not be thrown away, not minimized or devalued. On the contrary, it must be given its full due.

A subtle *deflation* precedes each transition. This *deflation* is the equivalent of the *plié* before the jump, in this instance, the *deflation* of the transition before the *inflation* of the actual pose.

The *deflation* during the transition empties the lungs, preceding the full intake of air for the golden Buddha position. The pose is then sustained (inflated), having been propelled by the preceding (deflated) transition.

One could say that the *deflation* of the transition into the *inflation* of the pose is, in nautical terms, akin to the downward gust of air which then flows upwards into the billowing sails.

Economy of gesture

Douglas Fairbanks, Jr. says it all when, in the *Conversations* section of this book, he describes his step-mother Mary Pickford's mastery in gestural simplicity.

I once saw an early silent film of the inimitable Italian tragedienne

Eleanora Duse. In it, she was an aged woman whose son had long since strayed from her loving fold. Lifting her arms slowly to the neglectful heavens, her gestures carried the weight of all those whose love is spurned and spat back by heartless ingrates.

Murial Stuart, one of my very early teachers, was one of the only eight girls in the world entirely trained by Anna Pavlova, later becoming a soloist in her company for eleven years. Miss Stuart had seen both Sarah Bernhardt and Duse. "Duse, unlike Bernhardt," she stated to me, "would be as great today because of her simplicity."

In the *economy of gesture* exercise, there must be simplicity for without it the gesture would be cluttered. The gesture would be extravagant rather than economic.

The students in this exercise must express offering, giving, bestowing. Think specifically what you are giving and to whom. Perhaps the intended recipient is hesitant in accepting. Then you must insist, not taking no for an answer. This insistence, with its touch of opposition, will add fervour to your offering.

Since *economy of gesture* is the essence of this exercise, say as much as you can with as little movement as possible. The inner monologue of offering is non-stop in its generosity while the actuality of the gesture is frugal, economical. Reduce the physicality to its bare essentials.

Get on your knees, sitting on your haunches, and with your arms, offer something to someone. Feel as if your elbows are glued to your sides so that the giving gesture becomes restricted.

Now, dramatically justify those instructions of the "glued" elbows. Are you tied up as a prisoner? Are you emotionally hesitant therefore physically shy? You supply the answer thereby justifying the instructions.

The actor who is given inexplicable stage directions cannot refuse to carry them out. He must resort to justification or finding the motive/reason for that particular activity. In locating that motive, he will bring clarity to the director's order.

Back to *economy of gesture*, the student has rid himself of superfluous movement, expressing the emotion in its barest physical essentials.

Oppositional states of mind: power/weakness, freedom/restraint, love/hate, innocence/sophistication

We are now going to express contrasting emotions, polarized moods. First, we'll express one mood then its exact opposite.

Power. The student, in a movement improvisation, conveys that all pervading force.

Weakness. Its debilitating opposite is then communicated in another improvisation.

Freedom. The exhilaration of liberty is imparted through the moving body and readable face.

Restraint. Its opposite and constricting mood is then revealed.

Love. The most ennobling of all emotions is shared by the student in eloquent action.

Hate. Its opposite, that most destructive of emotional maladies, is then expelled by the mind through the twisting body.

Innocence. The unknowing frame of mind is exposed in an improvisation of ingenuous movement.

Sophistication. Its opposite, knowingness, projected by the thought through the body.

The students, whether they know it or not, are writing confessional autobiographies in movement. As the reader learns as much about an author by what he leaves out of a book as well as what he has included, so does the teacher familiarize himself with the characters of his students.

The emotions the students keep covered are a key to their past environment. Few students care to keep the closets locked. They would much prefer to reveal without reservation. Consequently, they are delighted when their hitherto hidden feelings are able to emerge. There is no more lustrous discovery than stumbling across one's own covered gold.

Watching with activated interest

Many performers tend to cut off when not centre stage. They seem to think that, when not the focal point of attention, it isn't necessary to contribute to the over-all picture. This is a fallacious way of thinking for the audience's eye gravitates towards the single negative as surely as people notice a thread hanging from a skirt or an open shoelace.

There is no such thing as an unimportant detail. They all add up to the composite portrait painted communally by the author, director and other contributing artists.

Just as it is equally important to listen on stage as it is to speak, so it is no less obligatory to look as it is to be watched.

We know how pleasant it is to converse with someone who listens to us with complete absorption rather than to someone who is clock watching or person hopping at a party. On stage, acting seems more natural when the person or people about us respond to our motions with emotion, not staring through us while waiting for a cue either audio or visual.

In the exercise *watching with activated interest*, half the group sit on the floor in a loosely formed circle while the other half move around the circle in a danced improvisation. The sitting group sit up straight, not sinking into their spines, as they watch the group in action with a mental and muscular alertness.

The groups then change with the sitting group becoming the moving group and vice versa. As before, the sitting group watches with an attentiveness that brings them into the epicentre of the dance explosion. By watching with this kind of activated interest, the observing group's reaction becomes part of the action.

There are no snoozes or siestas on stage. The waiting person pulls his weight as much as the working one.

Movement: with effort/effortlessly

The purpose of this exercise is for the student to recognize the difference. It is surprising how many dancers, mimes and actors think they are moving effortlessly when they are, in fact, straining.

The improvisation will begin with movement that is consciously pushed, where the exertion is revealed rather than concealed. Keep up the muscular strain so that all of the improvisation is tensed.

Then repeat the improvisation, but this time, effortlessly. It is important that the improvisations are nearly identical in order for the student to be aware of the difference between the movement with effort and the movement without effort.

Just as the reality of happiness cannot be experienced without the familiarity of miserableness, true effortlessness in movement can sooner be achieved having strained against the leaden weight of difficulty. One's body soon feels the difference.

To create the impression of total ease in movement, one must, firstly, *be* at ease. Lifting the shoulder blades and foreshortening the neck destroy the image of facility. While you are improvising, distribute *throughout* your body the awareness of ease.

You have only one neck and it isn't very long so don't reduce its length. The neck is the suspension bridge between mind and body. Keep the pathway clear without reduction, tensed cords and nervous muscles. Think easy, be effortless.

Verbal to non-verbal communication: wonder, exasperation, depression, elation

Few people express themselves instinctively in movement. Thoughts are made concrete through words since that has been our lifetime conditioning.

So that the developing mime can honestly communicate, wordlessly, through the face and body, this exercise will begin with the verbalization of an assemblage of moods. Once having familiarized himself by expressing these moods through the everyday recognition of speaking, the mime-to-be will then eliminate the talking, concentrating his thought communication through speechless acting—theatre mime.

The emotions to be conveyed are the following: *wonder*, *exasperation*, *depression* and *elation*. Remember that each of the emotions is to be communicated firstly through verbalization (words, not sounds) then subsequently in silence (mimetically).

Dim, bright, brilliant: exercise in inner volume

The student starts to laugh at a moderate audio level. He then laughs again, still at the same external audio level. For the third time, he laughs, still at the unchanging volume level. Now, though all three laughing sections were at the same decibel level, that is, the same level of audible sound, the intensity of the laugh rose from *dim* to *bright* to *brilliant*.

In the first laughing section (*dim*), the sound is at its lowest intensity. In the second laughing section (*bright*), the sound rises in its intensity *though the volume has not changed*. In the third laughing section (*brilliant*), the sound reaches its highest peak of intensity.

The *inner* volume has been raised to its maximum though the *outer* volume has never increased.

This is an extremely challenging exercise to do correctly since the natural inclination is to laugh with increasing loudness during the three stages. Technical control will be attained when the student can increase his emotional power during each successive laugh while the volume of the laugh remains the same from *dim* to *bright* to *brilliant*.

The exercise is then repeated without sound, the laughter being distributed silently and instantaneously throughout the body. Remember that the silent laughter remains constant while the body's voltage increases.

Inmates: cackling laughter/aggressiveness/apathy

The characters to be brought to life are inmates of a mental institution. For virtually all the students, such an environment is completely unknown. How then, many may wonder, can they bring conviction to such a foreign situation? The solution is to bring out some aspect of your own sense of personal eviction, of withdrawal, of persecution. We all have within us the seeds of discontent that, if developed, could well expel us into an anti-social state.

It is this understanding that we must call upon when interpreting such characters. We take our own small scale disturbances and magnify them to fit within the scope of the given situation.

The students will now be inmates beginning with cackling laughter changing into aggressiveness changing into apathy. All in sound. No speech, just sound.

The cackling laughter should court hysteria while the aggressiveness stops one step short of assault. Apathy can present a problem in that if the actor isn't careful he can disengage the audience's interest. Before he knows it, the public can have been put to sleep! To enact the state of apathy is to already manufacture an atmosphere of lethargy. This is inevitable if one is a convincing actor. Yet within the accuracy of the interpretation there is the possibility of a sleeping pill effect on the audience.

What, then, can we do in such a situation? We wish to be convincing yet keep the people on the alert. The character may be bored but the audience mustn't be!

The answer is to introduce an element of opposition. In this particular context (an inmate's apathy), introduce the desire *not* to be apathetic, as if the inmate would like to rouse himself from his stupor but can't quite succeed. If the inmate is lying on the floor, he might be trying to get up but keeps falling back only to try again and then again to stumble. The apathy will in no way be diminished yet there will be less danger of deadening the audience. The actor, by introducing conflict, rivets our attention when it might otherwise wander.

After doing this exercise with sound, the students next do it in mime. The intensity of the vocal feelings are re-routed, silently, throughout the entire body.

As I write these lines my mind drifts back to the asylum sequences in my evening length ballet, *Marilyn*, based on the life of Hollywood's most magical and mythic star. The frenetic and frenzied movements of the inmates were further intensified by the enforced silence of their shrieking bodies. In mime, the vocal repression reinforced the emotional expression.

Caricature/characterization

With this exercise I will ask some helpful student to bring out my portable soapbox! If there's anything I really find insupportable in the theatre, it is the straggling foreign legion of mimes who caricature from their first pathetic entrance to their last grateful exit. I have said once and I will say many more times in the future, audiences do not tolerate this kind of gross exaggeration from actors, so why should so-called mimes believe they can get away with this kind of artistic felony?

This absurd mockery damages the seriousness of the art form and trivializes a mode of universal expression into a cartoon dimension. Mickey Mouse was delightful but Walt Disney made it clear he was a comic strip.

Mime, as a theatrical style, should not be an unending caricature. On specific occasions, caricature is appropriate and therefore necessary, but this is only on occasion as bombast and rhetoric are appropriate at certain times for the actor.

The student must know when he is doing which otherwise the result all tends to come out on the side of the caricature. When the student can differentiate between the two, there is little danger of confusion.

Caricature has its place in farce, in comic fantasy, in satire and in highly stylized forms of theatre, but as a sole and exclusive method of miming, I find it, aesthetically, an affront. Bear in mind that caricature belongs to those two M.M.'s-Mickey Mouse, an endearing little rodent and Marcel Marceau who once stated in *The Guardian* of London that when he dies, so will the art of mime. That erroneous thought, I may add, is as illusionary as his repertoire.

A form of human expression that has existed since Thespis' voice reverberated through archaic Athenian ampitheatres will survive the life and style of any single practitioner.

Stepping down from the soapbox, we will now do the *caricature/characterization* exercise. The following animals and people will first be caricatured then immediately after, characterized.

Hypnotist. Peacock. Newsboy. Seasick passenger. Landlord. Astronaut. Auditioning actor. Rickshaw boy. Hijacker. Model. Politician. Priest. Cowboy. Violinist. Olympic champion. Waiter. Headmaster. Opera singer. Ballet dancer. Archeologist. Prostitute.

I usually give no more than six characters when including this section in a lesson. I might say, "Politician—caricature!," and the students freeze in a pose denoting that personage. After some seconds I would call out "Characterization" and the students will then change their poses, stamping the persona with a recognizable reality.

And so on with some five other characters. In certain sessions I will ask the students to move as these characters, no longer to merely hold a stationary pose.

My kind of mime artist is an actor with a dancer's technique, not a fixed face buffoon who, wound up, goes through his mechanical paces.

Dramatic improvisation: the trap

The Trap used to be part of my repertoire. Never a spectacular item, it usually elicited a felt but muted response at its end. In Leningrad, however, where the public identified with its theme, there was rhythmic applause, the Russians' highest form of theatrical approval. This work is now in Kazimir

Kolesnik's repertoire. His definitive interpretation reveals yet another aspect of his remarkable talent.

The Trap is about anything we want very badly which initially intrigues us then subsequently ensnares us. For example, a medical career for which one studies many years only to discover is no longer of interest, or a long sought after marriage partner with whom one has three children, only to discover the relationship is a mistake, or a house bought, subsequently disliked then sold at a huge loss. These are traps not easily discarded as would be a shirt or blouse one doesn't like then leaves in the bottom drawer.

The students, in two or three groups depending on the size of the class, select any object they wish to use as the symbolic trap. It could be a pack of cigarettes, a ballet slipper, a mirror, a £5 bill, a piece of cake or something more generally symbolic such as the chair of my own choosing.

The scenario of the improvisation is divided into three sections:

1) the fascinated approach to the trap tinged with an iota of caution
2) the acquisition of the prize and the delirium of joy which follows
3) the subsequent disenchantment followed by the frenzied and ineffectual attempt at escape

This improvisation, to take no more than three minutes, is different than the pure movement ones in that not only movement but story line must be introduced and developed. Its dramatic structure must be adhered to so that the narrative doesn't wander but, instead, travels a straight path towards home, namely, the audience's understanding.

Progression exercise

ACQUISITIVE/GREEDY/GLUTTONOUS
GIGGLES/LAUGHTER/HYSTERIA
PLEASED/ENTHUSIASTIC/ENRAPTURED
OBSTINATE/RESISTANT/DEFIANT
ASKING/BEGGING/IMPLORING
DISCOMFORT/PAIN/AGONY
WHIMPER/SOB/WAIL
APPREHENSIVE/FRIGHTENED/TERRIFIED
MEDITATION/PRAYER/MANIA
IMAGES/VISIONS/HALLUCINATIONS
TEASE/MOCK/REVILE
IRRITATION/ANGER/FURY
SILLY/STUPID/IDIOTIC
CONSCIENTIOUS/AMBITIOUS/MEGALOMANIACAL
INDIFFERENT/RUDE/CONTEMPTUOUS

REPRIMAND/PUNISH/CHASTISE
ATTRACTION/DESIRE/LUST
TASTY/DELICIOUS/SCRUMPTIOUS

These above progressional triptychs are a vital key towards opening the bolted door of emotional release. They are immensely therapeutic as well as explosively theatrical. The inhibition that greets the first efforts are to be expected since these maximum emotions have hitherto been taboo if expressed even privately let alone publicly. For the person who dares to push his way to the forefront of personality expression (such as fury or hysteria), there is often in wait a punishment extracted by conformist society.

There are many students who have never even consciously experienced some of these feelings. There are other students who, though they have personally felt these moods, have never aggressively confronted another person with any of them (to be defiant or to revile, for example). Strangers as they are to such excessive expression within themselves and with others, these students believe it is almost impossible to do these exercises in the naked glare of theatrical lighting and, as well, in the presence of a teacher and even observers.

But it can be done and once achieved there is no looking back. The results are often extraordinary. Once the lid is off the rubbish bin of private demons, to fit it back on is like pushing a square peg into a round hole.

Since we are accustomed to camouflaging our feelings with words, the first expression of these progression exercises is made in sound. With words we can be devious. With sound it is harder to manipulate the truth. The second time we do the exercise we eliminate the sound and convey the thought in mime. The sound that was formerly concentrated in the vocal chords is at once redistributed throughout the body. The emotion, localized in the voice box, is re-routed until it shoots out of the head, hands and feet.

The thought, formerly expressed in sound, is now disseminated throughout all the body. The monopoly once known by the tongue is now equitably shared by the entire physical instrument.

In each of these progression exercises, a specific image must be nurtured by the mind. Personalize, don't generalize.

Acquisitive/greedy/gluttonous: When doing this exercise it may be of help to think of a collection of jewellery or, better yet, food. For most of us the need to eat is more urgent than the need to hoard rare gems. Though few of us know what it is to starve, all of us know what it is to be hungry. Use that knowledge and magnify it.

To do this and all the other progression exercises, the students begin sitting cross-legged on the floor. From this position the students can move about freely within their own area. I will call *acquisitive* and, in sound, the student begins having been ignited by his mental picture of hunger. Then I will say *greedy* and the student accelerates emotionally. Finally I will call *gluttonous* and the student goes beserk in his ravenous grab for nourishment. All in sound and movement.

The entire exercise is then repeated *without* sound, in mime. The energy that was pinpointed in the throat is immediately diffused through every other part of the body. This is a key principle in expressive mime, namely that the mental image is instantaneously released throughout the physical intrument.

Giggles/laughter/hysteria: Find the mental image of something which can precipitate giggles which can, in turn, lead to hysteria. As mentioned before, it is not easy to do this exercise well. After a young lifetime of restrictive responses, to so suddenly break out is, indeed, difficult. What we are aiming for is not bad behaviour privately but good technique, theatrically.

Pleased/enthusiastic/enraptured: Here we come across a positive progression exercise which in its own way is as difficult as the anti-social ones. This is due to the fact that even appreciative feelings are bottled in our emotion feared society. How often have you ever wanted to tell someone you thought them beautiful or wonderful or whatever, and refrained from imparting the compliment? How many compliments have you, yourself, never heard because others have nipped in the bud their own most responsive thoughts? Have you ever shouted a lone *bravo* in the theatre and seen quizzical heads turn sharply in your direction?

When doing this particular exercise, see yourself at a rock concert or at the opera or ballet, idolizing your favourite star. Let yourselves go and air the cupboards of your inhibitions. You are not committing a crime in giving vent to your profound appreciation. The sin is in keeping it a secret.

Obstinate/resistant/defiant: Select an image of adequate force that will carry you through the final progression. If you think, "No, I will not bring you a pint of milk," that thought is too tepid to escalate to the level of defiance. The chosen image must have the possibility of developing through three accelerating stages.

Asking/begging/imploring: What is it you require so urgently? This must be a request of utmost importance. Have your passport and money been stolen? Are you asking the hotel or restaurant to give you credit? Whatever it is that you are requesting must have a do or die sense of emergency.

Discomfort/pain/agony: Don't be afraid of an image that will incite suffering. It takes courage to be a true artist for in the process of shedding the protective layers, we expose ourselves to the slings and arrows of the painful past or present. Who, in their pleasure inclined minds, wishes to re-live the agony of an excruciating tooth ache or any of the other pains that unexpectedly visit us? Only masochists and actors digging through the debris most other people excise. But suffer we must if we wish to take the audience across the border from make believe to belief.

Whimper/sob/wail: This progression exercise is, perhaps, even more painful than the previous one in that it calls upon emotional distress. Sometimes mental anguish is harder to bear than its physical counterpart.

Locate a wretched memory of the past or employ one from the present. If one is so fortunate as to be exempt from grief, then that person must propel himself into some possible future misery. To shriek without meaning is to undo the cumulative benefits that have been accruing from the inner approach. So don't make noise unless that noise is the outer product of inside turbulence.

Apprehensive/frightened/terrified: In this exercise we come across too many students who, so fearful of such a situation, tend to indicate, that is, pretend. They imitate the emotion rather than enter into it. Watching these cowardly actors (cowardly because they are afraid to be afraid), we don't believe them any more than they believe themselves.

Everyone can call upon a situation of extreme fear and now everyone must have the nerve to re-create it.

Meditation/prayer/mania: Here we run into the problem of many students who cannot identify with the religiosity of the subject. This is the flimsiest of excuses for being unable to act a role. Where would we find the actors to enact the theatrical literature of Aeschylus to Wesker and from Aristophanes to Stoppard if only those thespians who had experienced murder, incest and other excesses were available for performance?

Familiarity with the experience, or its lack, is not the criterion for coming to grips with a scene.

If you've never meditated, you have certainly reflected quietly. If you've never prayed, you have certainly fervently hoped for the presence in your life of something then absent. And if mania is a total stranger to your experience, you have undoubtedly felt excessive emotion or a passion or a craze towards a person, sporting event or theatrical occasion.

Find some seed of identification and quickly water it. Now that you understand the reason for this exercise being difficult, it will be far less so. In fact, you may have no difficulty whatsoever.

Images/visions/hallucinations: Select a thought that is either very positive or else very negative. The in between image will not get off the ground; it will not take off. If, after a few seconds, the image escapes you, quickly replace it with another image. With immediate replacement, you will not want for mental pictures. And you must have a mental picture, either happy or horrible, to do justice to this exercise.

Tease/mock/revile: This is one of the hardest progression exercises in that to do it well negates all of the compassion and humanity of our upbringing. Not that the human race isn't quite capable of savagery. Any daily newspaper will attest to the fact that it is.

Teasing is remembered from childhood. *Mocking*, less common, is the cruelty often displayed by children to other children fatter, thinner or ethnically different. *Reviling* belongs to the mob syndrome of adulthood, grinding to a halt one step short of lynching. In *reviling*, if the student can't find an object of sufficient loathing, substitute a monster such as Hitler or other barbaric dictators of his ilk. The exercise, then, becomes surprisingly simple.

Irritation/anger/fury: Again we come across the barrier of extreme social prohibition, that is, publicly projecting acute hostility. As in many of the progression exercises, there are always a number of students for whom anger and fury are unknown emotional qualities. And even when those emotions are understood, they have, most often, never been released.

Parents and teachers do not take lightly to temper tantrums in childhood nor does society in maturity. Such long standing disapproval puts the lid on livid behaviour. For the actor, these restrictive shackles are not easy to remove. When the curtain goes up at 8 o'clock, he knows he should give forth but our social history of behavioural repression often interferes.

To act with passion requires the ability to let go at will and, conversely, to stop at will. This is technique as differentiated from self-indulgence.

Silly/stupid/idiotic: To do this exercise well is something of a minor achievement for all of our conditioning prevents us from behaving either silly, stupid or idiotic. If and when we do, we are commensurately reprimanded.

Girls, in particular, find this exercise a tricky one since they have been groomed to be as attractive as possible in order to land a man and legally reproduce themselves a few times. Though, nowadays, many dispense with the certificates, the fear of being publicly unattractive still prevails.

Think of this as an acting exercise. One's value on the love market is not at stake.

Conscientious/ambitious/megalomaniacal: The student's mental image is of doing a job or participating in an activity to the very best of his ability. He is being *conscientious*. Extending his desire to acquit himself with honour, he intensifies his efforts leading him into the further field of ambition. He is now *ambitious*. Going even further, he suffers delusions of grandeur, becoming *megalomaniacal*.

This exercise can be expressed while doing a literal activity such as addressing a crowd or it can be conveyed in an abstract fashion by communicating the moods through the entire body. If done in the latter manner, the thought in the mind must still be specific. Perhaps you are a film director's assistant (*conscientious*), then a fully fledged director (*ambitious*) and finally the head of a major studio (*megalomaniacal*). Advancement into power is the recurring image.

Indifferent/rude/contemptuous: We are often the first, occasionally the second and rarely the third. Quickly select the circumstances which could lead to your becoming contemptuous. Are you being asked to do something which goes against your ethical grain? If the person insists upon your doing what you have no intention of doing under any circumstances, would you then react in a contemptuous manner towards him?

Such a situation could take you through the three stages of this exercise.

Reprimand/punish/chastise: This can be an exercise in wishful thinking, the disciplining of someone for a wrongdoing committed against you or to others. Begin with a tongue lashing (*reprimand*) then inflict a penalty (*punish*). Finally, subject the offender to a whipping (chastise). The latter category falls into the realm of corporal or physical punishment.

Certainly everyone can think of someone they would like to penalize. By the time the student reaches this retaliatory progression exercise, his ability to tackle unsavoury emotions should be well within his grasp.

Attraction/desire/lust: This exercise is always given as the last of the progressions, for if it were given much earlier in the term, inhibition would rear its uninvited head. Two thousand years of religious indoctrination, both Christian and Judaic, have left their indelible imprint. Sexuality is sinful, so we're told, though profiteering from packaging carcinogenic cigarettes is not nor is gratuitous violence which splatters our cinema screens.

Considering the persuasiveness of such education, this exercise is understandably difficult. Prefacing my explanation to the students, I always point out that they must not indulge in graphic displays or text book illustrations of the facts of life. Economy of means. Say much by doing little. A strong thought with minimal movement adds up to genuine impact.

Anyone can procreate, but only a pro can create.

Tasty/delicious/scrumptious: Within this frothy exercise lies a concealed complexity. Outwardly, one's inner image could be of oneself plunging into a piece of birthday cake. Seemingly only sheer delight, but wait! As the student arrives at the *scrumptious* section, his pleasure is diminished by the knowledge that the chocolate gateau will soon be finished. The student's awareness of impending loss adds a bittersweet tinge to the otherwise delectable dessert. This exercise, then, becomes a symbolic miniature of life's silver dollar coin tarnished on its reverse and inevitable side.

Remember, the exercises are first done in sound and then in mime. Because the din is so pronounced during the sound section, I clap my hands to accentuate the command for the next progression.

On the beach

At first glance this exercise would seem to be as easy as falling off a log. As it happens, it is one of the most elusive for the student or even the experienced actor to grasp. For here we are leaving the mundane and the commonplace, replacing the prosaic with poetry. And poetry is that far off domain which many people have glimpsed but where few, at any one time, reside. It is the Shangri-La of singers, the Timbuktu of dancers, the Utopia of actors and the Never-Never land of mimes.

Few are issued passports to this most sacred of domains. Poetry, if part of one's persona, can be cultivated. It cannot be grafted or attached. The essentially elemental will reject the ethereal. If these seem like discouraging words, they are not intended as such, but the reality must be faced before the improbable becomes possible.

The student imagines himself to be on a beach of his own personal recollection. The passage of the years reverse and the student is once again a child, either building sand castles, throwing a multi-coloured beach ball, playing with a golden pale and shovel, splashing in the ocean, listening to a seashell or any other seaside diversion. He can select one or several of these activities.

The movement must be in slow motion, never relapsing into ordinary tempo. Simultaneously, the movement must have breadth and expansiveness, a generosity of reach. All activity must stem from a near full inflation, a quality which will suspend and float the images.

The tendency of the inexperienced will be to relapse into realistic tempo rather than sustaining the slow motion rhythm. There will also be the inclination to use literal movement rather than stylized movement. Don't be photographic, representational or depictional. Aim, instead, for the glistening pastels of a Renoir or Seurat. This can be achieved by generosity of movement, a reaching outside of oneself that physically begins at the waist while emotionally aiming for that irretrievable seashore of our vanished and banished youth.

Remaining in a state of nearly full inflation already removes the scene from gravity's reality. Real life settles, memories waft.

Over and beyond the slow motion, expansiveness of movement and use of inflation, there is the most important aspect of all—immersion. It is this ability or lack of it which separates the pearl from the shell. To be able to soar towards the ether of irreversible experience, to promenade along the sun-drenched esplanade of squinted memory, this is the first step in being, not a trespasser, but an honoured guest in the outer space domain of poetry.

Children's games

This exercise is similar to the previous one in that both are revivals of earlier periods of our lives. *Children's games*, however, concentrates on the diversions and amusements of children as enjoyed primarily in the street. One game, two or three can be chosen by the student.

Care must be taken that one doesn't *imitate* a child. Try, rather, to *be* a child. Relate to the game you are playing as if nothing else exists in the world. Whether flying a kite or playing hopscotch, return to that more innocent period when one's mother, a stone's throw away, was preparing her loving supper.

Carriage for theatre of the 17th to 19th centuries

In plays of Molière, Sheridan, Congreve, Shakespeare, to name only a few playwrights within this epoch, the portrayal of aristocratic characters demand an appropriate posture. You cannot wear taffeta skirts, lace ruffles and high starched collars with the caved in posture so popular in contemporary fashion advertising.

To begin with, the buttocks are gripped with the torso pulling out of the waist. The head is directly over the neck and the neck is directly over the spine. Only the buttocks are tightened. The torso, in its escape from the waist, is free and easy. If the backside is stuck out, the spine is pushed into a dangerous curve, unaesthetic as well as potentially injurious.

When walking with this posture of cultivated elegance, there is an attitude of disdain, a haughtiness, a sense of superiority. When one gazes downwards, one condescends to look down, doing the floor a favour. It is as if the nobility are looking down from the castle turret at the peasants in the field below.

The arm gestures emanate from the waist, not from the elbow which gives a piecemeal line. When gesturing outwards (in grand opera as well), let the arm or arms open in front of the chest, not the face as is so often the case. To gesture too high is to mask the facial expressions.

When sitting down or standing up, the same attention to verticality must be heeded. Don't walk around the stage with aplomb only to show tell tale signs of inconsistency by breaking the style in repose or while seated.

When standing, allow the weight to fall on one hip, leaving the opposite knee slightly bent. Let the wrists droop outwards, permitting the lace cuffs to droop decoratively.

For girls using a fan, let the head tilt obliquely, slightly front. The fan can be used as an indicator of responsiveness, or lack of it, to an ardent suitor. Opening it suddenly can express surprise. Closing it abruptly can convey annoyance. Fanning oneself rapidly can mean mounting interest, fanning slowly can communicate a decision in the making. Holding the open fan just under the eyes gives the owner an air of suggestive invitation. In these ways, the fan becomes an extension of the character's identity.

It is in period plays that the ballet trained actor has a decided advantage over his non-balletic colleagues. The ballet was nurtured in the glittering courts of France and Russia. It was the lavish plaything of pearl-encrusted royalty. The dancers mirrored the grand manner of their regal patrons, hence the nobility of fine classical dancers.

It is this nobility that must permeate the atmosphere in plays of that period when interpreting characters of regal or high born position.

Escape circle

The students hold hands in a very large circle with some four or five of the students placed within. The outer circle then drop hands and begin moving slowly to the right as the inner group of students try to break out.

The outer circle move in slow motion with high voltage obstructive gestures, preventing the inner group from escaping. The inner group trying to break out move *quickly* but also with high voltage gestures as they try to escape.

Then the speed is reversed. The "gaoler" group move quickly while the fugitives move slowly. Both groups, however, as before, exert themselves with high voltage energy.

This exercise must not degenerate into a football match free for all. Both groups confront each other with a stylized attitude of combat. There must be no grappling or actual wrestling. Though the thought of escape and imprisonment are literal, their realization is formalized.

To move slowly while trying to imprison or escape feels unnatural. The tendency in such a situation is to move quickly. So, though the brain is in a state of agitation, control is called upon to slow down the muscle response.

The opposing groups can touch each other when trying to keep in or get out, but care must be taken that literalness does not take over. Touch, but don't tear apart.

Silent screen characters: pleading heroine, betrayed husband, vindictive villain, Hunchback of Notre Dame, tramp, siren, cowboy, tango dancer, Charleston dancer, Indian chief, heroine tied to railroad tracks, Keystone Cops

When Greto Garbo was forced to talk, according to Alexander Walker in his book, *Garbo, A Portrait*, she remodeled her originally high voice on that of the deeper and more authoritative tones of the senior Swedish actress Naima Wifstrand, a great artist whose retardation of certain vowel sounds added to her distinctive style. I wonder what Naima Wifstrand's reaction was, knowing that though she was the original, it was her follower who reaped the universal rewards.

Had I known this information during the almost three months that I worked with Wifstrand in Ingmar Bergman's production of *The Bridal Crown* back in 1952 in Sweden, I would have asked her. Decades after Garbo learned from her, I did as well for never since did I share a stage with such an electrifying actress.

But let us return to the period before the advent of the talkies, when Garbo and other screen royalty reigned supreme.

Silent screen acting was a form of mime insofar as the exclusion of words demanded a compensatory communication through the face and body. The outstanding actors of the silent screen transcended the melodramatic frame which was required of them, leaving us with a legacy of highly stylized humour, charm and beauty.

To the accompaniment of appropriate silent screen music, the student becomes:

The pleading heroine—Take your choice, Mae Murray, "the girl with the bee stung lips," Vilma Banky or any other of those faded damsels in dire distress.

The student, whatever the gender, is the beautiful young wife found by her husband in a compromising situation. She begs for her life as he threatens to take it from her, proclaiming him to be her undying love, the other a passing dalliance. She kneels at his feet, she cries, she prays, but her proclamations merely feed the fuel of her husband's simmering fury.

The betrayed husband—The student, again gender notwithstanding, is now the cuckolded husband who equates sexual infidelity as the ultimate rejection. (This is the one lesson hammered into us that we have, alas, learned too well.) The pain of his discovery is compounded by his astonishment that he could have been so treated by the woman he so implicitly trusted. The virgin wife has become the vixen wench.

As a model, Rod La Rocque, John Gilbert or a host of other done by cinematic husbands.

The vindictive villain—This villain could possibly be the landlord who, when confronted by the beautiful tenant's inability to pay the rent, demands from her payment of another kind. Laughing at her with a mockery fanned by the fires of frustration, he orders her to give in or get out. The model? Emil Jannings or, Mr Evil personified, Erich von Stroheim.

The Hunchback of Notre Dame—Grotesque as the gargoyles adorning the famous church, he clears the path in front of him by the sheer horror of his appearance. Swinging the church bell, the misery of his existence is mournfully puntuated by the tolling chimes. The model can be none other than Lon Chaney, the man with a thousand faces.

The tramp—The tramp *is* Charlie Chaplin. I will leave the student his own choice of situations from which to draw upon for there is no scarcity of images within the world of Chapliniana.

The siren—Images of Theda Bara smoulderingly staring into the face of the tempted camera, with snakes circularly coiled to cover shameless breasts, such images come alive as the student reclines commandingly on a rug of tiger skin. Nibbling on purple grapes, she has just begun to feast as she beckons her lover of the moment to kneel down beside her.

The cowboy—Tom Mix or William S. Hart, gun-toting cowboys of the silent screen, heading a posse towards the local saloon; the wild west hero rides again in the galloping re-creation of the student.

The tango dancer—Who else but Rudolph Valentino comes to mind when thinking of the tango as an overture to conquest? The female partner snugly follows her partner's sweeping movements, their dance a prelude to her submission.

The Charleston dancer—Joan Crawford in *Our Dancing Daughters* or Clara Bow, the epitome of 1920's insouciance; select your model and dance the night away with a desperate gaiety that barely cloaks the inner dark. The frivolity must be at a fever pitch, camouflaging the yawning vacancy within.

Indian chief—Sitting Bull, or any of his other ill-treated ilk, goes on the warpath when the settlers invade his territory.

Heroine tied to railroad tracks—Coming immediately to mind is that most famous of all serials, *The Perils of Pauline* starring Pearl White. Thrilling rescues from train wrecks, automobile accidents, fires at sea, among others, kept audiences of 1914 on the edge of their suspenseful seats.

Keystone Cops—Mack Sennett, the name synonymous with the Keystone comedies, springs to mind as the creator of those racing, chasing policemen, forever turning corners at breakneck speed on one hopping leg.

When the student can quickly juxtapose the above assemblage, when he can be any of the above characters at random, out of sequence and for sustained passages of time, it is then apparent that the characters have been digested.

It is of interest to note that the overly emphatic gesture identified with that period of screen entertainment began to change in 1927. Just as the era of the silent screen was coming to a close, silent acting began to be more naturalistic.

The "indicating" style of acting was being replaced by the actor's use of inner monologue and interior approach.

When doing this exercise, the student must not yield to the temptation to "camp" or make fun of these characters. He must, instead, portray these figures with sincerity, the exaggerated style being a physicalized offshoot of that sincerity.

What couldn't be communicated verbally, in the days of the silent screen, was re-directed through the face and body, the consequence of which is the acting style of the silents.

In all of the aforementioned characterizations, both male and female students act all the roles, regardless of gender. To take a brief holiday from your own gender role can be considered an additional challenge as an actor. Need I add that silent films must be studied to absorb their singular flavour and style?

(For me, personally, my having known Mae Murray, one of the greatest stars of that era, afforded an insight not obtainable from either films or books. I knew her in the late 1950's, long after her reign had subsided into archival mustiness.

Her life was barely believable, so far beyond the borders of fiction did it travel. Discoverer of Valentino and initiator of his legendary career, her extravagant wealth taken from her by a bogus prince husband, her career terminated by L.B. Mayer whom she had unsuccessfully crossed, her son legally stolen from her in a stretched out court case, she was, in her old age, found dazed and destitute in a St Louis, Missouri park.

Her gilded cage closed in on her as, one year later, she lay bald and dying, protected by a wig of lemon-yellow curls, a pathetic imitation of her crowning glory when she was catered to as "the girl with the bee stung lips." The famous Merry Widow, her John Gilbert decades dead, had long been a restless queen in cruel exile, the spat out outcast of turncoat Hollywood.)

Michelangelo's Pieta

With the girls as the madonna figure and the boys as Christ, the students re-create the famous sculpture. Each girl sits on her haunches cradling the mortally wounded figure of Jesus. He responds, lying on her lap, with a strained arching of his back.

This is an essay in the potential power of stillness. Despite the movement being minute, there is a strong transmission between the two figures, so inter-related that the two bodies seem almost indivisable.

The student must learn to transmit the most potent thought through limited physical means. Ordinarily, powerful thought finds expression in powerful movement. In this case, great mental power is communicated through severely reduced movement.

To achieve this emotional force in near stillness, or even complete immobility, the student must have the sensation of some outer force obstructing his full muscular release. In other words, his physicality is trying to match the mentality, but cannot. This frustration of physical energy adds strength to the restricted movements of the couple.

Wanting to scream but not doing so can almost be more disturbing than the actual piercing sound. Anger barely repressed can be more menacing than anger released. With anger released, we know its confines. With anger suppressed, we can imagine it to be worse than it might well be.

Movement contained can often be more far reaching than movement that arrives at its expected destination. Let me remind you, however, that there must *be* a source of movement to contain. If there is no movement, the result is not stillness, but lifelessness.

Great acting has, at its base, stillness as well as activity. As the actor builds his role, layer by layer, he must marry the characteristics of the person portrayed to his own private understanding of those particular traits and emotions. The union produces, as its offspring, audience empathy and acceptance. What more can we ask for from the public?

Exercise: My name is . . .

In this acting exercise, the student places himself in a situation, remembered from reality or otherwise invented, where he is confronting officious officialdom at their most exasperating.

The character is passing through customs and finds that he is minus his passport. Was it stolen or did he lose it? Worse still, the character is in a foreign country unable to speak the language of that land. Added to this already considerable dilemma is the character's feeling that the official is prejudiced against travellers of his ethnic origin.

In this terrible situation, the character tells the official that his name is whatever the student's actual name is. His action is to convince, his attitude one of repressed impatience.

The student walks about the studio, varying his plea of truthful identity. As the inquisition continues, the character makes every effort to retain his politeness, without which, he realizes, he will be in even hotter water.

His sub-text is clear, nonetheless. Not stated but implied, are the following thoughts:

"Why don't you believe me? I'm telling the truth. I have a train connection to make. I'm not a criminal. I've done nothing wrong. Oh, for God's sake, let me pass. What can I say to convince him? Stay cool. Don't get excited. Things will get worse if I do."

The student can only state, "My name is John Smith" or whatever it is. No other text is allowed. Variations of message are expressed in the sole statement of the person's name.

This exercise cultivates a sense of definition in the personality of the emerging actor.

Building an improvisation climactically

Performances have to build. They should not aimlessly amble along. The student, though intellectually understanding this concept, finds it difficult to put into practice. The reason? He simply does not possess the force essential to successfully place climax on top of climax. Reaching his peak relatively early in an improvisation, he is hard put to supersede it.

His stamina deserts him and though try as he may, the current of his improvisation slips back to static. Volume build is not yet on the dials of his control.

When I structured my solo dance-mime performance or the duo performance I now share with Kazimir Kolesnik, I saw to it that two of the very strongest items concluded the first act and that two even more potent items concluded the second. The most dramatic, the most poetic or the most comic must bring to a conclusion the entire evening.

And as a journey of a thousand miles begins with one step, so must the student learn to build from a studio improvisation before its later stage counterpart. In attempting this exercise, the student must begin his improvisation with strength and then progressively build it. By the time he has concluded, there should be no doubt that it can go no further, either emotionally or physically.

Alphabet exercise

When Romeo tells Juliet he loves her, even if he is a bogus actor, we accept his declaration because of the indisputable meaning of the text. When

Albrecht offers Giselle his love-beyond-the-grave devotion, his spectral proposal is understood even if the Albrecht in question is no actor and only a dancer. The choreography of melting romanticism makes abundantly clear that here is a man who loves Giselle more in death than he did in life.

In the *alphabet exercise*, in order to ensure the veracity of the student's feelings, we will eliminate the text and eliminate, as well, any choreography. There will be no crutch to lean on, no support to prop up a flagging intention. The thoughts stands or falls on its own.

One student will command the other, using letters of the alphabet out of sequence. For example: DPWLU ... QP ... ZZA etc. The other student will refuse the command, also using disconnected letters of the alphabet. For example: KVQH etc.

Neither student is allowed to touch the other person. No shoving, grabbing or gripping. Such physical confrontation would be used as a substitute for the raw emotion, diluting the intensity of the alphabet interplay.

The commanding student must think of the most demanding task for the opponent to undertake. It can't be something as simple as, "Get me a cup of hot chocolate!" Such a simple request would never elicit such sheer force of will. The refusing student must think of an action that he simply could not see himself obeying; nothing as ordinary as "No, I will not close the door!" The refusal must be for an imagined command that is altogether abhorrent.

The students can move about the studio but again I remind you not to touch each other though the temptation in anger will be great.

Sometimes in the heat of the argument, a student gets his tongue twisted, stammering and stuttering before he utters the next letter. If and when this happens, use such a stumbling block to propel yourself with even further anger onto the next letter that manages to escape your lips.

The most exciting demonstration of this exercise I ever saw was the day Warren Mitchell was the refusing party. The pianist, a charming lady of indeterminate years, not owning a television set, didn't recognize Britain's great comedian-tragedian.

When Warren fell to the floor she thought (telling me this later) that some older man, participating in the class for the first time, was suffering a heart attack. Only when she fearfully looked in my direction and didn't see me unduly alarmed, did it begin to dawn on her that she was witnessing acting of Olympian level.

Expressing dramatically then comedically the following emotions: yearning, fear, enthusiasm, desire, anger

The same emotion takes on a completely different aspect when interpreted dramatically then comedically. Care must be taken during this exercise that truth remains intact in the comic version as well. Students when trying to be funny tend to externalize and exaggerate so that there is little semblance of the original reality.

Let us take a food analogy. The dramatic effort is a salad with no dressing. Unadorned. The comic effort is the same salad but with an abundance of dressing over it, so much so that at first taste it is difficult to distinguish the lettuce from the celery. Nevertheless, there is a salad underneath and it will be recognized as such shortly.

So it is with the same emotion expressed under the twin arches of drama and comedy. The comedy is the dressing, in this instance, but beware of using too much dressing for the salad (the dramatic truth) would then be obscured.

The student expresses, dramatically, *yearning*. He then communicates the same emotion comedically. This is followed by *fear*, *enthusiasm*, *desire* and *anger*, each of the emotions first expressed dramatically then comically.

It should be remembered that tragedy and comedy stem from the very same source and that comedy, very often, is merely truth in excess.

Improvisation based on set choreography

The students, as an ensemble of marionettes, learn 16 bars (two beats in a bar at a moderate tempo) of loose-limbed choreography. During the next 16 bars they do an improvisation thematically and choreographically related to the original. In the final repeat of the music, again 16 bars, they return to the set choreography.

The overall impression must be that of a cohesive unit of related movement, with no apparent difference between the set and improvised choreography. The improvised section must seem to emerge logically from the preceding set choreography. This improvised section must also seem to flow naturally into the final section which, again, is set choreography.

In other words, the set choreography/improvisation/set choreography must relate as one unit. The middle section, the improvisation, must logically evolve from the preceding set steps and just as logically evolve into the following and final set section of steps.

Sometimes the dreaded fear of forgetting choreography (or text) does happen on stage. If and when the nightmare occurs, the student must have the technique to cope with such an emergency. In the exercise just described, he learns what it is to freely weave from a pre-set pattern and then, when the crisis has passed, to return to it.

Improvisation is essential in developing the student's inner resources. I have seen, too often, marvellously skilled ballet dancers who, if their lives depended on it, could not put two steps together of their own. Their obedience to their teachers' and choreographers' wills have fossilized their once creativity.

The other end of the stick is the student who can improvise to his heart's content but without one iota of technique in any movement form. Exactly in between lies the ideal instrument for expressive movement.

Out of sequence narrative for filming: Little Red Riding Hood

Creating a role on stage is, in many ways, simpler than doing the same on film. In a theatre one begins a role and continues with it until its inevitable end is reached. When acting for the cameras, the usual method is to film out of sequence. This rather confusing out of order system is necessitated by the threatening economics of the film industry. All the scenes taking place on one set or on one location must be filmed one after the other since it would not be economically feasible to rebuild a set four times or travel with an entire company and crew three times, let us say, from Hollywood to Hong Kong.

Using our hypothetical example, the three scenes in Hong Kong might take place five years apart with many episodes in between, but for practical considerations must be filmed one after the other.

In the event that the student will one day be filming, either for the cinema or television, in such a back to front fashion, the following exercise will begin to acclimatize him to what otherwise could be a daunting situation.

Recalling the fairy tale *Little Red Riding Hood*, the boys are divided into two groups; as the wolf and the hunter while the girls are divided into two other groups; as Red Riding Hood and the grandmother. At first they do six scenes from the story in the sequence in which they happen.

a) Little Red Riding Hood strolls happily along the forest path, picking flowers for her grandmother.
b) She is accosted by the wolf but manages to escape him.
c) Entering her grandmother's bedroom, she presents her with the flowers.
d) Red Riding Hood is increasingly puzzled by her "grandmother's" sickbed behaviour.
e) The "grandmother" leaps out of bed to eat Red Riding Hood as the little girl realizes too late the duplicity of the wolf.
f) The hunter frightens the wolf away as Red Riding Hood is reunited with her grandmother.

Having gone through the fairy tale in its narrative order, the students are now called upon to act each of the scenes completely out of sequence. Despite the confusion caused by the narrative's upheaval, each scene must retain its original validity.

Here is an example of an out of order sequence:

a) The "grandmother" leaps out of bed to eat Red Riding Hood as the little girl realizes too late the duplicity of the wolf.
b) Little Red Riding Hood strolls happily along the forest path, picking flowers for her grandmother.
c) The hunter frightens the wolf away as Red Riding Hood is reunited with her grandmother.
d) Red Riding Hood is increasingly puzzled by her "grandmother's" sickbed behaviour.
e) Entering her grandmother's bedroom, she presents her with the flowers.
f) Little Red Riding Hood strolls happily along the forest path, picking flowers for her grandmother.
g) The hunter frightens the wolf away as Red Riding Hood is reunited with her grandmother.

By grasping the over-all contour of the role and the character's response to the ever changing situations, the student need not be thrown by the illogical order of events. Whether commencing in the middle, end or beginning, the actor is not diverted because of his total comprehension of the character in relationship to the script. He can, therefore, begin at any point and not be thrown off balance.

Of course, when acting in sequence one is aided by the logical momentum of preceding events. When acting out of sequence, it is far more difficult but the obstacle can be overcome.

The out of order sequence is repeated in varying tempi (some scenes very short, others longer) and further jumbled.

Petrouchka imprisoned in his cell

The hero of the Fokine/Stravinsky ballet is an appropriate character to bring to life for any dramatic mime artist. The anguished scene in the cell with Petrouchka unable to escape the narrowing confines of his existence can call upon both illusionary and expressive mime.

Illusionary mimes are ruled by the arithmetic of area. Here, for a change, is a situation where the touching of invisible walls is dramatically justified by the scenario, not an excuse for showing off that obligatory exercise.

What a wonderful role Petrouchka is. Like snapped branches dangling from a desolate tree by some unexpected hurricane, Petrouchka chops the air with his disjointed body. With his arms, legs and head flopping about, struggling to connect with his jerking spine, Petrouchka beats his fists against the enveloping walls, sound proofed from his unheard and dying cry. Now, alas, he is no more than strewn sawdust, the bitter remnants of his carnival of death.

When Sarah Bernhardt, the most celebrated actress of her time, first saw

Vaslav Nijinsky, the original interpreter, dance the role, she exclaimed, "I fear, I fear that I have seen the greatest actor in the world."

To dance this role was, for me, to know the true meaning of union, union with its great tradition, music and story. For those students not familiar with this Diaghilev classic of the tormented puppet with a human soul, call upon your own understanding of emotional restriction and enforced isolation. For who hasn't, at one time or another, frantically wanted to get out of something or some place somewhere?

Heroes and fans

As well as the prevailing problem of not being able to release our so-called negative emotions, our upbringing has been so constrictive that the vast majority of us can't even express our positive ones. As mentioned earlier in the progression exercise *pleased/enthusiastic/enraptured*, how often in the past have you wished to compliment another person, to tell him or her that he was wonderful, looked beautiful or anything else deserving of praise? And how often did you give vent to that impulse? In all probability the appreciative words never found utterance. What a loss for the receiver and, as much if not more, for the giver.

To be an actor, whether dramatic, operatic, balletic or mimetic, one must first remove the cork from the wine bottle of our stored emotions. We have to re-learn the spontaneous enthusiasm of the children we no longer are. People whose psyches are bound and gagged cannot be expected to generate emotion. As the legs are stretched into *penché arabesques*, so must the emotional instrument be stretched from all directions.

To begin this exercise of *heroes and fans*, the girls all sit together as an audience of teeny boppers while the boys go to the other side and become an ensemble of rock stars. Using sound to begin with, the girls shriek and scream as the boys sing, thump and bump, grinding and winding their way to insolent adulation.

The girls are not allowed to go past an agreed upon line, the boys as well, leaving a no-man's land in between. Without this divide, the pubescent hysteria would cause a stampede, encouraging the exercise to turn into a mass groupies' assault.

Having now made a tremendous amount of noise, both girls and boys repeat the exercise silently. The same frantic adulation is re-created but with the vocal hysteria of the girls channeled through the entire body and the aggressive wildness of the boys recharted physically. The wild sound is now the wild look.

Then the groups reverse so that the girls are the rock stars with the boys as the adoring fans.

Just today I singled out a boy who was particularly good as the rock star.

Immediately before I had him repeat his "performance" alone, I asked which singer had been his inspiration. No response. Helping him, I offered, "Mick Jagger? David Bowie? Iggy Pop?"

"Shirley Bassey," he sheepishly answered.

Distraction exercise

This is an exercise that would be hard to find in any theatrical text book yet it is as important as elementary *pliés* are for the would be dancer. Conditions in a performance are rarely as perfect as they can be in a classroom or rehearsal. Remove the ideal circumstances, as will happen in a theatre, and the flimsy armoury of the actor can collapse. This cannot be allowed to happen and so the actor prepares for battle with every means at his disposal. If not, *he* will be disposed of for the audience knows quite well how to make mincemeat of ham actors.

In the exercise, the girls, each one a Columbine, talk to an unseen Harlequin, imploring him to return. The coquetry of Columbine has been misinterpreted by Harlequin as mere infatuation where, in fact, her feelings are genuine and longstanding. Pleading with him to restore their former union, the Columbines continue their monologues of seeming no response.

As their verbalized monologues get under way, the boys of the class move about the studio consciously distracting each and every one of the girls. This is done by approaching them very closely (not touching them, though) and making gestures and/or comments to derail their mental coach. The girls, of course, must concentrate twice as hard in their efforts to regain their Harlequins, studiously ignoring the distraction about them.

The boys must be sure to disperse their "distraction" to all the girls and not just concentrate on a few. After a few minutes the boys, as a parade of Pierrots, replace the girls, begging their unseen Columbines to take cognizance of their love. As the boys proceed, the girls enter their precincts (about one minute after the boys have begun), starting to distract them with a running commentary of irrelevant nonsense and silly gestures. The boys, as the girls previously, focus twice as intently on their monologues.

The text of the Columbines and Pierrots is spoken in a stylized manner, almost as one would 19th century poetry. The accompanying music should be Schumann, Liszt or any other of their romantic contemporaries.

These monologues are extremely hazardous for it takes very little noise, let alone buzzing in the vicinity of one's ear, to lose one's concentration. A moving body within one's eyeshot adds a further and even greater obstacle. Note that there is no touching nor any physical contact between the "distractor" and the soliloquizing actor.

If there aren't enough boys in the class, then the group is divided equally regardless of gender. This would mean that the monologues are done by both girls and boys at the same time and that the "distractors" are, as well, male and female.

During the actual performance any number of distractions can arise; continuous coughing from someone in the audience, a missed lighting cue, a defective sound system, a costume coming apart, a late entrance of a fellow actor, a passing ambulance siren heard straight through the walls of the theatre, stage hands walking noisily about in the wings, the list can, painfully, go on and on.

Rarely are conditions backstage or on stage so perfect as to duplicate the sterile silence of rehearsal. The actor must learn how to withstand the onslaught of distraction, never loosening his grip on the teetering wheel of concentration.

To cite just one example from too many in my own background, the first row of the theatre in Madrid was inches away from the stage. Leaving the wings, I at once noticed the big feet of one young gentleman comfortably placed next to my placards and props which meant that the spotlight would pick up my hands and his feet always at the same time. Slouching in his seat, his feet defiantly perched on the stage, the insolence of his intention could not be ignored.

During the blackout I sharply slapped his shoes, pushing his feet abruptly off the stage. When the light came on again, his feet had returned to their former position.

As the minutes wore on, my concentration was split between continuing the performance or stopping it, then having the spotlight turned on the culprit until such time as he would leave the theatre at which moment I would resume the performance. However, I chose not to since as a Pentagon presentation, my ire might have had dire repercussions in Spanish-American relations.

As it turned out, the ill-mannered man managed to have his fill and left the theatre during the interval. (Adding to that considerable distraction was the realization that the trouble maker had tampered with my placards, necessitating immediate readjustment as I held them.)

Leaving that bull ring for the surety of the studio, the *distraction exercise* is to be done in three parts:

1) The monologue undistracted
2) The monologue distracted
3) The monologue again undistracted

After the extreme effort of the second section, the third section will present no difficulties whatsoever.

Tactile responsiveness: playful, aggressive, compassionate, erotic

We now come across one of the most stringent taboos in our society—touching. There are very few people we are permitted to touch, and in very few places. Touching is generally thought of as erotic though it can equally be sympathetic, friendly, combative or affectionate. We tend to equate any body contact as a sexual prelude. With this firmly entrenched attitude, men in Anglo-Saxon society tend to go no further than the hearty slap on the back, the exception being football players who give in to the natural inclination by hugging and kissing, using victory as the macho excuse.

For the actor, the inability to touch or be touched is a locked handcuff, shackles which prevent unlimited freedom of expression. Ballet dancers don't suffer this problem, having had extreme physical proximity with other bodies since middle adolescence when lessons in partnering begin.

For actors, both speaking and speechless, the hurdle of touch must be overcome in order to relate, without restriction, to another body. Touching another person, whether male or female, must be accomplished without mental clutter.

Neither the piano not the violin can become embarrassed unlike the actor whose instrument is himself. As such we must unravel the loose ends of disturbance which have accumulated through our growing years.

In the *tactile responsiveness* exercise we are about to do, each person takes a partner. The gender is immaterial. Or so I would like it to be. The person on the teacher's left initiates the touching while the other person responds.

Playful. The initiator touches his partner playfully. The other person responds naturally which may manifest itself in a giggle. Or that person may jerk with ticklishness. After a minute or so, the partners reverse, the other person initiating the playful touch.

All the responses are in silence. There is no sound.

Stop.

Aggressive. Next the initiator touches his partner in an aggressive manner, the other person reacting accordingly. Care must be taken that restraint goes hand in hand with the aggression. No free-for-alls or wrestling matches. The partners reverse and the "victimized" partner begins touching aggressively.

Stop.

Compassionate. This is the touch of commiseration and sympathy. In each of the above situations the student must, as always, choose a specific mental image until it grows on its own accord. If you have ever been touched compassionately in a situation of dislocation or loss, you long remember the comfort of that contact.

Finally we come to that most threatening of all tactile situations (or inviting, depending upon one's point of view), erotic touch. When doing this part of the exercise, pay heed that the gestures are mentally motivated with potent thoughts, but are realized with a stringent simplicity. To commit murder on stage does not make necessary the spilling of real blood. By the same token, physical passion on stage does not require a display of carnal calisthenics.

If two girls or two boys are matched together as partners, they must make every effort to do the exercise with the same conviction as the girl/boy combinations, assuming, of course, that the couple in question is heterosexual. If they are otherwise inclined, inhibition should be less in evidence.

One's innate sexuality must have no influence on the exercise. The student cannot be allowed to offer the direction of his own libido as an excuse for non-participation, anymore than an actor can be allowed to refuse the role of an alcoholic because he's never taken a drink. One's experience or lack of it is no criterion for the actor's expansion.

The erotic touch sequence must be no more intimidating than the playful, aggressive and compassionate sections.

The sexual instinct cannot be swept away under the rug. Such thinking, with all sue respect to the Pope, is a pipe dream. Orthodoxy, with its insistent dogma, restricts and suppresses, leaving the future actor tied up with the ropes of self-consciousness. The *tactile responsiveness* exercise helps loosen those unwanted bonds.

Raucous/refined behaviour at party: contemporary and courtly

In this exercise of contrasting social mores, we move back and forth from a Chelsea gathering, 1983, to a queen's garden two hundred years earlier. In the first, the guests consist of punk rockers, mods and related inhabitants of copycat identity. The guests grab food, drink and partners, making every effort to be as publicly obnoxious as possible.

Then a sudden change to the aristocratic environs of a royal ball where the palace guests cavort with orchestrated courtliness.

From Chelsea or Greenwich Village to Versailles, from lightning strobe lighting to candle glow, the students switch from the most raucous to the most refined behaviour, a see-saw of antithetical styles. To ape the sloppiness of the first is relatively easy because the media amplify all current crazes. We've been there. It's all around us. To recapture the lost splendour and exquisite elegance of the latter requires a familiarity with satin, lace and balletic grace, textures and technique not quickly mimicked.

Svengali/Trilby mime sequence

Mauritz Stiller was Svengali to Greta Garbo, Josef von Sternberg had the same relationship to Marlene Dietrich, similarly Howard Hawks to Lauren Bacall; Serge Diaghilev was the great artistic manipulator to Nijinsky and Massine, George Balanchine was the puppeteer to the dancing Trilby of Vera Zorina, Maria Tallchief, Tanaquil LeClerq among others; the list is as varied as the great practitioners of the performing arts who have blossomed under the obsessive tutelage of their devoted maestros.

I, myself, am no stranger to this kind of relationship, the role of adoring Svengali being one of my most enduring credits. Yes, I consider it a credit, the loving transmission of any art form from one person to another.

Trilby was a novel written by George du Maurier, grandfather of novelist Daphne du Maurier. *Trilby* deals with a woman of no discernible talent turned into the greatest singer of her time by her opportunist discoverer. When he dies, her phenomenal soprano reverts to its original croak. The creative umbilical cord has been severed, the brilliant offspring unable to survive without its link.

To compare a relationship to Svengali and Trilby does not necessarily imply that the Trilby is ungifted or that the Svengali has ulterior motives. In all of the previously named duos with the exceptions of Nijinsky (gone mad) and LeClerq (struck down by polio), each of the aforementioned Trilby's continued as a major figure after the break with their Svengalis.

In the exercise we are about to do, the boys are Svengali and the girls are Trilby.

a) Trilby enters, meeting Svengali for the first time. He assesses what he sees as her future and enormous potential.

b) Under his mesmeric influence she develops into a dancing divinity.

c) At the very apogee of her triumphs he suddenly dies, the beauty of her movement deteriorating into disconnected jerkiness.

This exercise affords an opportunity to explore and develop a dramatic relationship in mime. One has to relate to one's partner with an exclusiveness that eliminates exterior distractions. This concentration on each other, this emotional give and take acts as the magnet that draws out public acceptance.

Along the Via Dolorosa mime sequence

One of the most searing performances I've ever seen was not by an actress as such, but by a woman preacher who, in a room along the Via Dolorosa in Jerusalem, intimidated every member of the audience by her power to make us all feel that each and every one of us present was personally guilty of that most celebrated crime in history, the crucifixion. When she finished her tirade, visibly perspiring, we breathed a silent sigh of relief that her inquisition was over. Insofar as involvement is concerned, there is not an actor in the world who could not have learned from Sister Agnes, that possessed evangelist.

In this most dramatic of episodes, the students are cast as Christ, the Virgin Mary, two Roman soldiers and the populace. Christ stumbles along his final mile, the Via Dolorosa, carrying the present weight of the cross and the future weight of Christian consciousness. The crowd jeers at him, hurling epithets and mud, spitting and mocking at the figure barbed wired with the crown of thorns.

The Roman soldiers hold the crowd at bay as Christ plods along the street of sorrow, followed by the desolate pleas of Mary. The procession of pain grinds to a halt when the Roman soldiers lift Christ under either arm in the image of history's ultimate execution.

The entire sequence is done in mime with the exception of the Virgin Mary who audibly laments in the language of her country (I always pick a non-English speaking student for this role). There is one other moment when the silence of mime bursts forth into a frenzy of sound and that is during the lifting of Christ onto the cross. At that moment, the sound of pounding drums clefts the air as concurrently the previously muted crowd bursts forth in an orgy of blood lust triumph. The Roman soldiers then lower the martyred body into the weeping arms of the madonna. As she cradles the broken body, the screams of the crowd accelerate, framing her anguish with quenchless hate.

For those students who comprise the populace, be aware of establishing an individual character. Don't disappear into the general contour of the group.

The Seven Deadly Sins mime sequence

One of the male students is chosen as an Everyman figure, based on the famous 16th century morality play which flourished in England at that time. The morality plays were allegories, in which character traits such as goodness and evil were personified. Other personality aspects such as charity, faith and vice were also much in evidence. The morality plays contrasted the required morality of the church's teaching with its always in wait opposite.

In this exercise, a morality playlet of its kind, the seven deadly sins are each represented by a student. One by one, each of the sins entices the Everyman with his or her particular vice. At the conclusion, they all converge upon him in a battle he wishes to lose for the defeat of temptation in this instance is sweeter than the victory over abstinence.

As the Everyman wanders in, the sins are seen in frozen positions indicative of their character. A *pas de deux* (dance for two) approximately one minute long takes place between each sin and Everyman. In order of their entrance, they will be Pride, Covetousness, Lust, Anger, Gluttony, Envy and Sloth (laziness).

Some of the sins such as Anger, Lust and Gluttony are simpler to interpret because their characteristics are so obvious and overt. Others such as Pride and Envy are more difficult since those sins require greater subtlety.

Beware when doing Sloth (laziness) that you don't add inertia to what is already apathy. In other words, don't add laziness to laziness. The result could be soporific, a mass sleeping pill for the audience. When portraying an extremely passive emotion, go counter to its obvious qualities and inject an oppositional antidote.

In the case of Sloth, let us say the character is on the floor, wallowing in his own inactivity. Instead of just lying there, make the effort to rise from the floor, but to no avail. Each struggling effort collapses as the floor continues its hold on the sin of laziness. This struggle adds interest to a passive emotion without, in any way, altering its esential qualities.

After the final sin has completed his infection of the Everyman, the other sins join in so that the victim is violated seven fold.

The student as Everyman must enact his role with a duality of attitude. He feels acutely uncomfortable as a stranger in somewhat mysterious territory. Concurrently, he is drawn to the magnetism of each approaching character. What enticing wares are they offering him and dare he savour any or all of them? What price tag, if any, will be attached to the gift being proffered?

The Everyman begins physically to resist but inwardly he welcomes the ravishment. Only at the end, when he is finally overwhelmed by the deadly seven, does he realize he has paid an inflationary price, runaway prices from which there is now no escape.

Pied Piper of Hamelin mime sequence

In this most vindictive of fairy tales (precursor to the nastiness of comic books?), the students are cast as the Pied Piper, the City Council, the children and the rats.

In the first sequence, the sleeping children are disturbed by rats who nibble at them before disappearing back into the night.

In the second sequence, the city council discuss the problem of the city's infestation by the rats when the Pied Piper enters, proposing to them his musical solution. If he succeeds, the men of the Council promise to reward him with a handsome sum of money.

In the third sequence, the rats are scampering about when the Pied Piper enters beguiling them with the irresistible sound of his music. They follow him, unreservedly, as he leads them to a cliff from which they plunge into the sea.

In the fourth sequence, the Pied Piper returns to the City Coucil, reporting to them his successful mission. Their gratitude is short-lived for they now refuse to compensate the Piper though he has succeeded in fulfilling his promise. Furious that he has thus been treated he leaves, his revenge already formulated.

In the fifth sequence, he returns to the now unbothered children, playing the same magnetic music to which earlier the rats succumbed. Enchanted, the children follow the Pied Piper to the deep interior of a mountain cave. Thinking that all the children are inside the cave, he closes the opening, snuffing out the future of the unfortunate pawns.

Unknown to the malevolent musician, one of the children, lame, unable to keep up the pace of the others, has lagged behind, her infirmity saving her life since she was too late to enter the mountain cave.

In the final sixth scene, she returns, crying, to the City Council, telling them of the others' fate. The members of the City Council lament over the high cost of their false economy.

Visual imitation

Actors learn a role by memorizing a script. Dancers and mimes learn their roles by imitating the physical example of the choreographer. I am referring now to learning group work as differentiated from choreographing solos on oneself.

The *visual imitation* exercise is designed to help the student pick up choreography by copying the demonstrator. Being able to learn choreography begins in the dance class where the student visually assimilates the combinations be they ballet, modern or jazz. If and when a student enters a movement group, it will, by then, be second nature to him to learn dance passages. Whereas previously he acquired the skill of memorizing classroom exercises, in a company he extends that ability to memorize sections of choreography which when joined together become a full scale dance production.

All the students stand in a straight line, diagonally from one corner of the studio to the other. The student who is first in line, the leader, extemporizes, creating a continuous stream of movement. The improvisation now being created must consist of slow, extended movements so that there is time for them to register and be copied by the person second in line.

The third person in line then copies the person in front while the fourth person copies the person in front of him and so it goes until the very last person in the line. This means that while the second person is copying the first, the third person is copying the second, and the fourth person is copying the third and so on.

The teacher will thus see movement unfolding as a series of multiple photographs. Have you ever seen an aquacade where a line of swimmers dive into the pool one a split second after the other? This *visual imitation* exercise will give the same impression.

After some minutes reverse the line so that the tail end person becomes the leader while the previous leader is now last. Keep concentrating throughout upon the person directly in front of you, not on the leader.

In general, when participating in a class or rehearsal, clear the mind so that speed of absorption is developed. A slow learner is nobody's favourite.

Sirens mime sequence

In ancient Greek mythology the sirens were female creatures living in the sea whose irresistible songs lured unsuspecting seamen to their watery graves. The word *siren*, now long outmoded, suggested a woman who used her feminine wiles for manipulative and destructive purposes.

In the exercise about to be done, the girls, on one side of the studio, are the sirens and the boys, on the opposite side, are ancient mariners. The girls, perched on their knees or reclining on their sides, magnetize the boys towards them, actually singing and using intense physical gestures to accompany their voices.

The boys, placed as if in an archaic sailing vessel (in two lines with a captain at the helm), row towards their rapturous doom. As the sailors and sirens meet, the boat is overturned, the sirens intertwining with the men as they sink towards their watery bed of final passion.

The exercise is repeated without sound, the song still heard but only in the minds of the girls "singing" and the boys who still "listen." The emotion expressed by the earlier sound must now be re-channeled silently through the entire body.

When doing this exercise without the voices, remember that the vocal power was only local power. Now, nationalize the energy and "sing" with unity of feeling, using the entire body. With or without the voice, each girl's "action" (purpose, intention, aim) is to lure the seamen into their underwater domain. Each boy's "action" is to arrive there.

The rebirth experience

The French obstretician Frederic LeBoyer believes that when a baby is born the lights are too bright and the sounds too loud. On top of these initial shocks, the baby is then straightened out too quickly and the umbilical cord cut too suddenly. The major mistake is taking the baby away from its mother and isolating it in another room. This sudden succession of events constitute, in Dr LeBoyer's measured opinion, the first traumatic experience from which many of us never recover, our first environmental insult.

He, himself, delivers babies in dim light with hushed tones from the nurses, then places the baby gently on the mother's stomach, continuing in an opposite manner to the usual time honoured methods of speed, sound and severance.

Though none of us can consciously recall our entry into this world, who can say if this momentous experience is not, indeed, etched ineradicably in our psyches?

The students lie down on the floor and accompanying themselves with vocal sounds, re-live that most spectacular of entrances.

a) being born with lights too bright
b) with sounds too loud
c) severance of the umbilical cord
d) held upside down and slapped
e) immediate separation from the mother

The exercise is then repeated without sound, in mime only. As always, the emotional force is re-routed throughout the entire body.

St Francis feeding the birds

St Francis loved both birds and animals, not as inferior species to be harnessed for profit or as domestic adornments to be patronized, but as a noble nation of which he, himself, was an inhabitant.

With this understanding, the student, as St Francis, feeds the birds, radiating gentility and purity of spirit. Without visible transition, the student becomes the hungry and grateful bird, feeding at the hand and feet of the loving saint.

The "action" as St Francis is to feed. The "action" as the bird is to be fed.

Avoid bird-like imitations. Metamorphose your mentality into that of a bird.

A truly great actor must be filled with love to the point of overflow. If he isn't, his ability to identify is limited to his immediate family unit. How can you step into another's shoes, claws or paws if you feel no common denominator identity?

Yes, the very great artist has qualities akin to a saint. He is compassionate, giving, understanding and has consecrated his gifts and skills at the altar of arterial theatre, the unchanging church of man that has survived replacement rituals and shifting gods and goddesses.

The artist as divine messenger, paying penance for his gift, is he not the perpetual protégé of God?

Mirror exercise: reflecting one's most admired qualities, then the least desirable ones

Think of your most admired personal quality such as generosity, loyalty, kindness, sincerity and so forth, expressing that quality in movement. This part of the exercise can be a little more difficult that one would think at first since we are conditioned to cover our virtues with the cultivated mask of humility. Putting aside the social niceties, awareness of one's own attributes is essential, for this self knowledge is at the very base of confidence. And confidence is the wind filled sail that keeps our boat afloat.

Then think of the quality in yourself that causes you the most misgivings. What aspect of your character are you least proud of? Selfishness? Irritability? Impatience? Intolerance? Whatever it is, reveal it in movement.

When I give this exercise to students, I never tell them what I have learned from watching them. To do so would be to embarrass the student and send him recoiling backwards into the shell from which he is trying to emerge.

At all times the student must feel safe in exposing himself before the scrutinizing stare and glare of the teacher. To pull the rug from under his feet would be breaking, not his neck, but worse, his trust.

Listening exercise

The students sit in a long semi-circle stretching from one side of the studio to another. The first student begins a fictional tale on any subject. About a half minute later, the teacher abruptly interrupts the speaker and the tale just begun is then continued by the second person who continues in his own fashion. Again, approximately half a minute later the speaker is cut into, when, without pause, the story is continued by the third person.

And so it goes until the tale has travelled through the fantasies of the entire class. The very last person should finalize the tale definitively.

This exercise forces each student to genuinely listen because if he doesn't he will be unable to continue the narrative. No one, when it comes to their turn, wants to be found at a loss for words.

It is interesting to note the faces of the students as the narrative inexorably approaches them. They are glued to the words of the encroaching fiction as the sound of the speaker gets closer and closer. This quality of the listener as participant helps transform him, on stage, from a passive receiver to an active one. In this way the actor does not just wait for a cue, for he is involved in what he is listening to or watching.

Fanatical preacher/congregation exercise

One of the students (male or female) is chosen to be a preacher of evangelical fervour, the fundamentalist variety flourishing in southern American states.

The other students are the congregation, willing and ready to believe in the gospel, singing, chanting, swaying and praying in their ecclesiastic zeal.

This exercise with its preacher and congregation can be likened to a concerto for soloist and orchestra, the soloist being the preacher and the orchestra, the congregation. The orchestra must not drown out the soloist, instead, feeling the moment to chime in, to punctuate the declamatory statements, to answer affirmatively, en masse, the questions that beg instantaneous agreement.

The preacher wields his power over the pliable mass as a snake charmer controls his serpent, as a hypnotist his subject and as a demagogue his constituents. He knows when to retreat, when to attack, when to intimidate, when to caress, never for a second losing his grip on the group.

This is an exercise in the wielding of power and the yielding to it, in the beginning verbalized then later mimed.

Sub-text exercise

We often say one thing to a person while implying another. In acting this is referred to as sub-text, the meaning under the audible. For instance, if a student who is habitually late enters the class some thirty minutes after it has begun, the teacher may greet that person by saying, "Well, hello, how nice to see you! How have you been?" Clearly, the sub-text of that so-called greeting is, "How dare you keep making your own set of rules when everyone else adheres to them? You're late for the umpteenth time!!"

Not all sub-text need be sarcastic. A person may be seriously ill and a visitor seeing the invalid may say to the patient, "You're beginning to look like your old self again." The sub-text of the visitor's compliment is, "Don't be discouraged. Please get well very soon."

The use of sub-text in acting (be it theatre, opera, ballet or mime) borrows from the actuality of our own real life experience. Often the sub-text conveys more than the words that are being uttered.

At a party a husband is chatting up a woman other than his wife. When the husband eventually leaves the party with his wife, she says to him, "You seemed to have had a very nice time tonight," inferring in her sub-text that he had gotten too friendly with a woman clearly making herself available.

In movement drama (dramatic ballet or dramatic mime), sub-text is equally applicable. True acting doesn't change with the addition or absence of words. In my item *The Dreamer*, the harrassed husband cowers at the onslaught of his wife's verbal attack, his movements seeming to say that she's won, that he's heard enough. His sub-text, though, is a plea to be released from the solitary confinement that is his wretched marriage.

The Dreamer is a comic item, regardless of the aforementioned description. So while on the subject of comedy I must warn you of the danger of laughing at your own ability to amuse. Never share the audience's keen amusement at your own comic situation. You may well be riotously funny but as soon as you share in the public's mirth, the character collapses and in his place is just another stand-up comedian. Those kind of comedians have a fear of not being laughed at which is so acute that they often laugh at their own jokes knowing that the public is programmed to copy. This kind of attitude borders on desperation, alienating us from the characterization; good enough for Bob Hope but hopeless in situation comedy.

Entrances and exits: as Pierrot, Harlequin and Columbine

What is more important in performance than an auspicious entrance and a definitive exit and yet how often do we see their opposites? A preparation must be made in the wings so that from the very first moment on stage the characterization is at its peak level. Too many people warm up visibly in front of an audience whereas warm-ups should be done in private.

The first few seconds of a performance are, in a sense, even more important than the minutes that follow, for in those opening moments the audience makes its decision to accept or reject. From the point of view of the actor, a strong commencement gives a confidence that acts as a railing for the entire performance.

When it comes to exits I cannot believe what I too often see. Who has not sat on the extreme far right or left of an auditorium and seen outstanding ballet dancers slouch off and waddle into the wings? If that dancer continued his exit movement just a few short feet further, the enchanting illusion so carefully created earlier would not so suddenly be destroyed.

But even if the sightlines of the theatre prevent the audience from seeing the demarcation line between on stage and off stage, the dancer, for himself, should feel the necessity of completing the movement.

Even when exiting from a *curtain call*, I continue my run until *I* have completed it.

So begin *before* you commence and end *after* you conclude.

In the following exercise, *exits and entrances*, the students portray the commedia dell'arte characters Pierrot, Harlequin and Columbine. Pierrot is, of course, love's silken scarecrow, battered by the tempest of Columbine's intemperate whims; Harlequin is the bravura exhibitionist of the local piazza, the Mick Jagger of Renaissance Italy while Columbine remains the enchanting soubrette whose twirling parasol obscures her compulsive coquetry.

The students invent their own situations (why they are entering, what they are doing when they arrive and where they are going) and then begin with a powerfully clear entrance, a fine performance proper terminating with a truly conclusive exit.

The elements

This exercise draws upon the sense of unrestricted freedom found in children but lost with the advent of maturity. By identifying with the forces of nature, the student goes back to his roots of uncluttered innocence, thus facilitating his ability to identify with any character in any sphere of existence.

As each of the following elements is called out, the students spontaneously respond in movement to that particular manifestation of nature.

Waves Snow Thunder Sun Lightning Rain Volcano
Rainbow Sandstorm Eclipse Earthquake Clouds Fire

In the final sequence of *fire*, the students group together as a huge bonfire, rising and falling with flickering and devouring flames.

Positive answers

Almost without exception all of us have been educated in a system where fault finding is the norm and the compliment is the rare exception. The end result of this year in and year out carping and chipping away of our flimsy coat of self-esteem is insecurity at best and fear at worst.

It is essential for people to be aware of their virtues as much as they are aware of their failings. Consciousness of one's positive qualities consolidates those qualities so that they become visible and immediate assets. If a student is unaware of his developing ability, that emergent aspect of his talent will be hit or miss, a once in a while plus of lucky accident. Real technique, as we know, can be called upon in any weather, any place and at any time.

When a student knows he's good, he gets better. When he thinks he's bad, he gets worse. A simplistic but indisputable equation.

This exercise is designed to help counteract the erosion of our self-belief caused by parents and teachers in our most vulnerable years.

All the following questions put forward by the teacher are to be answered by the students en masse and out loud. Avoid a tongue in cheek attitude as a cover-up for self-consciousness. Answer seriously, never flippantly. Try to convince the interrogator as if he were something of a doubting Thomas and needed to be persuaded.

All questions must be answered in the positive even if within yourself you believe otherwise. When answering the questions, even if they seem difficult to respond to affirmatively, latch on to even a glimmer of the truth and expand upon it. Even the ugliest of ducklings has moments when he sees himself as a swan.

Are you talented? Are you handsome (*or beautiful*)? *Are you a fine ballet dancer? Are you a wonderful actor? Are you a great mime artist? Are you generous? Are you popular with your colleagues? Are you a good son or daughter? Are you physically attractive? Will you arrive at your goal?*

The answers to the previous questions have rarely, if ever, been set forth by the students, publicly, in such a blatant and arrogant manner. By answering in this fashion, one cracks the very outer layer of the ice which encases the frozen ego.

Ego must be commensurate with achievement or with the belief of inevitable arrival. Even then, the ego when thawed must not spill over beyond the good dictates of humility. No accomplishment can be achieved without prior belief (ego) but that belief must always be proportionate, not overtaking.

Meaningless/meaningful movement duologue

Each student extemporizes movement opposite a given partner, relating to each other in a superficial, surface manner. This is the *meaningless* section of the duo improvisation, familiar to all of us as the way in which most social interplay between neighbours and working colleagues is conducted. The weather, last night's television programme, a department store sale, any one of these safe topics that dares not poke beneath the psychological epidermis, all of this is grist for the meaningless mill.

Switch. The improvised duet takes on exclusive undertones as the *pas de deux* becomes *meaningful*. The communication between the couple leaves the infertile soil of safe subjects, delving, instead, deep beneath the self-protective covering. The subsequent conversation encompasses, perhaps, personal fears, a complex love relationship, trailing guilt that refuses to be side-stepped, an inner dream or any other topic of great personal importance that we do not share with all and sundry. This is the meaningful conversation at the party that retires all other guests to the buzz of the blurring sidelines.

Both the meaningless and meaningful aspects of this improvisation are expressed through movement only.

Garden of Eden mime sequence

Adam, Eve and the snake—the first ménage à trois?

Adam and Eve cavort without a care in their trouble free tract of land called Eden. The snake soon enters, the precursor of our present day commercial brainwashing. Buy this, eat that, in this case, the ignominious apple of lost innocence.

Eve succumbs to the super salesmanship of the snake who now realizes that temptation will never go out of style. If there were residuals for successful selling, then this snake would be the richest creature in the business for think how many of Eve's descendants have yielded to instant satisfaction at cost to longer term security.

Eve sinks her teeth into the juicy fruit to be followed by Adam who bites off more than he can chew. The end result is a double case of food poisoning from which orthodoxy has never let us recuperate. At once, unwelcome tenants, Adam and Eve are evicted from their once unpolluted paradise to the shame infested world at large.

Is there a moral to this story? Perhaps it could be that he who offers too much hospitality ends up in the hospital himself!

In this first cautionary tale the students are cast as Adam, Eve and the serpent. Depicting the path from public innocence to pubic shame, this biblical story is, arguably, history's first cover-up.

Characters from 16th century morality plays: Everyman, the Devil, Faith, Guilt, Charity, Force, Wealth, Sex, the Spoken Word

In France, Germany and England, a form of theatre developed during and after the 12th century in which mime was featured prominently.

These were the mystery, miracle and morality plays, all of them closely bound up with the Christian church. The source of inspiration for the mystery plays were happenings from the old and new Testament while the miracle plays dealt with the lives and deaths of the saints.

The morality plays did not deal specifically with biblical events, instead dramatizing the virtues and defects of man in an allegorical manner, namely representing such human characteristics as Good, Evil, Force, Wealth and other forces that forge our character.

It was in the 16th century that the most impacting of the morality plays came into being—*Everyman*. Mimed episodes assumed a greater place in the morality plays than in the mystery and miracle presentations. The Devil, as a predominant character, created hell for the increasingly larger audiences, now moved from the interior of the local church to the exterior of the village green.

In the following class exercise, the students represent such characters from the morality plays as The Devil, Faith, Guilt and Charity.

As a second exercise, they hold imaginary masks to their faces symbolizing Vice tempting Everyman. The hand-held mask, as always, must become an extension of self, steering the body into grotesque postures reminiscent of a Dürer woodcut.

Lastly, with another of the students cast as Everyman, the rest of the students are cast as Force, excessive Wealth, Sex and the Spoken Word, four potential danger areas of our existence.

From emphatic pose to definitive gesture and movement (completely expressed in mime), the characters of the morality plays revive the medieval war between good and evil in their symbolic representation of our conscience.

Remedial truth exercise

This is a most cathartic exercise, emotionally speaking, and a potentially precarious one if the teacher doesn't tightly hold on to the reins. All of us, at one time or another, have been victimized unfairly by someone, be it a teacher, parent, lover or employer. Often, we were not in the position to defend ourselves, or attack back as should have been the case, in some instances.

In this exercise, everyone recalls some incident from their recent or distant past, answering their assailant now with a whiplash sharpness that could not have been realized then. The defense, or the attack, is verbalized (everyone speaking at once, insuring the privacy of one's retort).

Here is the opportunity to make amends for unjustly inflicted wounds. For some students, this recall borders on the traumatic so the teacher, when noticing the spilling over of a long boiling cauldron, must call a halt to the proceedings lest a theatrical exercise turn into a do-it-yourself exorcism.

The purpose of this section of the syllabus is not to exhume the ghosts of the buried past but to loosen the restraints of the actor's instrument—himself. If the *remedial truth exercise* succeeds in opening the door to locked up pain, thereby easing it by freeing it, as well as tuning up the emotional attack of the actor, then a double bonus will have been achieved.

Circus mime

The clown, as the archetypal figure of external merriment and internal suffering, is chosen for a number of expressive mime exercises. In this *circus mime* exercise, the student learns the following choreography.

Assuming a turned in position, conveying the permanent insecurity of he who gets slapped without respite, the clown touches his chalk white face, irremovable stigma of the man without address or redress. He can no more remove the paint from his face than the former concentration camp victim, his tatooed number.

Fingering his frilly and silly cuffs on the left wrist then the right, his arms feel weighted as if by lead.

Clasping his heart, he is certain of the loving warmth he could, if given the chance, distribute, but circumstances decree otherwise. Hands still over his heart, the outer hand flutters against the other, the tremolo beating paralleling the quivering emotions within.

Extending his arms outwards to the non-existent recipient of his deep feelings, the clown continues to offer of himself to the multitude who singly and collectively ignore him.

Starting from the beginning, the clown soliloquy is intensified as the traditional circus melody (*Over The Waves*) is repeated with a commensurate acceleration.

Throughout the preceding mime aria, the student is fed by a continuing inner monologue. The silent words within the mind instigate the movements and gestures which are the result.

To summarize: Touching the face—4 bars
Fingering the left sleeve—2 bars
Fingering the right sleeve—2 bars
Hands over heart—4 bars
Pulsating hands over heart—2 bars
Arms extended to the absent beloved—2 bars

Few of us have been clowns in the circus but who among us can claim never to have experienced the bitter pill of rejection, estrangement and emotional isolation? It is this knowledge that is transplanted by the student to his adopted clown which must soon belong to him as if genetic.

At the circus: side show/main event

The class is divided into two groups; the first group being members of the side show, the second group, the performers of the actual circus itself.

The characters of the side show consist of the barker, the fat lady, Siamese twins, the sword swallower, the strong man, the midget, the snake charmer, the elephant man and the wolf boy. The characters of the circus proper are made up of clowns, tightrope walkers, bareback riders, acrobats, seals, acrobats, jugglers and the ringmaster.

There will be two areas of activity split down the middle of the studio by an invisible centre. The scene begins with the sideshow in performance while, concurrently, the circus cast are making-up supervised by the ringmaster.

The students must nurture their improvisations with a continuous image replenishment. The moment one mental image subsides, immediately replace it with another which in turn brings with it a host of further pictures until very soon one's mind is operating as a motion picture instead of a series of still photographs.

Keep the mouth of the subconscious open thus enabling a continuous creative feeding process.

Now the groups change. The side show group which was performing now removes its make-up while the circus group which was making-up then begins its performance.

All the movements must be enlarged, not exaggerated, with the life force surging through the arms and legs past the fingertips and toes. There should be concentric circles of energy, the furthest circles caused by the initial blast of the first.

Finally, both groups come together for their curtain calls, another performance in itself with the golden glitter, sparkling silver, spangled red, sequined blue and all the other garish colours of the Technicolor prison where animals are caged rather than men, where the ever present death sentence (by high wire and trapeze) has not yet been repealed and where the freaks pay penance for fate's cruel roll of the loaded dice.

Clown poses

Strike a clown pose, holding it for eight bars. Then abruptly change to another position, always in the style of the antic clown. The first count of each pose must be struck emphatically, the echo of the energy lasting through the entire position.

All told, the student will strike four sets of these eight bar poses (32 bars, four poses). Afterwards, the poses will be accelerated by doing eight sets of only four bar positions (32 bars, eight poses). This is to be followed by doing eight sets of 2 bar poses (16 bars, eight poses) and finally 16 sets of one bar positions (16 bars, 16 poses).

This exercise helps the student to count music while acting, no easy balancing act except for the trained dancer.

Each of the positions must be struck with a vitality that is repercussive in its reach, supersonic in its speed. You do not court the audience, you consume them.

Clown on a tightrope

This is the only illusionary aspect of mime that I ever teach. Note that I say *aspect of mime*, for that is exactly what it is, a part of the art, not its entirety.

In this exercise the mime as clown wavers on a tightrope, his attitude faltering between a shaky confidence and an all too real terror of the ground below. The quick steps forward and backward must be in an absolutely straight line, one foot exactly replacing the other in the advance or retreat.

Though few of us have actually walked a tightrope, everyone is aware of the fear of falling from the roof of a building, the top of a mountain ledge or a high rise balcony. Draw upon your knowledge of intimidating height then borrow from that awareness, thereby creating a convincing personage.

Clown entertaining children

Imagine an arena of thousands of tiny children responding with sheer delight at the silly and outlandish capers employed by you, the madcap clown. Repression and reserve must be tossed aside if the emotional freedom aimed for is to be achieved. To do this exercise well is to develop an expressive liberty unhampered by that arch enemy of communication, self-consciousness.

A child's delight is immediately contagious. Their joy revives the child still alive within us. By responding to their imagined excitement, we dust the cobwebs of our conformity, expanding our emotional range.

Clown blowing bubbles

Bubbles. The transparent prisms of our imprisoned hopes. In their circular perfection we see the fleeting reflection of our fragile aspirations.

Clown, the laughing Christ of the circus cavalcade, forever blowing bubbles that disintegrate as surely as the miracle before the doubting masses, the dream before awakening.

The student, as the clown, blows bubbles with anticipation, watches them float with an excessive joy, then sees them burst with collapsing sorrow. Each of the emotional stages must be clearly depicted. This exercise is a *pas de deux* between life and death, the life and death of a bubble, our beautiful but troubled world in microcosm.

Pierrot's declaration of dependence: miming/stillness/miming

In this improvisation, Pierrot, the Commedia's symbol of perrenial estrangement, rather than assert his freedom, declares his willingness, his need, to be the slave of love to his elusive Columbine.

With this thought pouring out throughout his face and body, Pierrot mimes. The thought continuing, his body stills, but the passionate need still permeates his immobile frame. So though his body is seemingly frozen, the message is as clear as when he was moving with emotion. Then he reverts to the earlier mime, his continuing need intensifying with his body again in motion.

This improvisation, expressive of Pierrot's unending search for a beloved, is a triptych of emotional torment. Throughout the three part portrait, Pierrot's upset spirit is never in doubt.

In the first part, he conveys his feelings while moving.

In the second part, he conveys his feelings while motionless.

And in the third and last part, he conveys his feelings, again while moving.

So though the muscles subside in the stillness section, the mind is roaming and roving without respite. The feeling is constant throughout. Only in the middle section does the physicality subside before resuming in the final part.

Clown: adagio/allegro/adagio

The public clown is traditionally an allegro figure in that his rhythm is usually sprightly and upbeat. The student, as a clown, improvises in contrasting musical moods; adagio, allegro and back to adagio.

When doing this exercise, the student must retain the merriment of the performing clown, not only in the obvious quick allegro section, but also in the contrasting slow adagio.

The music starts lyrically and though the movement of the clown must parallel the sound of the music, the personality of the clown is nothing less than dazzling. This, then, is the adagio section—slow music, slow movement but mercurial personality.

Next comes the allegro section in which there is quick music, quick movement and the continuing mercurial personality. This section is, of course, obvious. Bright music elicits bright personality.

Then the music returns to the adagio section. Again, there is slow music, slow movement while the mercurial clown is still ejecting his brilliant rays.

The big challenge of this exercise is to retain the allegro aura of the clown during the adagio sections. Be aware of not matching the lyric quality of the adagio with a lyric performing quality. In this exercise, the clown's sparkle never diminishes despite the seeming perversity of the musical accompaniment.

Circus mime: singing/speaking/mime

The student, now familiar with the choreography of the *circus mime*, will at this time approach the exercise from another direction.

In the first part of the exercise the students will accompany the mime by actually singing the melody of the music. In the second part of the exercise, the students will accompany the mime with a running commentary, an audible inner monologue. In the last part of the exercise, the students will do the mime on its own, unassisted by either singing or speaking.

What is the purpose of these additional responsibilities, one may well ask?

By singing as well as miming, there is a fuller participation of the interpretive instrument. By verbalizing one's thoughts while miming, there is a lesser risk of generalizing one's emotions. Speaking one's thoughts keeps the mime actor on the dramatic track.

By the time the student reverts to the original challenge of miming with no artistic additives, he will be intensely familiar with the emotional terrain of the character's habitat. He will not be an alien trespassing on someone else's property for he, himself, will have lived there.

Jack-in-the-box/clown/Pinocchio/Pierrot

The students will do a four part improvisation encompassing characters whose souls are encased in tinsel, timber, paint and powder. There will be jack-in-the-box, so eager to participate in the tantalizing world of reality, to escape his anchoring springs. Next there will be clown, publicly parading his manic mannerisms as a cover for his privately depressive demons. Then there will be Pinocchio whose eagerness for life is almost his undoing. Finally there will be Pierrot, apparent simpleton with a hidden wisdom, sufferer of unseen stigmata.

At first, the characters are realized in the above progression. Then they are given out of sequence, in varying time durations. Despite the speed of alternation and jump cut approach, the accuracy of each character must be instantaneously established.

Clown taking curtain calls: waving, blowing kisses, being funny, bowing

In this mosaic of a clown's conclusion, the student takes his reluctant curtain calls, reluctant because the bows foretell the finish of the night the circus closed.

When he waves, it is with the hurtful consciousness of no return. When he blows kisses, they are merely doomed tokens of affection, directed towards an audience no more to be seen. When he is funny, his humour is a camouflage which covers the empty arena of his own and barren circus.

And when he bows, he is the supreme impostor of high spirits, concealing his inner desolation with his comical mask and conical hat, amusing a world bloated by tasteless popcorn and drifting in a heaven of indiscriminate injustice.

Providing musical accompaniment for me in all the classes I teach either at The Mime Centre or abroad is Kazimir Kolesnik. Though, himself, a mime artist of exceptional theatrical strength, his versatility is such that as a musician he is able to play either the piano, Chinese flute or percussion (drums, bells and tambourine). For some of the exercises he plays three instruments concurrently, using at the same time his hands, feet and mouth. His musical inventiveness contributes enormously to the creativity and excitement of every lesson.

3. An Outline of 10 Classes

THE FATHER WHO SEARCHED
FOR HIS LONG LOST SON

I am alone.
My legs, like weeping willows,
remember you
and I ask everyone
why I no longer embrace you.

I cry out at night and during the day.
I cry out to the sun which, at every step
Incises deep rainbows on my shoulder.

Where are you, my son forever,
like a blow from a blunt instrument
on my smile,
like a kiss on greeting and
on saying goodbye,
like a shriek from within
my sluggish mind?

José Luis Naranjo Ferrer

The following 10 lessons are representative examples of my method. The classes are structured so that they begin with physical exercises which lead into the emotional exercises. The lessons always begin and end with *inflation/deflation.*

1st lesson

1. Inflation/deflation
2. Exercising facial muscles and hands
3. Tension/relaxation
4. Traction/withdrawal
5. Sequential movement
6. Stillness/activity
7. Ribs/armpit movement
8. Expansiveness of gesture
9. Distribution of energy
10. Flowing/fragmented movement
11. Energy/lethargy
12. Impetus/improvisation/conclusion
13. Progression exercise: acquisitive/greedy/gluttonous
14. Adaptation to partner: one person creates the movement, the other harmonizes: reverse
15. Feeling the centre of the light – improvisation
16. Merging into the ensemble/emerging as soloist
17. Clown poses
18. Inflation/deflation

2nd lesson

1. Inflation/deflation
2. Exercising facial muscles and hands
3. Tension/relaxation
4. Traction/withdrawal
5. Sequential movement
6. Articulate extremities
7. Circular/angular
8. Dynamics in movement: three levels – breeze, wind, tornado
9. Shifts in balance: strike a balance then while still balancing, shift axis
10. Compensation: standing up with rigid lower body and compensating with upper body; reverse – standing up with rigid upper body and compensating with lower body
11. Body stops/thought continues: fear, begging, encouraging, refusal
12. Symmetrical body line exercise (straight, curved then angular lines)
13. Progression exercise: giggles/laughter/hysteria
14. Greek tragedy and comedy masks: with tragedy masks invent language, with comedy masks, laughing and with screaming masks, wail
15. Communication through face only: begging, anger, compassion, enthusiasm, exasperation; through hands only, through feet only and then the above emotions expressed through all the body
16. The Elements: waves, snow, thunder, sun, lightning, rain, moon, rainbow, sandstorm, eclipse, earthquake, fire, cloud, volcano, avalanche, flood
17. Circus mime
18. Inflation/deflation

3rd lesson

1. Inflation/deflation
2. Exercising facial muscles and hands
3. Tension/relaxation
4. Traction/withdrawal
5. Sequential movement
6. Embracing space
7. Elasticity/control
8. Reaching out from a central impetus
9. Out of focus/in focus line
10. Spine/thighs
11. Elbows and knees coordination exercise
12. Conflict in movement: moving forward with alternate arms and legs
13. Progression exercise: pleased/enthusiastic/enraptured
14. Colour responsiveness: red, white, black, gold, pale blue, silver, green, grey, purple
15. Meaningless/meaningful movement duologue
16. Entrances and exits
17. Clown entertaining children
18. Inflation/deflation

4th lesson

1. Inflation/deflation
2. Exercising facial muscles and hands
2. Tension/relaxation
4. Sequential movement
5. Terrestrial/celestial movement
6. High voltage/low voltage
7. Run with activity/freeze lifelessly; reverse – run lifelessly/freeze with activity
8. Attraction/repulsion
9. Duality of concentration: as a marionette express happiness, apathy, anger and yearning all the while sustaining the unchanging allegro rhythm
10. Medieval stained glass windows
11. Weight and weightlessness in characterization:
    asylum inmate – heavy; drunk – light
    reverse; asylum inmate – light; drunk – heavy
12. Continuity of movement
13. Progression exercise: obstinate/resistant/defiant
14. Caricature/characterization: astronaut, hypnotist, newsboy, landlord, seasick passenger, model, prostitute
15. On the beach
16. Heroes and fans
17. Circus mime
18. Inflation/deflation

5th lesson

1. Inflation/deflation
2. Exercising facial muscles and hands
3. Tension/relaxation
4. Traction/withdrawal
5. Sequential movement
6. Articulate extremities
7. Mobility on one leg
8. Magnet exercise
9. Melting/percussive
10. Interplay of movement
11. Height levels: low, medium, high
12. Cause and effect balance
13. Progression exercise: asking/begging/imploring
14. Garden of Eden mime sequence
15. Empathy exercise: inner identification – elephant, lion, swan, cat, monkey, peacock, frog
16. Sirens mime sequence
17. Clown poses (changing counts)
18. Inflation/deflation

6th lesson

1. Inflation/deflation
2. Exercising facial muscles and hands
3. Tension/relaxation
4. Traction/withdrawal
5. Sequential movement
6. Distribution of energy
7. Ribs/armpit movement
8. Spine/thighs
9. Exercise: My name is . . .
10. Progression exercise: irritation/anger/fury
11. St Francis feeding the birds
12. Inner monologue: child with seashell (verbalize then in mime)
13. Carriage for theatre of the 17th to 19th centuries
14. Motivation exercise: run from one end of the studio to another; each of the runs is motivated by the following emotions – anger, compassion, fear, denial
15. Fanatical preacher/congregation exercise
16. Children's games
17. Circus side show/main event
18. Inflation/deflation

7th lesson

1. Inflation/deflation
2. Exercising facial muscles and hands
3. Tension/relaxation
4. Traction/withdrawal
5. Sequential movement
6. Relationship of feet to floor: suspicious, tender, confident, arrogant, resistant
7. Small gesture/low voltage; large gesture/high voltage
   reverse;
   small gesture/high voltage; large gesture/low voltage
8. Lifting/lowering upper arms with resistance
9. Attitude exercise: person scrubbing floor – fatigued, carefree, resigned, conscientious
10. Spatial patterns: paint a picture with space as the canvas and the body as the brush, making as many varied designs as possible
11. Movement: with effort/effortlessly
12. Conducting an orchestra: standing up, kneeling, lying on back, stomach, side, sitting, then again standing up
13. Progression exercise: silly/stupid/idiotic
14. Dramatic counterpoint: while lights and sound fade, final pose increases in intensity (a child calling for his lost dog)
15. Caricature/characterization: auditioning actor, rickshaw boy, politician, hijacker, archaeologist, opera singer, priest, cowboy
16. Inmates: cackling laughter/aggressiveness/apathy
17. Distraction exercise
18. Inflation/deflation

8th lesson

1. Inflation/deflation
2. Exercising facial muscles and hands
3. Tension/relaxation
4. Sequential movement
5. Motivated/meandering walk
6. Marching/waltzing: energetic then apathetic, all the while keeping the same rhythm
7. Responsiveness to sound/reaction to silence: Pierrot taking curtain calls
8. Heightened awareness in movement: an improvisation built climactically
9. Torso in constant motion while feet are rooted
10. Accelerando/rallentando movement (increasing then decreasing in tempo)
11. Punctuation in movement: comma, exclamation point, question mark, full stop, ellipsis (. . .), dash, signature
12. Speeds (slow, medium fast): person running after their loved one
13. Progression exercise: indifferent/rude/contemptuous
14. Mirror exercise: think of your most admired personal quality (generosity, loyalty, kindness etc.) and convey in movement; then think of your least desirable quality (selfishness, intolerance, possessiveness, etc.) and convey in movement
15. Oppositional states of mind: power/weakness, freedom/restraint, love/hate, innocence/sophistication
16. Silent screen characters: pleading heroine, betrayed husband, tramp, Hunchback of Notre Dame, siren, Charleston dancer, tango dancer, Indian chief, cowboy, heroine tied to railroad tracks, Keystone cops
17. The rebirth experience: a) lights too bright; b) sound too loud; c) severance of umbilical cord; d) held upside down and slapped; e) immediate separation from the mother
18. Inflation/deflation

9th lesson

1. Inflation/deflation
2. Exercising facial muscles and hands
3. Tension/relaxation
4. Traction/withdrawal
5. Sequential movement
6. Stillness/activity
7. Inflate/run
8. Impetus/improvisation/conclusion
9. Walking past each other with and without contact:

   a) walk past each other physically touching but without emotional contact

   b) walk past each other without touching but establishing emotional contact
10. Musical phrasing: gesturing with arms, use as many musical variations as possible within the given tempo
11. Submissive/assertive movement
12. Walking/trotting/running
13. Progression exercise: meditation/prayer/mania
14. Attitude exercise: a person is lying on the floor in a coma with the onlookers registering puzzlement, disgust, amusement, compassion
15. Transition exercise: golden Buddhas
16. Petrouchka imprisoned in his cell
17. Out of sequence narrative for filming: Little Red Riding Hood
18. Inflation/deflation

10th lesson

1. Inflation/deflation
2. Exercising facial muscles and hands
3. Tension/relaxation
4. Traction/withdrawal
5. Impose/recede
6. Tension in one arm/relaxation in the other/relaxation in both;
   reverse;
   start with the other arm
7. Allegro music: move quickly, move slowly;
   adagio music: move slowly, move quickly
8. Serene/disturbed movement
9. Compressed/expressed gestures
10. Relaxed/rigid balances
11. Contained balance/expanded balance
12. Tautness in lower body/plasticity in upper body;
    reverse;
    plasticity in lower body/taughtness in upper body
13. Progression exercise: images/visions/hallucinations
14. Empathy exercise: inner identification – blades of grass, meteor, drifting moon, eclipsing sun, foam, waterfall, weeping willow tree
15. Alphabet exercise
16. Express dramatically then comedically the following emotions: yearning, fear, enthusiasm, desire, anger
17. The Seven Deadly Sins mime sequence:
    Pride Covetousness Lust Anger Gluttony Envy
    Sloth (Laziness)
18. Inflation/deflation

4. Conversations

RESURRECTION:
THE NAZI AND THE NAZARENE

A flower riddled with bullet holes
presides over the familiar meal.
From among the motley dead
and separated lovers
a dove bears out
the weapons of the defeated.

José Luis Naranjo Ferrer

With Douglas Fairbanks, Jr.

On expressive movement and mime in the silent cinema

Douglas Fairbanks, Jr., born in New York City in 1909, is the son of Douglas Fairbanks, the undisputed king of the silent screen while his step-mother, Mary Pickford, "America's sweetheart," was the screen's reigning chaste goddess. Together they were the king and queen of Hollywood, the recipients of world idolatry never since equalled, not even, in their heyday, by Elizabeth Taylor and Richard Burton.

With such a family background, Douglas Fairbanks, Jr.'s entrance into the cinema was not unexpected. He, himself, carved out an illustrious career, having acted in more than 75 motion pictures, among them *Gunga Din* and *The Prisoner of Zenda*.

For his wartime, diplomatic and philanthropic services, he has been awarded innumerable honours, among them the Croix de Guerre with Palm (France), Knight Commander of the Most Excellent Order of the British Empire, the City of Vienna Medal and the American Image Award (simultaneously elected first member of Hall of Fame).

ADAM DARIUS: Your own career as a motion picture star began in silent films. What transition did you, personally, have to make as an actor from the silents to talkies?

DOUGLAS FAIRBANKS, JR.: Luckily, very little. I began in silent films but I also went on the stage shortly afterwards. I was doing both so when sound came in I was already well trained in drama, in Delsarte, in commedia dell'arte technique and well versed in the classics. I had done a lot of training before sound came in when I was quite young, in my teens, so actually I had less trouble than a lot of others.

ADAM DARIUS: Your father, Douglas Fairbanks, had a physical bravado that has never been matched in the subsequent history of Hollywood. Was he as dazzling to watch on the set as he was in the edited images on the screen?

DOUGLAS FAIRBANKS, JR.: Oh yes, because he had been equally dazzling, in a physical sense, on the stage before then. If ever he saw a fence he would prefer to jump or vault over the fence than walk around it. It just amused him to do it whether an audience was there or not. He just had this boundless energy. But it also interested him to create an image and a personality of that sort, first in the limited confines of a theatre and the proscenium arch but then in the relatively unlimited medium of the cinema. He learned more and more in the first years and then he took full advantage when he went into his classic period.

He didn't really think of himself so much as an acrobat either. He was not so much acrobatic as athletic. In a way he thought of it more as dance.

ADAM DARIUS: And speaking of dance, your father took the only known film footage of Anna Pavlova dancing some of her repertoire during a break in the making of *The Thief of Baghdad* in 1924. Was he amusing himself or was he aware of documenting the world's greatest ballerina for posterity?

DOUGLAS FAIRBANKS, JR.: Both. She was staying at the house, as a house guest, and he invited her to come down one time, saying, "Don't you think it would be a good idea for posterity for you to do just a few snatches of some of your more famous dances?"

In the silent days, on the sidelines, they always had music. Depending on the size of the budget, they'd sometimes have a two piece group, maybe a violin and an organ or somebody playing a squeeze box of some sort. But if you had big budgets in classics, you might have a whole quartet or quintet playing. So my father always did have that kind of orchestra standing by.

I don't remember the circumstances clearly myself because I wasn't there though I knew about it. And I was really too young. But that is what happened. So Pavlova arranged to do just a few minutes. The entire film runs ten or fifteen minutes. They did it on the set of *Thief of Baghdad*, and I think it was on a Sunday, you know, when nothing else was happening.

In those days there were six 10 hour days a week, sometimes 12 hour days and sometimes seven days a week.

ADAM DARIUS: There were no unions then to call a halt.

DOUGLAS FAIRBANKS, JR.: No.

ADAM DARIUS: According to your step-mother Mary Pickford's account, written 40 years after the event, your father once asked her, "Do you know who are the outstanding artists in pantomime?" He then named them – Mary Pickford and Charlie Chaplin. Your father is further quoted as saying to her, "You mastered the art through a great economy of gesture. You do less apparent acting than anyone I know and because of that you express more."

What, Mr Fairbanks, are your personal recollections of Mary Pickford, not on screen, but as relatively few saw her, actually acting for the cameras?

DOUGLAS FAIRBANKS, JR.: I very seldom saw her working. It was a long, long time ago when I was quite young. But I had talked to her about it and I was with her just the day before she died. I had been seeing a lot of her in recent years. Recently, I saw a retrospective of her films, which I presided over, at the Museum of Modern Art in New York.

She was one of the masters of very subtle understatement and yet knowing exactly the distance between the camera and herself, how much there was to do and how little there was to do and how a flicker of one eyelash would convey practically the same meaning of a speech two paragraphs long. I'm exaggerating, of course, to make my point, but it was very carefully and studiously worked out. As with Lillian Gish. They were both conscious masters of the economy of movement, of projecting meaning in what needed to be said. And they knew how to do it.

They had what Noël Coward called star quality. Some people have star quality and little technique. Some have a lot of technique and no star quality. When you find it all, you have a Mary Pickford and a Lillian Gish.

ADAM DARIUS: Now Lillian Gish was the embodiment of the immaculate heroine. What was the main difference, as you recall, between Mary Pickford and Lillian Gish?

DOUGLAS FAIRBANKS, JR.: Lillian Gish was not her own creator. She worked for the most part under Griffith and was rather like Liv Ullman with Ingmar Bergman, a magnificent artist guided by another major artist.

Mary had some good directors and some not so good but she was like my father and Chaplin in that she created things from the word go. She decided what she wanted to do, how she wanted to do it, who was to do it with her, everything. I mean, she was the complete creator, not just the interpreter. She was the composer, the conductor, the soloist all in one. So that was the difference between them. But when it came to interpreting they were about the same except that Mary was the complete boss while Lillian was never the boss.

ADAM DARIUS: Didn't Mary Pickford also play more child-like roles?

DOUGLAS FAIRBANKS, JR.: Oh, yes, but that was to satisfy the popular demand. But not always. Sometimes she'd get away from it. There's a famous story about an Anglo-Indian named Sir Philip Sassoon and he had a very crisp way of talking with his r's in his throat—like that. He said when he met my step-mother, "At that time she was a stretcher case with rage. Her teeth were chattering like dice in a box because for years she'd been playing little girls of 11 and was now being forced to play little girls of 12."

Mary, herself, laughed at the story. I mean she was fully aware of it because she was also a very shrewd business woman.

ADAM DARIUS: Yes, I've heard. Was she reclusive in her older age, towards the end?

DOUGLAS FAIRBANKS, JR.: When she was ill, yes. Very. She didn't like being seen because she had been in bed for a very long time. She was reduced to just skin and bones. And she couldn't walk and couldn't see. Nearly blind.

So only very few members of the family could see her and then it would depend on what mood she was in that day and how long she took to prepare herself. I could see her but I was a very favoured figure. Even then, however, not every day. Certain days she would be with it and certain days she wouldn't.

ADAM DARIUS: Which roles in your own long career have afforded you the most satisfaction?

DOUGLAS FAIRBANKS, JR.: It depends on the category. If you asked which of all the costume dramas, which one of all the adventure films, of all the high comedies? There are almost too many to say. I tend to like the ones that were the most successful. But that's not always the case. Sometimes the public was just too far behind the times and we were too far ahead of them.

ADAM DARIUS: That often happens, unhappily. In these many categories of films in which you've appeared, whose work among your co-stars have you most admired?

DOUGLAS FAIRBANKS, JR.: Well, they say there are no indiscreet questions, only indiscreet answers.

ADAM DARIUS: Fred Astaire, as well, doesn't like to state his favourite partner.

DOUGLAS FAIRBANKS, JR.: Well, I knew Garbo very well and played with her as her younger brother in Michael Arlen's *The Green Hat* which was later re-titled *A Woman of Affairs*. This was in 1928. But I wasn't aware of her greatness, only of her being very nice. We were very great friends. She was a few years older than I. It's only in looking backwards and seeing the film again that I realize how really terribly good she was. She had excellent training before she came here.

Looking backwards I would say that Irene Dunne was a very, very fine technician. Bette Davis was a good technician but she was very young when she started with me and we didn't know she was going to become as good as she became later on. Katherine Hepburn was always a striking personality and you didn't know where the personality stopped and the talent began. But she was wonderful and had that star quality. She has improved in technique since those days.

Elizabeth Bergner, from Germany, I felt was all technique and very excellent technique but you could see the machinery going around. Well, obviously the general public didn't or she wouldn't have been so widely recognized in Germany and elsewhere. But another pro could see it.

ADAM DARIUS: In which film did you work with her?

DOUGLAS FAIRBANKS, JR.: Catherine the Great. Gertrude Lawrence, of course, also had a fine technique and certainly great star quality. But the technique was erratic. In one performance it would be incredibly wonderful so that you couldn't believe your eyes and ears and the next day it would be just terrible. There was no consistency to it. In fact, Noël Coward, who knew her better than anybody, would scold her. I didn't have the nerve to but he had known her since childhood. Both went to the same school as children. He could say things to her that nobody else could. He even slapped her once, I believe, for being inconsistent.

But I don't suppose the public was aware of the great difference because of this incredible personality that she projected. Wonderful she certainly was.

ADAM DARIUS: Going back to the silent era, where in the scale of importance would you place sub-titles?

DOUGLAS FAIRBANKS, JR.: The purest form of film making was the film with the fewest sub-titles. This was the best use of the medium. Obviously they tried to minimize the need for sub-titles, although funnily enough, it was often insisted that the actual lines be spoken, which was for the benefit of lip readers, I suppose.

The sub-titles were reduced to as little as possible so that they could be read very quickly. They entertained the theory that what was noted visually had a greater impact than what you heard. The eye was the more important recipient of the message than the ear. That was appreciated and known by anyone who took the medium seriously. Those that got ahead were those who knew this.

Once in a while there would be an experiment by doing an entire film without sub-titles. It wasn't always successful. Pictures that had an excess of sub-titles were generally classified as programme fillers, turned out like sausages on the assembly line.

Often, great companies like Paramount, who would have maybe three to five prestige films a year over which they took great care, would find a comedy and change the whole story around by altering the sub-titles. The action would come out in a completely different way. If they found themselves with a dud, an overly done drama, they might make it into a comedy by the sub-titles. There were some famous examples of this from time to time. But everyone knew, the fewer the titles, the better the film.

ADAM DARIUS: How did the advent of sound technically affect film making?

DOUGLAS FAIRBANKS, JR.: When the talkies came into being, it became less of a requirement to tell a story visually than in silent films, obviously. For all intents and purposes, talking films were just that, relying on talk, talk, talk. But the better directors, producers and the more conscientious stars, particularly the Germans, had an eye to the visual and continued to keep speech to a minimum.

The films, then, were also as realistic as possible. They didn't go into fantasy like you do and, let's say, Marceau.

Later on, von Sternberg, von Stroheim and Lubitsch made a great point of letting the camera tell the story. In fact, there are many more erotic scenes done by Lubitsch, in my view, than those we see today. His were by suggestion. He would merely have a door close and that closing door told a much greater story than all sorts of people doing all sorts of things blatantly.

Little by little, talk became, at times, just noise on purpose. It's the visual which is the more important and noise is an adjunct.

And speaking of the visual, black and white is perfectly beautiful and should be brought back for certain films. It's like doing something in pen and ink as opposed to watercolour. Really though, a good picture is a good picture.

ADAM DARIUS: Where, in the creative heirarchy, do you place the director?

DOUGLAS FAIRBANKS, JR.: It's a three cornered collaboration between the principal actors, the director and the cameraman that is most important, regardless of when these cults say, "Oh, the great so and so." That's all a lot of nonsense. It is greatly exaggerated to think that such and such director is worthy of a cult when it is such a teamwork job, such a collaborative operation.

The cameraman who is the least praised, the least known, the least respected by the public, is also the most important, the one who technically has to know more than anyone else and the one upon whom everyone is ultimately dependent. So it's a combination. If you have a gifted, wise, creative producer behind you, that's a fourth leg. Instead of a triangle, you have a regular table. They are very, very rare in the whole of the history of film making.

A person like David Selznick is an example that comes to mind. He was a literate, cultivated, intelligent, civilized figure as opposed to just a shrewd businessman who has the smell of who's good and who's bad but without really being able to know.

Funnily enough, they make a lot of jokes about Samuel Goldwyn but only because he was never able to be fluent in the language. He certainly had taste and knowledge and he knew what he was about. He was a strange character, an eccentric character and unconsciously funny but when he got down to business the results of his life's work proved that he knew what he was doing. All his films had quality.

ADAM DARIUS: How would you explain the fact that movie stars, as the world once knew them, have virtually ceased to exist in the contemporary cinema?

DOUGLAS FAIRBANKS, JR.: Well, there aren't companies any more to prepare, create and sustain them. They have to take what happens to come along or what they can package themselves. Being self sufficient isn't always possible. A lot of first class stars have made films that have been put on the shelf and never released.

Outside of Brando as he used to be, Dustin Hoffman and half a dozen others, the rest, along with the women as well, are not as thoroughly trained or as conscientious as they are in Britain or in Europe in general. There are too many who expect success yesterday afternoon. They're not prepared to put in the time and effort to learn their jobs, to realize that it's like studying law or medicine.

You just damn well have to apply yourself and know what the hell you're doing. Going on with either just a pretty face or personality can be managed in certain types of things but it's very limited and short-lived. When that time has passed and those attributes are no longer in fashion, to then go on is proof that you must know your job as well as in any other profession.

ADAM DARIUS: Do you mean to imply that silent screen stars approached their work with greater dedication than the current harvest of film actors?

DOUGLAS FAIRBANKS, JR: No, I wouldn't say that. It's just that circumstances made them work harder. Because it was visual a lot more people were there for their looks. A lot of beauties were there just waiting around to be rescued in the last reel and a lot of men were there because they could look stalwart and handsome and look like they could rescue them. Those actors, themselves, looked on it with a giggle. Look what we're getting away with. Aren't we lucky? Underneath, though, they wondered how long it was going to last.

ADAM DARIUS: With little precedent behind them, why didn't they believe such luck could go on indefinitely?

DOUGLAS FAIRBANKS, JR.: There were many people after the same job. There was a great deal of insecurity. All contracts ran for 40 weeks, but only if it was a long term contract. The options were on the side of the company. Nobody was able to plan what he or she was going to do next year. If they were free lance they didn't know what they were going to do next month. There might have been two jobs a year, each one at three weeks apiece.

Even if they were big stars with big studios they never knew. It was entirely up to the studio whether or not they would build someone else up and let the other star go for one reason or another. Yes, there was a lot of insecurity.

ADAM DARIUS: You commute very much nowadays between America and England. Is there a difference, intrinsically, between the actor's attitude towards his work there and here?

DOUGLAS FAIRBANKS, JR.: In Britain one is far more aware of the fact that people are devoted to their jobs. I remember when I was producing a whole series of television films, in one of which was Dame Sybil Thorndyke. Then in her eighties, she was also playing in the West End. Although doing a play at night, she was the first one way out in Boreham Wood at seven o'clock in the morning for make-up.

She would leave the studio at night with the help of a very speedy car which got her to the theatre bang on time. I remember meeting her a few months later at a dinner party.

She said, "Oh, Douglas, you haven't asked me to come back, to play in another one of your television plays." And I answered, "But Dame Sybil, I just haven't had anything worthy of you," which was the truth. The minute I would have, I'd have been honoured.

And she countered, "You mean you have nothing at all?"

"Well," I answered, "in about six weeks there's something coming along but it's only a two or three day small part. You would be right for it but I wouldn't have the nerve to suggest it."

To which she retorted, "But is it good?" and I said, "Oh yes, it's very good."

"Then," she added, "I don't care if it's only one or two days. No more questions asked. I'll do it." A woman in her eighties. That's dedication.

I remember when Larry and Vivien were having a very rough time financially. They had an offer from Hollywood which would have solved their problems. I was spending a week-end with them and had just come from a meeting with the Royal Shakespeare Company.

I told them that the RSC was interested in having them do something but, of course, I wouldn't recommend it since the top salary figure in those days was 60 quid a week. And it didn't matter who you were, the billing was alphabetical. My advice to them was not to pay any attention to it.

Well, they thought about it and felt it was their duty so they went further into debt, spending the better part of the year, ten months, at Stratford. And that's dedication. You'd find very few people in the

States who'd do that, but you'd find a lot of people who'd be prepared to do that here in Britain.

ADAM DARIUS: Douglas Fairbanks, Jr., thank you very much for your fascinating reflections.

With Dame Alicia Markova

On expressive movement and mime in ballet

Dame Alicia Markova, the greatest Romantic ballerina of her era, was born in England in 1910. At the age of 14 she joined the Diaghilev Ballet when the average age of the corps de ballet was 30. Despite the blow of Diaghilev's death, her subsequent and illustrious career led to her becoming the first great English ballerina. Prima ballerina of the Vic Wells Ballet, she then became star of her own company, the Markova-Dolin Ballet. Afterwards she was one of the crown jewels in the star-studded roster of the Ballet Russe de Monte Carlo before joining the American Ballet Theatre where she reigned for many years. More latterly she was the founding prima ballerina of the London Festival Ballet. Amongst her many roles she will always be remembered for the legendary beauty of her *Giselle*.

ADAM DARIUS: Dame Alicia, people who were privileged to see you dance witnessed a gossamer lightness, the likes of which have not since been duplicated. What technical explanation can you give for this phantom lightness?

ALICIA MARKOVA: That's a very difficult question to answer because, I, myself, never felt light. I think, maybe from my point of view, it would be breathing. I always found breathing terribly important. Perhaps it was a matter of breath.

ADAM DARIUS: Did you inflate, did you particularly breathe in while dancing?

ALICE MARKOVA: Maybe yes but never consciously.

ADAM DARIUS: And what of your remarkable *relevés*? No one ever rose on pointe or descended with your effortlessness.

ALICIA MARKOVA: I think that was probably just from hard work and strengthening the feet in a certain area – through the ankles.

ADAM DARIUS: Why were you not able, as an 11 year old, to accept the invitation to appear in Diaghilev's historic production of *The Sleeping Princess* at the Alhambra, a production that boasted the artistry of dancers such as Trefilova, Egorova, Spessivtzeva and Nijinska? Weren't you supposed to have appeared in that ballet as a child?

ALICIA MARKOVA: Yes, definitely. That was the first great disappointment in my life. I was taken ill with diphtheria and of course in those days it was a very dangerous illness. It took a long time. Sometimes one never really recovered. So that kept me out completely because I think it was about six months. I had to start back very slowly with training because often it affects the heart.

By the time I had recovered and been out of isolation, the production of *The Sleeping Princess* at the Alhambra was over. That was the first great disappointment of my life and I thought something as great as that would never happen to me again.

ADAM DARIUS: As young as you were, you realized the significance of the production?

ALICIA MARKOVA: Oh yes. In fact at that time, well I think even since then, I don't think I've ever seen a presentation to equal that for production, music, design and dancers. Maybe I was very fortunate. You see, I saw all the great dancers. It gave me such a standard.

ADAM DARIUS: When you did eventually join the Diaghilev Ballet at the age of 14, what were your feelings when rehearsing in the presence of such people as Picasso, Ravel, Karsavina and Diaghilev?

ALICIA MARKOVA: Strangely enough, I wasn't nervous. It sounds very odd because I was a very shy child and I was, how can I say, not very much at ease with a lot of people. And yet when I arrived there, there I was amongst the great and yet I never felt any nerves. Somehow I felt at home and I was able to do what I was asked to do and go ahead with my work.

It was a very strange feeling. I felt like that with Pavlova when I first met her and the same with Diaghilev. I felt they understood me, that I didn't have to explain or make any excuses.

ADAM DARIUS: You trained with both Cecchetti and Princess Astafieva. What was the difference in their methods?

ALICIA MARKOVA: Well, I was a pupil of Astafieva first. She was the Russian school, coming from the Maryinsky. Then when I joined the Diaghilev Ballet I was put with Maestro Cecchetti so then I had the Italian school. I think that, again, that was where I was very fortunate, having had both schools and being able to take the best of each.

ADAM DARIUS: Probably, the Cecchetti gave you some of the speed and brilliance while the Russian, the lyricism.

ALICIA MARKOVA: The Cecchetti was also marvellous for placing, for foundation and endurance. And of course for the Russian school, naturally you needed freedom and temperament. And shall we say, soul?

ADAM DARIUS: Who were the greatest dance actors you ever saw?

ALICIA MARKOVA: Oh, that's very difficult because during my time there were many different artists in different ballets. Certainly, Spessivtzeva in the first act of *Giselle*. She was fantastic. Not that when I took over the role I would copy her at all because somehow I didn't feel the same. But her performance was magnificent.

Then, of course, in the Diaghilev company we would have people like Tchernicheva performing in *Sheherazade*, in *Cleopatra* or as the queen in *Thamar*. Again I was fortunate. When I joined the company I think *Cleopatra* was in the repertoire for one season before it was taken out.

So I can speak firsthand of those productions which, today, many people talk and write about when they, I hate to say, never saw them.

ADAM DARIUS: Aside from your celebrated partnership with Sir Anton Dolin, who would you consider your other favourite partners?

ALICIA MARKOVA: Oh, there again that's quite difficult because I had many great partners and it really was a matter of which ballets. For instance, in the Tudor production of *Romeo and Juliet*, I felt Hugh Laing was a marvellous Romeo with me. And then Massine in *Rouge et Noir*. Youskevitch was wonderful in the first movement and in the third movement I think it was Marc Platt as the menacing one.

Then Massine choreographed *Aleko*, creating the leading male role for Skibine who was fantastic with me in that ballet. And while in the Ballet Russe de Monte Carlo, Eglevsky partnered me a lot in *Petrouchka*, *Spectre*, *Bluebird*, *Sylphides*, *Nutcracker*, *Swan Lake* and one could go on.

ADAM DARIUS: And Erik Bruhn in *Giselle*, a notable partnership.

ALICIA MARKOVA: Oh yes, and later also in *Sylphides*.

ADAM DARIUS: Who did you dance with in the Diaghilev production of *Le Rossignol*?

ALICIA MARKOVA: I was alone. That's why it was so suitable because I was alone except for the marvellous *pas de deux* with Death. When it was first produced Death was Sokolova. When Sokolova became ill, Doubrovska took it over. Balanchine had a wonderful *pas de deux*, a fight between the Nightingale and Death.

ADAM DARIUS: The first time I saw you dance was in New York in 1944 in the Broadway musical revue *The Seven Lively Arts* for which Igor Stravinsky wrote music especially for you. Did you find it difficult to repeat the same two ballets nightly as differentiated from the repertoire alternation in a ballet company?

ALICIA MARKOVA: No, that never bothered me because, you see, I go back much earlier in England doing that kind of format when we were trying to get ballet established. I often would appear in music halls dancing twice nightly or at the Palladium twice nightly and a matinee, three shows a day.

And the Coliseum would be the same programme twice a day. Also in that period I used to appear at the big movie theatre, the Regal

Cinema at Marble Arch, three shows a day, similar to the Roxy, so I had always been accustomed to repeating the same repertoire if that was required. And so later when it came to *The Seven Lively Arts* on Broadway, that was the very first time I danced consecutively like that in America.

People in Britain, though, didn't realize that in America you have performances on Sunday. So I used to do my performances at the Zeigfeld Theatre, in the Stravinsky and the Cole Porter, and on Sunday evenings when that theatre was dark I used to dance at the Met with Ballet Theatre in *Romeo and Juliet*, *Pas de Quatre* and *Giselle*. So I had a marvellous balance but of course you can imagine how hard it was. I didn't have one free day.

ADAM DARIUS: I was going to say, you didn't have one night off.

ALICIA MARKOVA: Well, I couldn't do it every Sunday.

ADAM DARIUS: You needed one day to recoup your energy.

ALICIA MARKOVA: Yes.

ADAM DARIUS: During the past few years you've directed revivals of the classics as well as coaching today's principal dancers in interpretation. What importance do you place on the drama in dance as opposed to the accent on merely flawless execution?

ALICIA MARKOVA: The complete feeling is most important because I think even if one is going to dance something which people call abstract, it's still, if you analyze it, not really abstract, since we're still human.

I think the most important thing is that it all stems from the music. I know there are many dancers who often don't really hear what music they're dancing to. That, to me, I must say, is amazing because first of all I always had to hear the music before I could start to move. I would then immediately know how I felt and which direction to go.

I think even if one is doing just exercises, say for instance in the studio, the muscles in the body can still be what I would call alive. When I'm teaching this is something that I'm always rather interested to find. So many dancers think of exercises or classes as a bore. But they shouldn't be. Surely you can put just as much into those as you would if you're going out to dance a variation. It's the same thing. You're using the same body.

And of course when it comes to, as you say, mime, this also is very important.

ADAM DARIUS: Did your interpretation of *Giselle* change much over the years? Did you alter it as time went on or was it more or less constant?

ALICIA MARKOVA: I would say it must have altered, though perhaps never consciously, because I didn't stay the same. So without realizing it

I think things had to evolve. Also there were different companies that I would dance with, different partners, different mothers, it had to alter. That's why I never worried about changing casts because I always felt that with a different mother it would be a different relationship.

ADAM DARIUS: Of course.

ALICIA MARKOVA: With the changing casts, it would always be alive. Naturally I would always keep the steps and the musical structure. But they were just the foundation.

The interpretation also depends a good bit on how one feels too because sometimes one felt happier than at other times. In cases like that I would call upon a lower key.

ADAM DARIUS: The first time I saw you do *Giselle* was in October, 1945. During the curtain calls Dolin moved front to the audience and said, "Ladies and gentlemen, tonight you have seen a performance of *Giselle* danced by the greatest ballerina in the world in memory of the greatest Spanish dancer in the world who has just died, Argentinita. Would everyone please stand up for a minute's tribute?"

Do you remember that performance?'

ALICIA MARKOVA: Oh, that's right, yes.

ADAM DARIUS: Dolin told me that they transcribed that speech for Spanish Radio because they thought it so touching.

ALICIA MARKOVA: Yes, she was a marvellous person. Although I knew I was never going to do Spanish dancing on stage, I had private lessons with her because I always wanted to know how one should move in different styles.

ADAM DARIUS: Didn't Ana Ricarda choreograph a solo for you?

ALICIA MARKOVA: Oh yes, she did the classical *Bolero* for me.

ADAM DARIUS: The 19th century's greatest Romantic ballerina Marie Taglioni, in her retirement, helped mold the remarkable young dancer Emma Livry. Taglioni's inscription to Livry on the opening night of *Papillon* is both moving and revealing, "Make me forget but forget me not."

Have you never felt the need to have the equivalent of that kind of protegée or do you prefer to give of your enormous experience to the many?

ALICIA MARKOVA: I think for me it's been for the many because you see, again, perhaps I'm very fortunate. When I'm coaching or teaching I can coach the professional artist, the established dancer, if they need help in the roles that I once danced. Then at the Royal Ballet School I usually take the first year students as they come from White Lodge.

That is when the management seeks out their future potential for the company. It is in this period that I have them.

Then when I go to Ilkley for the Yorkshire Ballet Seminar, I have the 10 year olds who would just be starting, again to look for potential talent that can later be sent to the Royal Ballet school. So, perhaps I'm very fortunate like that, being able to come in at any stage.

ADAM DARIUS: You were the stellar attraction in both the Ballet Russe de Monte Carlo and the American Ballet Theatre. What were the differences, as you recall, in working atmosphere between those two companies?

ALICIA MARKOVA: Well, Ballet Russe de Monte Carlo was really a Russian company. It was, I suppose, about the last because they were mostly dancers born in Paris of Russian parents whereas Ballet Theatre was the first American company. So again I had really crossed the bridge, the same as in England when I had crossed the bridge from the Diaghilev, the Russian company, to the Vic-Wells and Rambert, the first English companies.

In both circumstances, when people had ideas and wanted to try and create something new, I'd always been interested, encouraging them, willing to go along with them in trying to achieve something fresh.

ADAM DARIUS: Throughout your career you seemed to have often paved the way, to have been first. For example, you had your own company in Britain in the 1930's.

ALICIA MARKOVA: Yes, I've always been a pioneer. I was the first ever to be televised in this country. I did all the experimenting with them including make-up.

I think it's good to know how things work. I studied lighting because I felt it would be so much better if you wanted to ask somebody in the theatre for an effect. In that way it was like speaking their language. Then, you know, you can get along.

Maybe I preferred to do that instead of going to parties. Those never interested me. To sit and listen to an orchestral rehearsal conducted by a great conductor, that was much more interesting. We all have our choice. This is not to say that when the performance was over I couldn't go with my colleagues and have coffee somewhere. I could enjoy that too.

ADAM DARIUS: So you do believe in the value of unwinding.

ALICIA MARKOVA: Yes, I think everybody needs time to catch their breath, to meditate a little. So many people become ill because they're all the time in tension. I think, if I may say, that's part of the trouble today.

There is nothing more precious than time.

ADAM DARIUS: There is a thought, Dame Alicia, that every word spoken on this planet reverberates throughout the universe. If such is the case and there could be a parallel in movement, then your dancing deservedly goes on forever. Thank you for the rapturous moments you gave and still give to so many.

ALICIA MARKOVA: Thank you.

With Kate Bush

On expressive movement and mime in rock

Born as recently as 1958, **Kate Bush** has established herself as not only the top, but the most original recording star in Britain. Her first single, *Wuthering Heights*, was proof of a singular voice accompanied by a distinctive manner of moving. The creativity she then displayed as a songwriter has since been consolidated with her four albums, *The Kick Inside*, *Lionheart*, *Never for Ever* and *The Dreaming*. As manager, designer, arranger and choreographer of both her live and recorded presentations, she has ensured that no aspect of her work can be diluted by those less caring than herself.

ADAM DARIUS: Kate, you are a singer who incorporates movement as an integral part of your performance. Who were your very first influences in mime and movement?

KATE BUSH: I think probably my very first influences were the things that I saw on television because as a very young child my first instincts were to dance to music that was being televised. When I hit the age of about five or six, I stopped, straight away, because I started becoming inhibited. I think my dance world wasn't really opened again until a much later age which was when I left school.

I knew that I wanted to dance when I saw the ad for *Flowers*. So I went there. Then I began studying with Lindsay Kemp but after six months of me having found him, he went away to Australia. Technically I had nothing. It was all emotion without any kind of technique. So, The Dance Centre was the place. There I began doing modern dance and jazz.

And then I came to you. I mean I found you, initially, at The Dance Centre. I thought I'll try it out, I'll see. And when I came to your class I really felt in many ways that what was called mime and movement was misleading. Other classes that I had been to that were called mime were the ones where you pretend to make walls and tilt like the Leaning Tower of Pisa. And though I found those classes analytically interesting, they weren't what I was looking for. Those kind of classes didn't use the body as an emotional implement. They were more like a piece of architecture.

It was incredible to suddenly walk into the usual warm-up spots at The Dance Centre, waiting for the class to begin. The vibes before a teacher comes in are always a giveaway what that teacher is like in the way the pupils are reacting before that teacher's entrance. There was automatically a great feeling of respect, a feeling of it's begun as soon as you walked in as opposed to when you said, "We're going to begin."

ADAM DARIUS: At which stage do you create the movement for your

lyrics? Is it after you've memorized the lyrics or while you're learning them?

KATE BUSH: Yes, that's a lovely question. I think 90% of the movement, if not even more, is after the lyrics have been composed. I think, though, that the more I write the more I'm starting to be able to subconsciously link the choreography with the lyrics.

The movement does tend to come at a separate stage when I sit myself down and think that now is the time. I literally use the lyrics to tell me what to do and the mood of the song to tell me who I am. So once the lyrics are written it becomes a script.

It would be lovely to be able to write the words while seeing the dance but my creative energy doesn't seem to be able to channel that. Not yet, I'm still very much concentrated on one thing at a time. I suppose if I were doing it the other way, the choreography would have a greater freedom.

ADAM DARIUS: Why do you think so many rock singers today are fascinated with mime and movement unlike earlier blues and jazz singers who settled for the ill-defined gesture?

KATE BUSH: Well, I think jazz and blues singers were very much the kind of people who came from homes where they'd always been surrounded by music. They had a big emotional release in singing their blues which were very negative and very sad. Very black and very poor they felt oppressed. In their music they became free again but their music didn't involve performance. It was much more the singer just completely letting himself or herself feel completely free. By the time the songs reached the clubs, the performance level had already been reduced.

I think today rock singers are very aware of the visual aspects, that they're being seen as well as heard. They're conscious of their image, of how you can express by having control of your body.

ADAM DARIUS: In the popular fields of entertainment, derivative competion is extremely commonplace. Originality is rare while copycat creation is rife. Do you find this particularly so in the recording field?

KATE BUSH: Well, I think in any artistic field you're going to have people that are always trying to snatch ideas. I think anyone who creates is, somewhere along the line, not actually stealing but sifting things they've seen, they've loved, they've experienced. They must do because when you create you're pulling from the past, from your own and other people's experiences. So really it's a mass theft compilation that becomes your own. As long as people are aware that they're stealing and they don't do it directly, then I think it's good.

ADAM DARIUS: How do you, Kate, personally cope with the unbalancing

temptations of fame and fortune that have been thrust so early at your feet? How do you keep your stability, your leverage?

KATE BUSH: I think so much of that is due to the preparation, the study that I managed to get between school and actually becoming famous, inverted commas. From the period that I left school, which is the time I became famous, I was almost like a student of my job-to-be without even knowing that I was going to be in it. The three years within that period were spent just writing songs and dancing all day. I was working and obsessed with the two of them and so though they were something I was doing very much for pleasure, there was a lot of discipline that became the foundation for everything that followed.

I think that had I gone straight in, I would have been drained so quickly and been unable to cope. Being strong and stable is the basis of life, being real rather than start thinking, "Oh, gosh, I'm a star," which is unreal. No one is ever a star. They're a human being. Stars twinkle in the sky.

I think that balance inside is so important.

ADAM DARIUS: As a songwriter you are clearly expanding in your creative output. In the area of movement, what are you doing to sustain and develop this vital aspect of your work?

KATE BUSH: Again, that's a very, very interesting question which I think only someone as involved as you are in this field would be able to understand. It's amazing how many people who don't dance think that routines are just thought up, literally on the spur of the moment.

I'm terribly aware of not being as fit as I should be. I ought to be in a very prime condition. This is something that worries me a lot.

There was a stage when I became very involved with dancing and I almost thought about putting my music second to the dancing. I realized I had to make a decision, to choose between one or the other because they both require so much dedication. And so I had to decide that music is my first priority and dancing is second.

But you know what my problem is? When I'm doing an album, the recording session sometimes go on until three or four o'clock in the morning. A few hours later I crawl into my dance class. Morning after morning the sessions would get later and later until my dancing was like this (demonstrating collapse).

ADAM DARIUS: Did you become a singer by accident or design?

KATE BUSH: Interesting that you should use those two words, accident or design. I think it was accident although from the minute I started liking music I hoped so much that it would be design.

I think eventually it really was accident and just pure bluffing my way through the situation. When I first started writing I was very young.

Although I could sing in tune I really didn't have any quality in my voice. It was very straight.

Because I was working my voice it gradually started to change, developing a bit more quality and becoming a bit more personalized.

I don't think anyone had ever even seriously thought of me singing any of my songs because my voice, though in tune, was then very boring. Everyone had made very clear to me that they didn't really regard me as a singer but rather as a songwriter. And I thought I really, really hoped that I'd be able to sing because though writing the songs meant so much, it was my interpretation of them that made me want to write them.

ADAM DARIUS: One feeds the other.

KATE BUSH: Yes, absolutely. And so I was just praying that my voice would get better one day and that I'd be able to get away with singing them.

ADAM DARIUS: Do you ever feel the temptation to repeat what the public has applauded rather than venturing into new directions?

KATE BUSH: No, no I don't. As far as the song that was *the* hit, if I could write a formula like that again, one would presume that again it would be a big hit. But, really, what is the point? It would be wrong because I'd know that in my heart I was cheating myself, that I'd sat down and instead of trying to push myself creatively, was just copping out. I would just be playing all the chords of *Wuthering Heights* backwards and also singing the words backwards so that I wouldn't have to use any effort. Everyone would recognize the song and it would be a big hit. It would be cheating not only them, which is terribly important, but also myself.

I feel this is the key factor in everyone's life. You do what is right by your code. Then, that way you never regret anything. And if you do regret something, then try not to do it again. I really believe you have to feel right about things you do, that your intuition will tell you when it's wrong or dangerous.

ADAM DARIUS: To avoid what causes regret.

KATE BUSH: I think it's very important to regret as little as possible.

ADAM DARIUS: Aside from your music, what other aspects of our world are of interest to you?

KATE BUSH: There are lots of things but, unfortunately, the ones that are really up front are the ones that worry me a lot.

You know, music for me is everything. So many of the things that affect me outside of music go into my songs. I'm worried about the human race not thinking enough, not seeing into the future, the consequences of what could happen. It's very, very frightening.

We, as a huge mass of individuals, have no control over any sort of governmental decisions at all. And that's very scary because it means that millions of innocent people have no choice, not knowing anything about what's happening.

ADAM DARIUS: I'm sure that many people identify with the feelings you've just described as realized in your music. They feel the same insecurities that you do otherwise you wouldn't have such a mass response to your songs. You are putting into words and music what many people similarly feel. That's one of the great functions of the artist in society.

KATE BUSH: Yes, and I often think that a songwriter in conversation would not be able to express what they've expressed in a song. It's almost like something very holy happening at the conception of a song.

ADAM DARIUS: And finally, Kate, towards which new frontier are you moving nowadays?

KATE BUSH: Well, I suppose the frontier I'm moving towards is trying to get away from the things I find unnecessary for my career. When I first started I spent at least 90% of my time creating, dancing, reading and going to the theatre. Now, that percentage has gone right down so that I'm spending only 40 or 50% of my time creating and the rest on promotion.

Unless you start peeling away the things that get in the way, you spend all your time on unimportant things. Life's too short. This is very important for me, this plan to get back to creating as much as possible.

ADAM DARIUS: There's a tug-of-war, isn't there, between being an artist and all the window dressing that obscures it.

KATE BUSH: Yes, it's true, yes. I think that although you don't like doing it, it's a very realistic attitude towards being business-like in your job. But once you've experienced it and you've had that discipline, it actually becomes time consuming. So that's what I'd like to do, to get down to the actual performance and recording without all the interruptions so that it's all on a much purer level. Because that's where it is, isn't it?

ADAM DARIUS: Absolutely.

KATE BUSH: On the pure level, yes.

ADAM DARIUS: Thank you Kate. I've so enjoyed meeting with you again and hearing your most relevant thoughts.

With Warren Mitchell

On expressive movement and mime in theatre

Warren Mitchell, born in London in 1926, is one of Britain's most brilliant actors. Trapped by his success as Alf Garnett in the hugely successful television series, *Till Death Us Do Part*, later expanded into two films, he abruptly changed course by playing the leads in the Australian productions of *King Lear* and *Death of a Salesman*. For his role as Willy Loman in the National Theatre production of the Arthur Miller play, he was the recipient of three awards—the Critics Award from the magazine *Plays and Players* for the best actor of the year, the *Evening Standard* award, again, for the best actor of the year and the Society of West End Theatres award for the best actor in a revival.

Clearly, Warren Mitchell's turnabout from comedian to tragedian had more than succeeded.

ADAM DARIUS: Looking back at your own student days at the Royal Academy of Dramatic Art, would you say, in retrospect, that the movement training was sufficient for the subsequent demands made on you in your career?

WARREN MITCHELL: The training hardly existed. There was no overall policy anyway in the training. Looking back retrospectively I remember there was a very good voice teacher and one or two of the directors weren't bad. But certainly as far as movement was concerned it was pathetic.

We did fencing which was useful if you're going to do fights. Some of the actors would, of course, join the Royal Shakespeare company or the National Theatre. We did a bit of ballet which is useful if you happened to be asked to do a minuet. But I mean how many times do you have to do a minuet? You can imagine me doing a minuet in *Death of a Salesman.*

But actually, training of the organ, you should pardon the expression, it didn't happen. RADA seemed to concentrate on the voice and I would say that's really almost endemic in the English theatre. Many times you could close your eyes in the theatre in this country and you would hear very good radio plays being done in the theatre. But as for being able to see the body being used to express anything at all, it's very rare.

Generally speaking as a student, no, I had no movement training. Obviously, though, my powers of observation were there so when I was going to play an old man, my eyes told me certain things.

ADAM DARIUS: Yet you have a natural facility for movement. In addition to your instincts, was it never actually cultivated?

WARREN MITCHELL: No, not at all. We did formal mime, representational mime, like picking up a glass of water to depict the shape of the glass but it didn't help very much. It didn't help our problems as actors. There was no way it connected with anything to do with acting.

ADAM DARIUS: **All ranking ballet dancers, opera singers and classical musicians practice regularly. Why do you feel that so few actors do the the same? Obviously, you, Warren, are the exception.**

WARREN MITCHELL: Well, I'm not all that much of an exception. This morning I was laying cement around the pool when I should have really been doing a voice class, a movement class and studying my script for *The Caretaker*. Also studying my script for tonight when I'm going to do Chairman Alf.

Why? First of all there's a tradition that actors are lazy, I guess. Actors, when they're out of work, sit around in coffee bars and moan about their agents. And because, I'll tell you this confidentially, I wouldn't tell everybody, acting is very easy up to a certain level compared to the art of the dancer, the musician and the instrumentalist. You know, you can't be a dancer without doing a barre every day. Every single day. But there are actors who saunter in front of a television camera or even onto a stage and they can be themselves quite convincingly.

So who needs to go to class? They can lay cement around the pool. No, it's never been a tradition in the English theatre for the actor to be trained to that extent, to use all the talents. Recently, we've seen a slight change. I remember *Godspell* being quite an innovation. One saw actors required to sing, to dance, to play instruments and everything else.

My son has been to a drama school, The Drama Centre, where there is a very different sort of training to the training that I had at RADA. But nevertheless, if you were to do a survey of the actors at the National Theatre, where I am at the moment, and ask them how many hours during the last seven days they spent in any training of any kind, you'd come up with a tiny number of hours.

ADAM DARIUS: **I think you hit the nail on the head a little earlier in the sense that everybody can talk and we do talk all day but not everybody pirouttes all day. And, of course, those who don't pirouette all day certainly can't do it in the evening on stage.**

WARREN MITCHELL: It's difficult to act all day. I mean it's a psychological process and it can be very tiring to work on one's inner psyche in the way that the dancer works on his muscles, sense of balance and so forth. But, of course, there are all the technical classes which the actor could be doing which don't require that degree of mental absorption.

Actors all say, "Oh yes, I'd love to go to class." I do it myself. I've been to lessons with you and then I get involved in a hundred other things and I don't come to class. And it's sad when I do this because I miss it, I miss it very much. Many actors pay lip service to training. The dancer can't pay lip service. He wouldn't work if he wasn't in top form. It's as simple as that.

ADAM DARIUS: How essential do you believe expressive movement is in the actor's armoury?

WARREN MITCHELL: Well, there are different categories of actors, of course. It's not quite the same in the world of the musician or dancer. There are those actors who play themselves and play themselves very reasonably and people pay money to see them. One musn't be entirely dismissive of show biz.

I would like to think of myself in the category of a character actor, someone who is prepared to change himself, his voice and his body to suit the part he's playing. There is a tradition of that in this country.

You know, this week we've seen the death of perhaps one of the greatest chameleons of all time, Peter Sellers. And he didn't train. He was just one of those geniuses who could do it. I may be speaking ill of the dead but I don't honestly think Peter Sellers ever agonized over a part. I mean, I think he thought about it. He opened his eyes, he opened his ears and then it all came pouring into him.

ADAM DARIUS: Enormous intuition and instinct.

WARREN MITCHELL: A genius in that way. But as far as I'm concerned, if I'm going to change my body then I have to have the facility to change it and I can't possibly do that unless I've trained those muscles to obey. When one sees a company like the Berlin Ensemble or the Georgian Company doing Richard III, one sees actors who are using their voices and bodies in a total form of expression. One is completely taken in.

Let's face it. With *Richard*, we didn't understand a word. It wasn't even in Russian, it was in Georgian. And yet because there was this amazing picture to look at the whole time, we didn't need to understand the language. We knew roughly what the play was about. I happened to have walked out of the National Theatre production of *Richard III* when it was in my own language. It was boring, dull!

I would say the answer is quite simply that with the Georgians we saw a trained group of performers as opposed to what I saw at the National Theatre which was an ad hoc mishmash of not very exciting actors.

Expressive movement for the actor is of supreme importance. The youngsters, in particular, are getting a little bit more discerning. When you can see people being themselves in mediocre rubbish on television every night, who needs to go to the theatre to see more rubbish? You can stay home and see it. If you want to have an experience, to come away from the theatre enriched, it has to be something special.

ADAM DARIUS: From the physical point of view, how did you approach the comic role of Alf Garnett in the phenomenally popular television series *Till Death Do Us Part*?

WARREN MITCHELL: It was the text. The man was a bully, arrogant, pushy and forceful. That sort of said to me, shave your head. I mean I don't have much hair anyway but what I had at the back didn't seem right. I wanted a bullet head.

The clothes were terribly important for the physical representation of the part. He always seemed to me to be a man who was aspiring towards sergeant major like smartness but, in himself, was a *schlump*.

ADAM DARIUS: Translate the word *schlump*.

WARREN MITCHELL: Untidy. Dirty. Unhygenic. I wanted the clothes to represent the hypocracy of the man. He was always on about cleanliness and smartness but in fact cut his toenails in the kitchen and the bits of nail shot into the sugar bowl. He was a *schlump!*

But to get back to the physical preparation. The lines dictated that this man points and gesticulates. The gestures needed a kind of arrogance about them. But having said all this, I don't remember ever having consciously worked on a pattern of movement.

ADAM DARIUS: That's because you're an actor of spontaneous empathy. Your subconscious understanding is the equivalent of most actors' worked out analysis. Warren, in essaying dramatic roles such as *King Lear* in Australia, what were the emotional and physical means you employed in your interpretation?

WARREN MITCHELL: Well, for *Lear*, I started working on it here. I started working with you a bit and then certainly with Doreen Cannon. I used some things that we did in acting class such as "Your legs are made of lead" and "Your lips are made of Venetian glass." That was a great aid to character, you see, because if your lips are made of Venetian glass you don't want to bang them together.

(During this last sentence, Warren illustrates his point by speaking with a pursed lip brittle awareness.)

ADAM DARIUS: That changes your entire face.

WARREN MITCHELL: Sure. This is a marvellous thing which comes from the Method, from the modern American adaptation of Stanislavski. We call it endowment, endowing parts of the body. For instance, you can endow your legs with the quality of lead or feathers or your heels with springs.

With Lear, I started off with a sense of weight. I thought I won't go for the age straight away because you can finish up playing a corny old man. I looked at my father who's 79 and he doesn't stagger about. People don't. But on the other hand if you're 54 and playing 80, you have to exaggerate a little bit.

I tried using animal images. I'd go to the zoo and watch them but I never found an animal that I could use for my concept of Lear. I watched a lion for some time but he wasn't particularly old. I wanted something that once had great strength but no longer had it.

In the play Lear goes hunting. So I worked on the premise of someone who had been athletic and had hunted. His joints would be arthritic and his back would be damaged. He'd probably fallen a great deal when he was a young man.

ADAM DARIUS: Did you do anything about the royal aspects of the character, the kingly quality?

WARREN MITCHELL: No. One of the things I said to the director was, "I don't think I want to play or can play a regal man. What I can play is a pretty tyrannical tribal chieftain." As it happened, no one in the opening scene of *Lear* was even allowed to look at me until I gave a certain signal. If anyone was caught looking at me, they really would have been in serious trouble. So I looked for the real tyrannical qualities, not Alf's empty paper tyrant.

Trying on the costume of fur, skin and leather, I knew my physical life exactly. It was all there. I didn't have to do anymore. It was a harsh climate, ancient Britain, you know. There was no central heating in that palace. Arthritis, rheumatism, all those things would be there. People who live and work outside develop a physical way of coping with the elements.

I worked on the idea that my make-up had a lot of broken blood vessels in the face because the man would have been out in the cold.

ADAM DARIUS: How did you approach your multi-award winning role of Willy Loman in *Death of a Salesman*?

WARREN MITCHELL: Well, there's a marvellous thing about the play in that you're playing Willy jumping about in time. He goes backwards and forwards from the age of 30 to 60. I stand upright as the young Willy, very ebullient with my gestures. I wanted those physical attributes of confidence that go with salesmanship.

I said to Arthur Miller, "What is Willy Loman selling? What's in those cases?" And he said, "Dreams." He never ever specified what it is that Willy sells.

The play shows us that his exterior is not what's inside. Inside is a very frightened little man who very rarely lets his cover down. I had the old and young Willy to work on. As Willy gets older it's very uncomfortable to play every night because I have to stand for lengthy periods with my shoulders very stooped and my knees very bent. People say, "Christ, you shrink in that last scene."

ADAM DARIUS: Well, when I saw you as the curtain went up, you were unrecognizable to me. It really was a transformation with a minimum of make-up and costume.

Would you describe Willy as a failed hero, an anti-hero? What would you call him?

WARREN MITCHELL: He was a symbol for Miller, a very powerful symbol of what Miller thinks about American capitalist society and what happens to people within that society. He's a symbol, the means whereby Miller puts his ideas over.

The play is a very human play, nevertheless. It's about fathers and sons. It's a love affair. It's devastating for a father and son to see that play together.

It doesn't matter, anyway, how we label Willy.

ADAM DARIUS: Tell me, in what way did your body share the responsibility of your portrayal of Shylock in the forthcoming BBC television production of *The Merchant of Venice*?

WARREN MITCHELL: The man lives in a ghetto. He's an outcast. The whole society that Shakespeare presents is elegant and aristocratic. Shylock, though, is denied the opportunity to learn the social graces, having spent most of his life in business. The only kind of business that he's allowed into is money lending.

Since he's spent a lot of time indoors, he wouldn't be a very healthy man. He'd be stooped, I figured, from sitting there at his table counting his ducats. I hope the physical side shows a kind of desperation. A cornered animal would be the image I use very liberally.

ADAM DARIUS: How do you manage to endure the gruelling schedule of approximately one year in *Death of a Salesman*? To watch it for one evening is an ordeal for the spectator.

WARREN MITCHELL: Well, there is an advantage in that we don't do it every night. We do it for perhaps nine or ten performances and then we have a break while other plays go in the repertory at the Lyttelton.

I think most actors are condemned for most of their lives to playing in rubbish. I've done my fair share of it. You have to, to earn a living. You do commercials and so-called comedy shows.

The relief when you climb out of that mire and suddenly find yourself, in one year as I did in Australia, playing Lear, Willy Loman and Alf Garnett. In one year to play three such magnificent roles. They give you such rewards because you don't have to struggle to make them credible.

They are. They have the mark of genius if you just sit down and read them.

So you have that to buoy you up. And then I train a great deal. I keep very fit, well, I smoke a bit, I eat a bit more than I should, but I swim and I do my yoga so I'm not exhausted physically by the role.

I don't think there's any great problem in coping with it. You'd better ask an actor who's in a piece of mindless rubbish in the West End which goes for eight performances a week like *Not Now Darling*. Ask him how he feels doing it every night for a year where there are no rewards coming from the script, where he has to invent. You can picture 20 commercial vehicles in the West End which would be boring in the extreme for the actor. That, I would say, is a much bigger problem. What I have is no problem at all.

ADAM DARIUS: And finally, Warren, no one is more humble in their approach to learning than you when you participate in my classes. In what safe deposit box do you place your protective actor's ego when making, so easily, the transition from star to student?

WARREN MITCHELL: I'm a very willing pupil. I realized a long time ago it's a waste of time to argue with teachers. You go to a teacher to listen. You may reject some of the stuff. But you must do that subsequently. If I go to classes, I go and open myself totally.

And when I came to you it was a relevation to me. When I witnessed your first class and saw you teaching, I had never been to a lesson where one applauded the teacher at the end. You got your applause and you deserved it. This is the truth.

I love the experts in all the fields. I love to see, in my own profession, Nicol Williamson, Derek Jacobi, I can name you 20. I love to watch these people work.

And I love to watch you. You're a pro. You're a great performer but you're also a really inspiring teacher. So for me it's no effort to put aside my own ego. I'm in the presence of somebody who's highly knowledgeable in a subject I know very little about. Self interest motivates me. We're all motivated by self interest. I'm going to be a better actor by putting aside my ego and becoming a genuine pupil.

I've been given, perhaps, a few gifts. It's nothing to do with the hard work that I can do. I look this particular way and I'm able to do voices and maybe change my body. That's a bit of a gift from a creator of some sort. I wouldn't like to spit in that creator's face and say I'm going to let those talents go rusty. I think I have to keep trying to develop them.

ADAM DARIUS: Warren, thank you very much for shedding so much light on the actor's intangible art.

Epilogue

AT A CERTAIN POINT IN TIME

To Adam Darius

Having once seen your face
and your hands which
enfold me in the dance,
I am suddenly appalled
at having grown up
without knowing you.
Since a certain point in time
you have inhabited my skin
and I am happy to have
the breath of your God
eternally near,
and the curve
of your shoulder
and your art, wiping the tears
from my face, saying:
Don't suffer, for true life
is a cry which encompasses
this new form of existence.

José Luis Naranjo Ferrer
Havana, Cuba
December, 1982

It was in Damascus, 1976, when I met Adam Darius for the first time. His performance was impressive and showed a supreme talent in mime, but only the next day when I interviewed him for Syrian Television did I realize how articulate he was in expressing his own original ideas on the subject. Almost six years passed before we met again. I visited him at his school, The Mime Centre, in London, intending to write about him, and was heartily exhilarated to know that he has finished what I wanted and expected him to do—a third book explaining his method. I did not just sit waiting for the book to appear; I joined his intensive course to explore personally and practically the man and his work.

Adam Darius has not evolved an exclusively mime technique. His system has in mind a wider range of benefits for dancers, actors and mimes in their careers. The training system Mr Darius developed under the title *expressive mime* is only comparable in its field to what Stanislavski accomplished in the realm of acting. Actually, though the two men differ in means, they share the same aim and work for the same result, a strong coordination between the internal and external, between soul and body, to reach the standard of the total performer. One might not be easily convinced until he sees Adam Darius performing on stage for Adam Darius is virtually the poet of mime.

Coming to the "purgatory" of mime from the "inferno" of ballet, Mr Darius linked both techniques. The result is a real innovation; using the body with the maximum of poetic energy and sustained control of physique while liberating the power of mind, emotion and psyche. The idioms of his body language are very wide and different between one person and another, yet always eloquently expressive.

In Adam Darius' method, acting is no longer an imitation; it is a state of being. The image in mind and the pulse in heart are what motivate movement. He gives us the secret golden key for the treasure of a modern performing art. I find Adam Darius' system valuable to both student and professional, young and old performers, instructors of acting and even for directors.

Naturally, Mr Darius is considered a heretic by the standards of the French school of illusionary mime. He has transcended pure mime and intermingled it with other genres. True. But didn't all innovations come from such unorthodox revolts? From Isadora Duncan to Martha Graham, from Laban to Béjart, from Tomaszewski to Alwin Nikolais, any birth of a new artistic trend has its hazards yet its glories.

In his last performances of an old piece (replacing it with a new work),

Adam Darius realized a possible improvement. He added it without hesitation for creation never stops. The experimental spirit should always be fresh and on the alert. Nothing is fully realized while the artist is still alive.

Today, Adam Darius is the ambassador to the world of a new mime form, a prophet who dedicates his life to his exhausting art, his humanitarian, ritualistic, narrative and universally symbolic themes.

In this book, the bell of many chimes is rung for his creation's birth.

By Riad Ismat
Damascus, Syria
1983

Post dedication

A Loving Eulogy
by Adam Darius

NATHANIEL

October 27th, 1946—July 9th, 1983

Friends,

As all of us here today well know, Nathaniel was a personality who, once met, imprinted himself on everyone's consciousness. Charming, brimming over with a special humour, he was a beautiful young man who beautified his every environment.

He was blessed with a multiplicity of talents, rarely found together in one human being. To single out a few is to exclude the others but I will, nevertheless, touch upon some of his major gifts. The costumes he designed and made could not be improved upon for impeccable craftsmanship, his interior house design could well have been featured in specialist literature, his superior capability with animals and plants attested to his deep affinity with the simpler creatures and creation of our earth, while his extraordinary ability in mask making left us all in humble admiration.

But above all, I am bereft of words to describe Nathaniel as a mime artist. He was as brilliant as a many faceted great diamond; searingly dramatic and incomparably comic. His first appearances in London in 1969 created a veritable sensation. Subsequently, he was seen and much applauded in Hong Kong, the Philippines, Yugoslavia, Portugal, Germany and America among many other stages.

I, personally, have heard the tributes to Nathaniel from such theatrical giants as Britain's first great male dancer, Sir Anton Dolin, from India's greatest dancer, Ram Gopal and from France's greatest actor, Jean-Louis Barrault, star of the film *Les Enfants du Paradis*, *Children of Paradise*. Yes, Nathaniel, one of *our* beloved children has now found *his* paradise, unencumbered by our earthly calendar.

Among the many people who loved Nathaniel, I will include his loving mother and family, his beloved friend Christian Gardiner and his little dog Baby, a lesson to us all in the constancy of love.

As *The Little Prince* was Nathaniel's favourite book, I will close with excerpts from that touching tale.

"And now, here is my secret, a very simple secret: It is only with the heart that one can see rightly; what is essential is invisible to the eye ... As the little prince dropped off to sleep, I took him in my arms and set out walking once more. I felt deeply moved and stirred. It seemed to me that I was carrying a very fragile treasure.

In the moonlight I looked at his pale forehead, his closed eyes, his locks of hair that trembled in the wind, and I said to myself: What I see here is nothing but a shell. What is most important is invisible.

The little prince then added, 'In one of the stars I shall be living. In one of them I shall be laughing. And so it will be as if all the stars were laughing, when you look at the sky at night.' "

NATHANIEL
the unforgettable

"an unforgettable evening of mime ... captured the spectator within moments of his appearance ... great expressiveness ... shattering starkness ... a continuously responsive relationship with the public"—*Dnevik*, Ljubljana, Yugoslavia

"admirable plasticity ... remarkable bodily discipline, control and expressiveness ... distinctive and often witty ... extremely amusing ... conveyed uncommonly wide background, imagination, creativity and, what was obvious from the start, the keenest sense of the absurd"
—*Philippines Daily Express*, Manila

In addition to Nathaniel's own international stage appearances which began in 1968, he travelled throughout the world as costume, props and lighting designer for Adam Darius' tours from 1969 through 1975.

At left, Nathaniel off stage; At right, on stage in a cavalcade of roles; Top left, The Puppet Rebellion; Top right, Narcolepsy, photograph by Norman Taylor; Centre, The Comedian; Bottom left, The Drag Queen; Bottom right, The Gigolo.

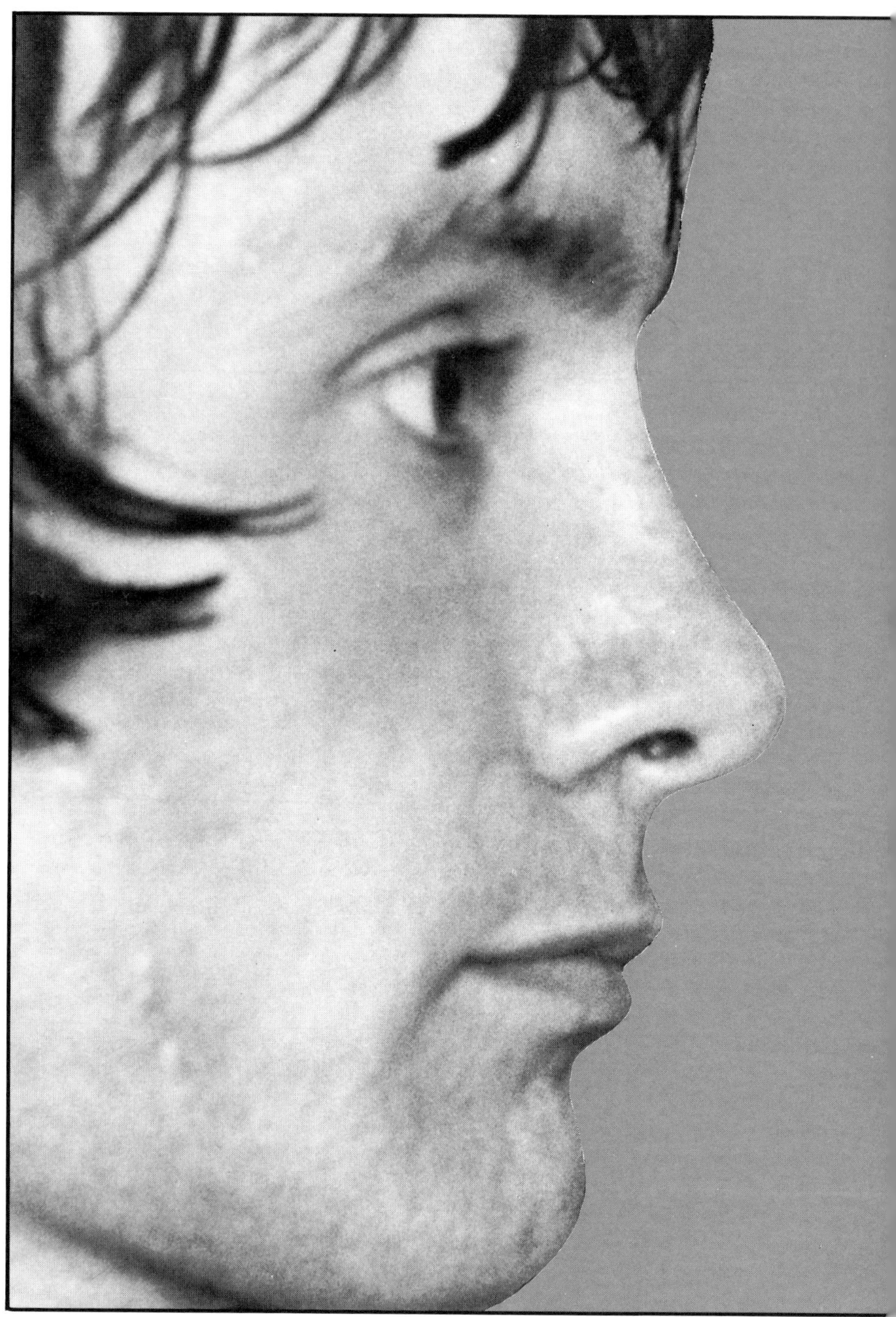

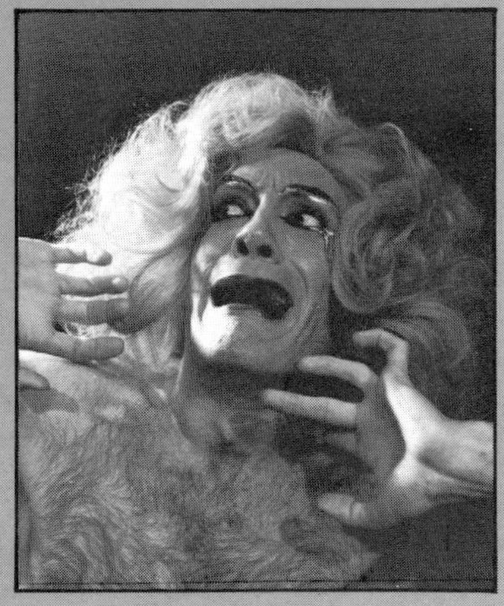

World press

"such first rate entertainment . . . Adam Darius is a genius who holds the key to tears and laughter"—*The Examiner*, Launceston, Tasmania, Australia

"rare and brilliant entertainment . . . as great mimes are among the rarest of performers, it will probably be many years before his like is seen again"—*Morning Bulletin*, Rockhampton, Australia

"magnificent . . . audience spellbound . . . a capacity audience of invited guests were privileged indeed by being exposed to the aesthetic, artistic and emotional greatness of this unique artist . . . even when comic he hurts with the tragedy of the humour; when pathetic there is hope and when ugly and shocking in concept there is beauty . . . brings a freeing, exorcising and cleansing of the emotions that is the very essence of theatre and it is magical . . . His performance reflected the colour of our lives and times. This is his strength and his greatness"—*The Cape Times*, Cape Town, South Africa

"electrifying . . . one admires and is enraptured, carried away, fascinated . . . Darius' gesture is not just technical; it is a profound science of humanity, an evocative sorcery, poetry"—*La Presse*, Tunis, Tunisia

"a wonderful opportunity for Damascus audiences to see a great and supreme artist and to observe a new kind of art . . . Absolutely alone he dominated the emotions and feelings of his audience for some two hours, eliciting our applause and admiration . . . he reached the highest level of perfection . . . a true creative artist who believes in what he does and does what he believes"—*Al Thawra*, Damascus, Syria

"blazes a new trail . . . may be the inspirer to the development of a new phase of theatre arts in Hong Kong . . . Herald the new age in miming. Enter Adam Darius"—*Hong Kong Standard*, Hong Kong

"Genius is a word I seldom like to use because it means the ultimate. However, there are occasions when it should be used as in the case of young Romanian athlete Nadja Comenici who received the very rare top score of 10 points for her performance at the last Olympic games in Canada. In the same manner, top marks should be given to Adam Darius, the world famous mime virtuoso who is currently performing in Brazil"—*Brazil Herald*, Rio de Janeiro

"a true and impressive master . . . not only did the muscles vibrate, but also the nerves and even the arteries, prepared and attuned to an unsurpassable degree ... certainly one of the greatest artists in this genre"—*Diario de Noticias*, Lisbon, Portugal

"it would be necessary to exhaust a dictionary of adjectives in attempting to recreate for those who weren't present, the two evenings of American mime artist Adam Darius at the Maison de la Culture. Even so, it wouldn't be more than a very pale approximation. What a far cry from traditional mime when one still thinks, too often, of darning an imaginary sock with invisible thread, to the sketches of Adam Darius where he succeeds in establishing within two or three minutes the failings of society ... and with what genius of movement, what supreme science of detail! ... Adam Darius' performance is one of the most perfect to be found in all the art of mime. It is also the most staggering"—*Ouest France*, Brittany, France

"creates a magic world ... He uses his hands with extraordinary mastery and is without question one of the world's foremost leaders of this art. Perhaps the greatest"—*Milliyet*, Istanbul, Turkey

"Darius, of course, is still the master of contemporary mime and his performance on Monday was ample evidence of his amazing talent"
—*Hampstead & Highgate Express*, London, England

"Adam Darius is undoubtedly the greatest living mime ... his range is wide; comic, tragic, pathetic, ecstatic ... he exploits his unorthodoxly beautiful body like a conductor controlling a sensitive orchestra, extracting from each part the ultimate residue of meaning ... so great is his hypnotic strength that he can evoke in his audience an emotional response as intense as that experienced in the last act of a Verdi grand opera. He has moved a long way from the whimsical, visual pun of the traditional mime"—*Synthesis*, London, England

"hands of phenomenal expressiveness ... a master of the mime art ... he has power over a diversity of emotions beginning with the spontaneous gaiety of childhood through the universal suffering of mankind ... an artist of technical perfection ... the public unanimously embraced on different levels the complex art of Adam Darius—*Soviet Youth*, Riga, Latvia, U.S.S.R.

"Possessing a superb technique and a style completely divorced from the other schools of mime, Darius enraptured the audience"—*Dance Magazine*, New York City, U.S.A.

"they offered an example of their repertoire in which dance and mime reach down to undreamed of roots in order to make us laugh or cry, as they comment upon the great sorrows or little joys which affect all men, equally, everywhere"—*Cuba International*, Havana, Cuba

Chronology

1930 Born May 10th in Flower Fifth Avenue Hospital, New York City

1938 Appeared in title role of school play, *The Clown of Doodle Doo*, New York City

1939 Interviewed on experimental television at New York World's Fair

1940 Danced in children's performance at the Rainbow Shell, Manhattan Beach, New York City

1941 Repeat appearance at the Rainbow Shell

1942 Winner of amateur theatrical contest in Evans Kiamesha Hotel, New York State

1944 Performed Indian war dance solo in Boy Scout Camp, New York State

1945 First ballet lesson on March 3rd at Ballet Arts, Carnegie Hall, New York City; subsequent teachers in NYC included Anatole Oboukhov, Pierre Vladimirov, Felia Doubrovska, Igor Schwezoff, Nathalie Branitzka and Elizaveta Anderson-Ivantzova;
in Paris, Olga Preobrajenska and in London, George Goncharov

1946 First appearances in professional productions as a supernumerary at the Metropolitan Opera House, NYC, in presentations of *La Bohème* with Jan Peerce and Dorothy Kirsten, *Lohengrin* with Lauritz Melchior and Astrid Varnay, *Carmen* with Risë Stevens, Raoul Jobin and Licia Albanese and *La Giaconda* with Zinka Milanov

1947 Further appearances as supernumerary with Ballet Theatre in *Petrouchka*, both at the Metropolitan and Broadway Theatre, the cast including Michael Kidd, André Eglevsky and Lucia Chase

1948 First foreign appearance in Mexico City, dancing *Muñecos Mexicanos* in open air performance sponsored by the National University of Mexico;
Entered Columbia University, New York City

1949 First ballet, *Delineations*, sponsored by the Columbia University Ballet Workshop, Brander Matthews Theatre, NYC;
at same theatre danced in new opera, *A Drumlin Legend*

1950 Choreographed ballet *Antigone* for Barbara Bocher of the New York City Ballet, produced at Weidman Studio Theatre, NYC;
Nationwide television debut on the Jack Carson Show, NYC

1951 Choreographed ballet *Oblomov* with cast including Ruth Sobotka of the New York City Ballet, presented at Weidman Studio Theatre, NYC;
Choreographed ballet *Robin Goodfellow* with cast including former Sadler's Wells Ballet member Eric Hyrst, presented at Carnegie Recital Hall, NYC; choreographed, danced, acted at Peaks Island Playhouse, Maine in *Roberta*, *Detective Story* and *Charlie's Aunt*

1952 Choreographed ballet *Cortège*, produced at the Kaufmann Concert Hall, NYC then later that year in Holland by the Ballet der Lage Landen and in Sweden by the Malmö Stadsteater;

also at the Malmö Stadsteater acted and danced under the direction of Ingmar Bergman in Strindberg's *The Bridal Crown* as well as appearing in *Finian's Rainbow* and *Lilla Helgonet*

1953 Danced in *Wienerblod* and *As You Like It* at the Malmö Stadsteater; guest ballet teacher at the Cologne Opera House in Germany;
Joined Mona Inglesby's International Ballet for a tour of the British Isles, dancing in *Les Sylphides*, *Gaité Parisienne*, *Capriccio Espagnol*, *Sleeping Beauty*, *Coppélia* and *Swan Lake*

1954 Joined the Royal Winnipeg Ballet for a 50 city tour of Canada and the USA, dancing in *Swan Lake*, *The Shooting of Dan McGrew*, *Finishing School*;
Engaged to appear weekly on General Electric Showtime, Canadian Broadcasting Corporation Television in Toronto

1955 Continued appearances on CBC Television;
Wrote, choreographed and acted in play *Augustina*, seen at Arts and Letters Theatre, Toronto;
Choreographed and danced title role in CBC Television ballet *Pierrot*, *The Wanderer*, partnering prima ballerina Melissa Hayden;
Appeared in Cabaret Concert Theatre, Hollywood;
Taught movement at Warner Brothers Studio, Burbank, California

1956 Studied acting in Hollywood with Raikin Ben-Ari, formerly of the Moscow Habimah Theatre;
Guest teachers and lecturers included Shelley Winters, Anthony Quinn, Nicholas Ray, Dore Schary and Ernest Borgnine

1957 Appeared in Las Vegas in Cole Porter's *Can-Can*, starring Denise Darcel;
Choreographed the Tournament of the Roses pageant in Pasadena; choreographed and danced in *The Fantastic Toyshop*, a children's television ballet

1958 Choreographed the ballet *Quartet* for the future prima ballerina Cynthia Gregory, San Gabriel Mission Playhouse, California;
First complete evening of own works seen at the Wilshire Ebell Theatre, Los Angeles, including first performances of *The Crystal Gazer*, *Dr. Libido* and *Moscow-Paris-New York!*

1959 Choreographed *The Anne Frank Ballet*, its world première taking place in Long Beach, California;
The Day The Circus Closed given its first performance on Bermuda Television; *Myth*, *Fin de Siècle*, *The Idol* seen for the first time at The Kaufmann Concert Hall in NYC in a programme also featuring *The Anne Frank Ballet*

1960 Creator and leading performer in musical revue entitled *Jack-in-the-Box* at the Seven Arts Theatre in NYC;
Season of summer stock in Connecticut and Rhode Island appearing in *Annie Get Your Gun* with Ginger Rogers, *Silk Stockings* with Geneviève, *Redhead* with Gordon MacRae and *Firefly* with Anna Maria Alberghetti; Toured American midwest and New England with Nelle Fisher's *The Littlest Circus*

1961 Danced title role in concert version of *Petrouchka* with New Haven Symphony, New Haven, Connecticut;
Performances on Swedish Television in Stockholm;
Joined Stora Teatern in Göteborg, Sweden appearing in *Fledermaus*, *Tiggarstudenten*; danced Peter in *Peter and the Wolf* during Stora Teatern ballet season which also included *The Anne Frank Ballet;*
Dutch première of *The Anne Frank Ballet* on N.C.R.V. Television, Hilversum;
Appeared as Puck in Scandinavian

première of Britten's opera, *A Midsummer Night's Dream*, the cast including singers of the Royal Danish Opera, the Royal Swedish Opera and Stora Teatern

1962 Joined Elsa-Marianne von Rosen's Scandinavian Ballet for performances in the Canary Islands, dancing in *The Virgin Spring* and *Helios* by von Rosen, *Classical Symphony* by Bartholin and a solo from *La Sylphide* by Bournonville;
Married Marilyn Mather in Mölndal, Sweden; *Narcissus in Blue Jeans*, *The Net*, *Girl in Paradise*, *Abortion by an Unknown Doctor*, *Révérence*, *Man On A Leash*, *The Intriguer*, *Beachball From A Forgotten Summer* among new works given at the Stadsteater's intimate theatre in Göteborg;
Appeared as Puck in *A Midsummer Night's Dream* at Bergen Festival in Norway;
Appeared as Pierrot in Offenbach's *Madame Favart*, also in Lehar's *Land of Smiles*, *Violen från Montmartre*, *Oh Mein Papa* and *Kiss Me Kate*;
The Earth Men, *Audition Time*, *Broadway*, *The Insomniacs* and *Patterns* among new works created by Adam Darius at Stora Teatern

1963 Choreographed the dances for the opera *Carmen* at Stora Teatern;
Choreographer, ballet master and principal male dancer of The Israel National Opera, Tel-Aviv, choreographing the dances for the operas *The Pearl Fishers*, *Don Giovanni*, *La Traviata* and *Carmen*, all starring Placido Domingo, in the latter two, dancing as well;
Record breaking ballet evenings at the Opera included first performances of *Aurora Borealis*, *Nightmare* and *Fans*

1964 Formed own company, The Israeli Ballet touring Tel-Aviv, Haifa, Jerusalem, Beersheba, Tiberias, Eilat, Sodom and the principal kibbutzim of Israel;
new works included *Strangers*, *Décolleté* and the Israeli première of *The Anne Frank Ballet*

1965 Choreographer and dancer for the musical *King Solomon and the Queen of Sheba*, Eilat, Israel;
Appeared with singer Jacques Brel in his tour of Israel; choreographed and appeared in musical version of *Peter Pan* at the Haifa Municipal Theatre;
First appearances of excerpts from future full length mime performance

1966 First full length solo mime performance at the Arab-Jewish Cultural Centre in Haifa followed by performances in Nazareth, Tel-Aviv and other Israeli cities;
Divorced in Juarez, Mexico; staged *The Anne Frank Ballet* for The El Paso Regional Ballet in Texas

1967 Solo performances given in Rehovot, Israel;
The Anne Frank Ballet filmed for Italian Television in Turin;
Death of a Scarecrow and *The Day The Circus Closed* seen on BBC Television, London;
Solo performance seen in Italy at the Spoleto Festival and Assisi Festival; in Göteborg, Sweden at Folkteatern and Chalmers University, in Stockholm at Stadsteatern, in Dublin at Radio Telefis Eireann (Death of a Scarecrow) and in Belfast at the Belfast Festival;
Lecture-demonstration at the Royal Ballet School

1968 Solo performance in Milan and Turin, Italy;
First London performances; appearances on the ship R.M.S. *Queen Elizabeth* during Atlantic crossings;
Appearances at Edinburgh Festival, Scottish Television and Ulster Television;
Tour of Scotland in dance/mime programme in which Nathaniel made his first appearances;

Co-authored and starred in the film short *Stigmata* made in northern Ireland

1969 Double bill of solo performance and *Narcolepsy* given during two seasons in London;
Double bill of solo performance and *Vultures* given during two seasons in London and one in Bristol, both plays written by Adam Darius and co-starring Nathaniel; solo performance seen in Leicester, Corby, Belfast, Oxford and Benjamin Britten's Aldeburgh Festival;
Solo performance in Lanciano, Italy and Sardinia;
Narcolepsy and *Vultures* both presented in cabaret in Berlin, again with Nathaniel

1970 Conclusion of Berlin engagement of *Narcolepsy* and *Vultures*;
World première of film *Stigmata* at Arsenal Cinema, Berlin;
Solo mime appearances on BBC Television series *Whatever Next*;
Solo mime appearances on Swiss Television, Lugano;
Double bill of film *Stigmata* and a new play *Umbilical*, written by Adam Darius for Nathaniel and Chrissy Roberts, given during two seasons in London;
Solo performance in Liverpool, St Albans and Leicester;
Solo tour of southern Africa; Cape Town, Pretoria and Johannesburg, South Africa;
Mbabane, Swaziland; Lourenço Marques, Mozambique; return visit to Africa for performances in Roma and Maseru, Lesotho

1971 Solo tour of Australia and Papua/New Guinea; 68 performances in Hobart, Launceston, Devonport, Ulverstone and Burnie in Tasmania; Canberra, A.C.T.;
Cootamundra, Cowra, Parks, Coonamble, Wellington, Mittagong and Sydney in New South Wales; Brisbane, Dalby, Toowoomba, Buderim, Gladstone, Rockhampton, Mackay, Townsville, Innisfail and Cairns in Queensland;
Port Moresby, Lae, Goroka and Madang in Papua/New Guinea;
Darwin, Tennant Creek and Alice Springs in the Northern Territory; Adelaide and Millicent in South Australia; Melbourne in Victoria;
Excerpts of repertoire seen on Australian television;
Solo performance tour of Bulgaria; Sofia, Stara Zagoura, Bourgas, Varna and Plovdiv;
Solo performance tour of Russia; Vladimir, Leningrad, Riga, Tallinn, Tartu, Vilnius and Moscow

1972 Solo performances in Rome and L'Aquila, Italy;
In Nicosia, Cyprus;
Excerpts of repertoire seen on Cypriot television;
Dublin season presented by the Abbey Theatre;
Performance at the Théâtre Récamier, Paris, under the aegis of Jean-Louis Barrault;
Further French appearances in Firminy, Rennes, Juan-Les-Pins and Beaulieu;
Guest mime instructor for Rosella Hightower's Centre de Danse International, Cannes; appearances in Copenhagen and Holstebrö in Denmark;
Guest mime instructor for the Royal Danish Ballet, Copenhagen;
Performances in Oxford and Hull, England

1973 Publication of autobiography *Dance Naked In The Sun* by Latonia Publishers, London;
Solo performance in Asnières, France;
Appearance on Thames Television, London;
Solo performance in London, Crewe, York, Kingston-on-Thames, Abingdon, Skegness, Basingstoke and Cardiff, Wales;
Solo performance at Teatro San Luiz in Lisbon, Portugal;

Guest appearance as The General in the ballet *Graduation Ball* with Nathaniel as The Headmistress; Teatro San Luiz, Lisbon

1974 Solo performance in Winchester, Brighton, Stevenage, Norwich, Southampton, Hastings and Brimington, England;
Solo performance in Fort Lauderdale, Florida, U.S.A.;
Solo performance tour of Spain;
Madrid, Barcelona, Soria, Cuenca and Salamanca;
Solo performance tour of Austria;
Vienna, Bregenz and Innsbruck;
Appearances in Split and Ljubljana in Yugoslavia;
Excerpts of repertoire seen on Yugoslav television;
Guest mime instructor at the International Academy of Dance in Estoril, Portugal

1975 Choreographer of evening length ballet *Marilyn*, with Tessa Bill-Yeald in the title role and featuring Nathaniel, sponsored by the rock group Jethro Tull, produced at the Arts Theatre, London for a five week season;
Solo performance in Bishop's Stortford, England;
Budapest, Hungary;
Athens and Thessaloniki, Greece;
Cologne, Germany;
Lausanne and Geneva, Switzerland;
Brussels and Turnhout, Belgium;
Montclair, New Jersey, U.S.A.;
Fort Lauderdale, Florida, U.S.A.;
Guest mime instructor for: The English National Opera, London;
The Hungarian State Opera House, Budapest;
The Rallou Manou Hellenic Chorodrama, Athens, Greece;
The International School, Geneva, Switzerland;
The Cologne Opera House, Germany

1976 Solo performances in London, Oxford and Derby, England;
Solo performance tour of the Middle East: Teheran, Isfahan and Shiraz in Iran;
Kabul, Afghanistan;
Damascus, Syria;
Cairo, Egypt;
Istanbul and Izmir, Turkey;
Television appearances in Iran, Egypt and Turkey;
Performances in Belgrade, Yugoslavia;
Town Hall in New York City;
Minneapolis, U.S.A.;
Solo performance tour of the Orient: Singapore;
Manila, the Philippines;
Hong Kong;
Bangkok, Thailand;
Dacca and Chittagong, Bangladesh;
Jakarta and Surabaya, Java;
Medan, Sumatra, Indonesia;
Television appearances in Bangladesh and Indonesia;
Solo performance tour of Africa: Tananarive, Madagascar;
Johannesburg, Cape Town, Durban and Pretoria, South Africa;
Bangui, the Central African Republic;
N'Djamena, Chad;
Yaoundé and Douala, Cameroon;
Bouaké and Abidjan, the Ivory Coast;
Monrovia, Liberia;
Freetown, Sierra Leone;
Tunis, Sousse, Le Kef, La Marsa, Tunisia;
Bamako, Mali;
Television appearances in South Africa, the Central African Republic, the Ivory Coast, Liberia and Tunisia;
Guest mime instructor throughout tours of Europe, Asia and Africa

1977 Solo performances in Coleraine, Northern Ireland; Norwich, England;
Solo performance tour of Brazil;
Rio de Janeiro, Porto Alegre, Belo Horizonte, Curitiba, Vitoria, Salvador and Brasilia;
Solo performance and *Vultures* at Chichester Festival Theatre, England, *Vultures* co-starring Adam

Darius, Marita Phillips and Nathaniel;
Guest choreographer and dancer for The Rio de Janeiro Ballet in Brazil, staging *The Anne Frank Ballet* and *The Net*;
Solo performance in Cooper City, Florida, U.S.A.; appearance on Florida television

1978 Solo performances in Rio de Janeiro, São Paulo, Brazil and Brazilian television; awarded Florida television Emmy;
Guest choreographer and dancer with The Rio de Janeiro Ballet staging new work, *The Risk*, as well as reviving *Fans*, *The Net* and *The Anne Frank Ballet*;
Solo performance in Teheran, Iran; Thames Television, London; BBC Television, Manchester;
Opening of The Mime Centre, London

1979 Solo performance in Milford Haven, Wales;
Publication of second book, *The Way To Timbuktu*;
Directing and teaching at The Mime Centre;
Preparation for the projected filming of *Flicts* including trips to Paris, New York and Hollywood for discussions with Peter Ustinov, Danny Kaye, Valery and Galina Panov, Peter O'Toole, Princess Grace, Hedy Lamarr and Joan Fontaine;
Began writing third book, *The Adam Darius Method: a technical and practical handbook for all performing artists*

1980 Duo mime performance with Marita Phillips in Rome, Italy, Llantwit Major, Wales, Chester, Eastbourne, Leicester and Greenwich, England;
West End season with Marita Phillips at the May Fair Theatre;
Duo mime performance with Marita Phillips in Brazil; Salvador, Petropolis, Rio de Janeiro and Belem;
Directing and teaching at The Mime Centre, London;
Continued writing *The Adam Darius Method*;
Began creating repertoire for mime artist Kazimir Kolesnik

1981 Appeared at charity gala at Sadler's Wells Theatre;
Duo mime performance with Kazimir Kolesnik in Sundsvall, Sweden and Copenhagen, Denmark;
Duo mime performance with Marita Phillips at the Newbury Festival, England;
Guest choreographer and dancer with The Dublin City Ballet, staging *The Anne Frank Ballet* in Dublin and Dun Laoghaire, Ireland and Belfast, Northern Ireland, Kazimir Kolesnik featured as Peter;
Duo mime performance with Marita Phillips in Richmond, Yorkshire, England;
Duo mime performance with Kazimir Kolesnik in Stockholm, Sweden; Hong Kong; Taipei, Hsinchu and Kaoshiung in Taiwan, the Republic of China;
Belfast Festival, Northern Ireland;
Fort Lauderdale, Florida, U.S.A.;
Created new repertoire for the duo performance with Kazimir Kolesnik;
Directed and taught at The Mime Centre as well as guest teaching in Scandinavia, Ireland and America during the aforementioned tours;
Continued writing *The Adam Darius Method*

1982 Westminster Theatre gala, London, appearing with Marita Phillips;
Directed and taught at The Mime Centre;
Duo mime performance with Kazimir Kolesnik at the Istanbul International Festival in Turkey;
also in Hereford and Richmond, Yorkshire in England;
Duo mime performance with Kazimir Kolesnik in Havana, Cuba at the 8th International Ballet Festival under the aegis of Alicia Alonso;

Coached *Petrouchka* for the National Ballet of Cuba;
Taught the National Mime Theatre of Cuba;
Continued writing *The Adam Darius Method*

1983 Duo mime performances with Kazimir Kolesnik in Miami, Florida, U.S.A., Elephant Fayre Festival in England;
Hong Kong;
Tokyo, Japan (including television appearances);
Directed and taught at The Mime Centre;
Completed *The Adam Darius Method: a technical and practical handbook for all performing artists*

Technical Index